Women and Justice for the Poor
A History of Legal Aid, 1863–1945

This book reexamines fundamental assumptions about the American legal profession and the boundaries between "professional" lawyers, "lay" lawyers, and social workers. Creating a dialogue between legal history and women's history, it demonstrates that nineteenth-century women's organizations were the first to offer legal aid to the poor, and that middle-class women, functioning as lay lawyers, provided that assistance. Felice Batlan illustrates that by the early twentieth century, male lawyers had founded their own legal aid societies. These new legal aid lawyers created an imagined history of legal aid and a blueprint for its future in which women played no role and their accomplishments were intentionally omitted. In response, women social workers offered harsh criticisms of legal aid leaders and developed a more robust social work model of legal aid. These different models produced conflicting understandings of legal expertise, professionalism, the rule of law, and, ultimately, the meaning of justice for the poor.

Felice Batlan is professor of law and associate dean at IIT/Chicago–Kent College of Law. Her groundbreaking work, which explores interactions among law, gender, history, and the legal profession, has appeared in numerous law reviews, history journals, and anthologies. She is a book review editor for *Law and History Review* and was an associate editor of the *Encyclopedia of the Supreme Court* and *Continuity and Change*. She has been a New York University Golieb Fellow, a Hurst Fellow, and a Freehling Fellow, and she received the Coordinating Council for Women in History (CCWH)/Berkshire Women's History Dissertation Award.

In memory of my mother, Syrene R. Batlan,
Who stood with me on the starting line
In dedication to my husband, the Honorable Robert Balanoff,
Who took each step with me

Studies in Legal History

Editors

SARAH BARRINGER GORDON University of Pennsylvania
HOLLY BREWER University of Maryland, College Park
MICHAEL LOBBAN London School of Economics and Political Science

Felice Batlan, *Women and Justice for the Poor: A History of Legal Aid, 1863–1945*
Sophia Z. Lee, *The Workplace Constitution from the New Deal to the New Right*
Michael A. Livingston, *The Fascists and the Jews of Italy: Mussolini's Race Laws, 1938–1943*
Mitra Sharafi, *Law and Identity in Colonial South Asia: Parsi Legal Culture, 1772–1947*

Women and Justice for the Poor

A History of Legal Aid, 1863–1945

FELICE BATLAN

IIT/Chicago–Kent College of Law

CAMBRIDGE
UNIVERSITY PRESS

CAMBRIDGE
UNIVERSITY PRESS

32 Avenue of the Americas, New York, NY 10013-2473, USA

Cambridge University Press is part of the University of Cambridge.

It furthers the University's mission by disseminating knowledge in the pursuit of education, learning, and research at the highest international levels of excellence.

www.cambridge.org
Information on this title: www.cambridge.org/9781107446410

© Felice Batlan 2015

First published 2015

Printed in the United States of America

A catalog record for this publication is available from the British Library.

Library of Congress Cataloging in Publication Data
Batlan, Felice, 1965– author.
Women and justice for the poor : a history of legal aid, 1863–1945 / Felice Batlan.
pages cm. – (Studies in legal history)
Includes bibliographical references and index.
ISBN 978-1-107-08453-7 (hardback) – ISBN 978-1-107-44641-0 (paperback)
1. Legal aid – United States – History.   2. Women – United States – History.   I. Title.
KF336.B38   2015
362.5′8–dc23   2014046191

ISBN 978-1-107-08453-7 Hardback
ISBN 978-1-107-44641-0 Paperback

Contents

List of Plates   *page* ix
Acknowledgments   xi
Abbreviations of Primary Organizations   xv

   Introduction   1

PART I. A FEMALE DOMINION OF LEGAL AID, 1863–1910

1 The Origins of Legal Aid   17
2 The Chicago Experience: The Maturation of Women's
   Legal Aid   47

PART II. THE PROFESSIONALIZATION OF LEGAL AID, 1890–1921

3 Of Immigrants, Sailors, and Servants: The Legal Aid
   Society of New York   87
4 Reinventing Legal Aid   123

PART III. DIALOGUES: LAWYERS AND SOCIAL WORKERS, 1921–1945

5 Constellations of Justice   157
6 Compromises   185
   Conclusion   215

Index   225

Plates

Plates follow page xvi.

1. Working Women's Protective Union: "Complaint Day"
2. "The Waiting-Room in the Building of the Workingwoman's Protective Union"
3. Cover of pamphlet published by the Legal Aid Society of Chicago
4. Advertisement in Legal Aid Society of Chicago pamphlet: "Regulate the Loan Sharks!"
5. Legal Aid Society of New York, main office waiting room
6. The Chicago Legal Aid Bureau: "Poor Man's Portia"

Acknowledgments

I consider myself the luckiest person in the world to be surrounded by my actual and fictive families. It was in Linda Gordon's kitchen, over a cup of well-brewed coffee, that she encouraged me to write a book, even though I had just snippets of archival documents. She read the prospectus and then the manuscript – twice. I went from Linda's home into Sarah Barringer Gordon's orbit. She has been one of my heroes since she sat on my dissertation committee many moons ago. I cannot imagine a more involved, hardworking, or committed editor and advocate, and she pushed me to do more than I ever thought possible. I am a better person and scholar because of her.

My truly wonderful friend Richard Bernstein has been my constant source of encouragement. He read, commented on, and edited this manuscript with his "special pen," more than once. No matter what time of day, Richard was willing to listen to my frustrations, as were my dear friends Tristin Kirvin, Jennifer Anderson, Marjorie Kornhauser, Martin Drell, Carole Balin, and Jancy Hoeffel.

A number of my colleagues read drafts of chapters at many different stages, and I am grateful for their comments and ideas. Thank you, Norma Basch, Karen Tani, Alfred Brophy, David Tanenhaus, Joanna Grisinger, Mary Ziegler, Christopher Schmidt, Linda Kerber, Jill Norgren, Leon Fink, Susan Levine, Gwen Jordan, Tracey Thomas, T. J. Boisseau, Henning Grunwald, Kenneth Ledford, Thomas Bender, Katharine Baker, Nancy Marder, Ron Staudt, Steve Heyman, and Carolyn Shapiro.

The NYU Legal History Symposium has been my home away from home for many years, and William E. Nelson has provided me with every kind of support imaginable. I will be forever grateful to him. Those attending the symposium have read various chapters over the past couple of years, and then the near-complete manuscript. All of their comments and criticisms have been enormously helpful, including those of William LaPiana, Harold Forsythe, Lloyd Bonfield, Daniel Hulsenbosch, Lauren Benson, Brad Snyder, Gautham Rao, and William Forbath. Likewise I thank my colleagues on the faculty at Chicago–Kent College of Law for the many times they have listened to and commented on my work at faculty workshops.

Kenneth Mack, Susan Carle, and Tamar Carroll are three of the most generous scholars I know. They shared their own archival documents and took the time to discuss with me a number of frustrating questions. Martha Jones has been a constant source of inspiration, and her comments always have been right on target. At just the right moment, she invited me to the legal history seminar she taught with William Novak at the University of Michigan, and the feedback that I received there helped me to reach the next level. At an early stage, Mary Anne Case, Amy Dru Stanley, Lisa Bernstein, and the participants in the University of Chicago's Sex and Gender Workshop and Scholarship Workshop provided me with excellent critiques and questions that sent me in new directions, as did attendants at the University of Pennsylvania Social History Conference, including William Eskridge and Michael Katz. Participants in the American Bar Foundation Legal History Workshop, the Vanderbilt Legal Culture Workshop, and the Newberry Symposium on Women and Gender have been supportive and their comments and critiques generative.

I am indebted to our former associate dean, Sarah Harding, and our dean, Harold Krent, for their patience, support, and funding. Becoming a Freehling Scholar was crucial to my completing this project, and I thank Norman and Edna Freehling.

I also had wonderful research assistants, including Alexander Rabanal, Sylvia St. Clair, Asa Naiditch, Lauren Crawford, and Christina Ziegler-McPhersen. Tom Gaylord is one of the most knowledgeable, patient, and hardworking librarians I have encountered. Laura Caringella, like a magician, has put together this manuscript and assisted me in too many ways to count.

I cannot thank my husband, Bob Balanoff, enough. He has done everything imaginable to help me complete this book. He has been my cook, chauffeur, photographer, citation checker, official staple person, IT guru, proofreader, and the one always ready to listen to half-baked ideas. He has encouraged me daily to push on, and when my spirits were low he made me cakes and cookies and caramels. I have also benefited greatly from our many conversations about his own role as a judge on Chicago's Juvenile Court and how he spends his days surrounded by social workers, women lawyers, and mothers hoping to have their children returned to them. He reminds me that what I write about is not just the past.

Parts of this book draw from material in Felice Batlan, "The Birth of Legal Aid: Gender Ideologies, Women, and the Bar in New York City, 1863–1910," *Law and History Review* 28, no. 4 (2010): 931–71.

Abbreviations of Primary Organizations

ABA	American Bar Association
BLAS	Legal Aid Society of Boston
BoJ	Bureau of Justice
CLAS	Legal Aid Society of Chicago
CWC	Chicago Women's Club
LAB	Legal Aid Bureau (Chicago)
NALAO	National Association of Legal Aid Organizations
NYLAS	Legal Aid Society of New York
PAWC	Protective Agency for Women and Children
UCC	United Charities of Chicago
WEIU	Women's Educational and Industrial Union (Boston)
WWPU	Working Women's Protective Union (New York)

PLATE 1. Working Women's Protective Union: "Complaint Day." From *Good Words for the Working Women of New York* (New York: Working Women's Protective Union, 1878). Courtesy of Felice Batlan.

PLATE 2. "The Waiting-Room in the Building of the Workingwoman's Protective Union." From *Frank Leslie's Illustrated Newspaper*, February 5, 1881. Illustration by Georgina A. Davis. Courtesy of Felice Batlan.

PLATE 3. Cover of pamphlet published by the Legal Aid Society of Chicago, ca. 1905. Illustration by Ralph Wilder. Courtesy of Chicago History Museum.

PLATE 4. Advertisement in Legal Aid Society of Chicago pamphlet, ca. 1905: "Regulate the Loan Sharks!" Courtesy of Chicago History Museum.

Main Office, Legal Aid Society, 239 Broadway, Manhattan

PLATE 5. Legal Aid Society of New York, main office waiting room. Photograph appeared in the program for *The Bartered Bride*, presented for the benefit of the Legal Aid Society, April 29, 1909. Courtesy of New York Public Library.

PLATE 6. The Chicago Legal Aid Bureau: "Poor Man's Portia," *Chicago Daily News*, November 20, 1943. Courtesy of Chicago History Museum.

Introduction

This book began in New Orleans amid the debris and destruction of Hurricane Katrina. In 2005, when the storm struck, I was living in New Orleans and teaching at Tulane University. The weeks after the storm were a confusing jumble of friends' couches, searches for clothing, and a growing sense that this would not end soon and that I would need to occupy my time until the university reopened. Doing something in New Orleans seemed better than passively watching the continuing disaster on CNN, so I moved back into my damaged but still standing home. As someone actually living in New Orleans when much of the city was unoccupied and in ruins, I received constant calls from acquaintances, friends, and friends of friends who were unable to return to the city. People needed help with insurance forms and mortgages, with locating relatives, procuring housing, finding documents, and, above all else, dealing with the Federal Emergency Management Agency (FEMA) and its arbitrary and changing policies and procedures. In the wake of such an enormous catastrophe and the haphazard response by the government, many people needed a witness and advocate on the ground.

FEMA established a series of disaster recovery centers in and around New Orleans that were intended to function as "supermarkets" for hurricane aid. In these centers, victims could apply for FEMA benefits; procure information on repairing a roof; speak to the Army Corps of Engineers; receive a disaster tax rebate; find a Bible, a hot meal, a friendly ear. In theory, the centers were an excellent idea; in practice, they resulted in hundreds of people waiting in long lines for hour after hour. One day I approached a FEMA manager, handed her my résumé, and asked if I could set up a legal-information booth. She allowed me to do so without asking a single question. The "booth" consisted of a folding table and my cell phone. I organized a handful of attorney friends, and we staffed our station six days a week for two months.

I noticed that of the thousands of people who stopped by, few needed anything that I understood to be legal advice. A series of complicated emergency rules temporarily allowed volunteer attorneys like myself to practice law. Yet I had no clear understanding of whether I was covered by those rules or for whom I worked. Nor did I have the resources or expertise to practice law in any traditional sense. Instead, I functioned as a sort of mediator, personal advocate, legal educator, and social worker.

People came to our booth because they were desperately frustrated and needed help in whatever form it would come. Victims would call their insurance companies and be put on hold indefinitely; by the time somebody answered, the callers would be too infuriated to speak and would hand the phone to me. I would try to argue that a policy covered a particular type of damage, but often all I could do was schedule an appointment for an agent to inspect a damaged home. At times I had to document that a check from an insurance company or FEMA could not be mailed to a victim's address because that home no longer existed.

More often I mediated between FEMA representatives and people applying for benefits, and tried to understand how FEMA was interpreting its ever-changing rules. I informed inexperienced FEMA workers what the agency's policies were on that day, and alerted FEMA employees, all working in the same room, that they were interpreting policy in diametrically opposed ways. Most of all, I listened to people's stories, as the storm produced as many stories as there were survivors. Narrating their stories seemed crucial to those who were trying to process events that had happened so quickly, and people needed someone to hear and validate their experiences.

As time went on, those still seeking assistance were even more desperate for housing and funds. These were people who were poor before the storm but now were destitute. I spent time procuring FEMA trailers for those still homeless. Even if FEMA approved, shipped, and notified an applicant that a trailer was at a particular location and ready for occupancy, it did not mean that in reality the trailer was present or habitable. I tracked down missing trailers, asked why plumbing did not work, why the key did not fit the lock. At the very end, I simply tried to find vacant motel rooms – paid for by FEMA – but this did not provide a permanent solution for victims. On the worst days, I helped people obtain relatives' death certificates.

This work made me reflect on what I was doing and whether I was using my legal knowledge, legal skill, or anything else that I had learned in law school or during my decade as a legal practitioner. In the FEMA center, law and social work bled together. My work seemed similar to that performed by many women's organizations in the late nineteenth and early twentieth centuries.[1] I was doing what had to be done. I was helping because people needed help. I certainly had no sense that my work had anything to do with justice; there was little that was just in the entire situation.

I want to believe that I made some people's lives a bit easier for a brief amount of time, yet I was the greatest beneficiary. During the hours that I spent in the center, I was transformed from a hurricane victim into a professional with authority and expertise that made other people, especially inexperienced FEMA personnel, pay attention. I also understood that this authority was partially an illusion based on my status as a lawyer and law professor, my whiteness, and my class. My legal-assistance project made me reflect broadly on volunteer work, charity, lawyers, social workers, and the ambiguities of what the practice of law means in an environment of massive and aching need.

The development of organized free legal aid for the poor in the United States has a rich history that has been overlooked, even buried. *Women and Justice for the Poor* uncovers the enormous role played by women as legal aid providers in the late nineteenth and early twentieth centuries. It explores how ideologies of gender shaped and constructed what legal aid was and who would be its providers and clients. This book exposes the "real" history of legal aid, a story that the predominantly male leaders in the field of legal aid intentionally masked.

By beginning this history with nineteenth-century women's organizations, we see how they played central roles in the creation of urban legal institutions and how their leaders understood that legal aid needed to be part of a wider reform agenda. In the past, historians of women have brilliantly explored how such organizations engaged in significant and wide-ranging social-reform activities, from suffrage and temperance work to the creation of settlement houses, kindergartens, reform schools, benefit programs, and playgrounds.[2] This body of work is large and rich,

---

[1] On gender and Hurricane Katrina, see the special issue of the journal of the National Women's Studies Association, *NWSA Journal* 20, no. 3 (2009).

[2] The literature on women's clubs is enormous. Just a few examples include Anne Firor Scott, "Most Invisible of All: Black Women's Voluntary Associations," *Journal of Southern History* 56 (February 1990): 3–22; Anne M. Boylan, *The Origins of Women's*

but it does not explicitly see such organizations as crucial and innovative legal institutions. On the other hand, most legal historians have paid little attention to such women's organizations; from the perspective of traditional legal history, they are largely invisible. This book frames a dialogue between the all-too-separate fields of women's history and legal history. It is simultaneously a much-needed institutional history of legal aid.

We begin by exploring how, in the later decades of the nineteenth century, women's organizations pioneered the provision of legal aid in major cities such as New York, Boston, Chicago, and Philadelphia. Although the actual everyday delivery of such aid was carried out primarily by upper- and middle-class women who were not professional lawyers, their work eventually created a female and feminized "dominion" of legal aid.[3] These early organizations specialized in claims on behalf of poor women – first addressing mostly wage claims against employers and then expanding to domestic relations cases and other legal problems. Such organizations defined legal assistance broadly, to include multiple kinds of advice as well as the provision of material aid. They also situated legal assistance within a wider agenda that included equality for women in the workplace, the home, and the public sphere. As practiced by women's organizations, the provision of legal aid intentionally entailed the legal

---

Activism: New York and Boston, 1797–1840 (Chapel Hill: University of North Carolina Press, 2002); Nancy Schrom Dye, *As Equals and as Sisters: Feminism, Unionism, and the Women's Trade Union League of New York* (Columbia: University of Missouri Press, 1980); Ellen Fitzpatrick, *Endless Crusade: Women Social Scientists and Progressive Reform* (New York: Oxford University Press, 1990); Sarah Deutsch, *Woman and the City: Gender, Space, and Power in Boston, 1870–1940* (New York: Oxford University Press, 2000); Maureen Flanagan, *Seeing with Their Heart: Chicago Women and the Vision of the Good City* (Princeton, NJ: Princeton University Press, 2002); Sara Monsoon, "The Lady and the Tiger: Women's Electoral Activism in New York City before Suffrage," *Journal of Women's History* 2 (Fall 1990): 100; Landon Storrs, *Civilizing Capitalism: The National Consumers' League, Women's Activism, and Labor Standards in the New Deal Era* (Chapel Hill: University of North Carolina Press, 2000); Karen Blair, *The Clubwoman as Feminist: True Womanhood Redefined 1868–1914* (Teaneck, NJ: Holmes and Meier Publishers, 1980); Sandra Haarsager, *Organized Womanhood: Cultural Politics in the Pacific Northwest, 1840–1920* (Norman: University of Oklahoma Press, 1997); Lara Vapnek, *Breadwinners: Working Women and Economic Independence, 1865–1920* (Urbana: University of Illinois Press, 2009).

3 Robyn Muncy's canonical *Creating a Female Dominion in American Reform, 1890–1935* (New York: Oxford University Press, 1991) describes the work of a series of women's organizations and the reforms that they sought. Although Muncy does not discuss legal aid, her concept of creating a female dominion – in this case, one in child welfare that existed in an otherwise male empire of policymaking – is particularly apt in describing the history of legal aid and how female volunteers and social workers negotiated with a variety of male legal institutions.

equivalent of a laying on of hands. That is, the connections and interactions between poor women and women lay lawyers helped heal class rifts, and they took place in an environment in which poor women could freely tell their stories. With time and experience, women lay lawyers acquired legal knowledge and positioned themselves as experts in the law, a stance that some male lawyers, and judges, accepted and even respected.

Following the creation of women's legal aid organizations, a second generation of legal aid associations developed in the late nineteenth and the early twentieth century. These societies generally were controlled by men, they primarily employed professional male lawyers, and they provided legal assistance to both men and women. As a number of male legal aid lawyers gained prominence, they sought to professionalize legal aid and transform it from its status as a charity – with its female dominion of lay lawyers – to something more akin to the private practice of law.

The history of legal aid thus fits into a much larger pattern of men professionalizing women's work and then using that professionalism to exclude women.[4] These new legal aid leaders redrew the conventional image of the legal aid client; rather than a poor woman with a domestic relations claim, the client was now a working man with a wage claim. Such manly clients were entitled to legal aid as a means to establish their independence. Many clients of second-generation legal aid societies were immigrants, and attorneys imagined that the provision of legal assistance to these men served as a lesson in citizenship. This process of reconfiguring legal aid obscured women's presence as clients, lay lawyers, and even professional lawyers. Moreover, new legal aid organizations began to reject the types of claims, especially those involving domestic relations, that women typically sought to bring.

Picking up on and synthesizing what was already occurring within legal aid, Reginald Heber Smith's *Justice and the Poor* (1919) was the first extended "history" of legal aid. It was written to curry favor with bar associations and to disassociate legal aid from philanthropy, women's

---

[4] The paradigmatic case of this phenomenon is in medicine. See, e.g., Regina Morantz-Sanchez, *Medicine on Trial in Turn-of-the-Century Brooklyn* (New York: Oxford University Press, 1999); Leslie J. Reagan, *When Abortion Was a Crime: Women, Medicine, and Law in the United States, 1867–1973* (Berkeley: University of California Press, 1998). In connection with nineteenth-century charity work, see Michael Katz, *In the Shadow of the Poorhouse: A Social History of Welfare in America*, 2nd ed. (New York: Basic Books, 1996), 65; Eileen Boris and Jenifer Klein discuss this appropriation in relationship to the care of the disabled as medical doctors pushed out social workers, in *Caring for America: Home Health Workers in the Shadow of the Welfare State* (New York: Oxford University Press, 2012).

organizations, and lay lawyers.[5] Moreover, Smith believed that lawyers (especially graduates of elite law schools) had unique skills and training far beyond anything possessed by women lay lawyers or even women professional lawyers, no matter their experience. Smith hoped, further, that allying legal aid with bar associations would place legal aid in a manly sphere of law and thus generate prestige and financial support. *Justice and the Poor* succeeded in part – it essentially became scripture, providing legal aid with a usable past and a blueprint for the future. Generations of scholars have accepted *Justice and the Poor* as an accurate account of the history of legal aid.[6] Within legal aid circles, Smith's work is still hailed for its originality and thorough research.[7] That legal scholars have missed the connections between women's organizations and the development of legal aid is proof of how well Smith and others hid them. Moreover, unlike later male-led legal aid organizations, the documentation of legal aid organizations run by women is sparse, buried in archival material seemingly unrelated to law, and consisting primarily of annual reports.

In the midst of the reconfiguration and professionalization of legal aid, social work first appeared as a profession, and at least some women lay lawyers began to consider themselves social workers.[8] Male leaders

---

[5] Reginald Heber Smith, *Justice and the Poor* (New York: Carnegie Foundation, 1919).

[6] See, e.g., Michael Grossberg, *Counsel for the Poor? Legal Aid Societies and the Creation of Modern Urban Legal Structure, 1900–1930* (Vancouver: University of British Columbia, 1994); Jerold S. Auerbach, *Unequal Justice: Lawyers and Social Change in Modern America* (New York: Oxford University Press, 1977); Martha Davis, *Brutal Need: Lawyers and the Welfare Rights Movement, 1960–1973* (New Haven, CT: Yale University Press, 1995); Phillip Merkel, "At the Crossroads of Reform: The First Fifty Years of Legal Aid," *Houston Law Review* 27 (1990): 1–44; Earl Johnson Jr., *Justice and Reform: The Formative Years of the American Legal Services Program* (New York: Russell Sage Foundation, 1974); Jack Katz, *Poor People's Lawyers in Transition* (New Brunswick, N.J.: Rutgers University Press, 1982); Deborah L. Rhode, *Access to Justice* (New York: Oxford University Press, 2005); Mark Spiegel, "The Boson Legal Aid Society: 1900–1925," *Massachusetts Legal History* 9 (2003): 17–48; Richard L. Abel, "Law Without Politics: Legal Aid under Advanced Capitalism," *UCLA Law Review* 32 (1985): 474–642.

[7] See Earl Johnson Jr., *To Establish Justice for All: The Past and Future of Civil Legal Aid in the United States*, vol. 1 (Santa Barbara, CA: Praeger, 2014).

[8] On the development of social work, see Daniel J. Walkowitz, *Working with Class: Social Workers and the Politics of Middle-Class Identity* (Chapel Hill: University of North Carolina Press, 1999); Elizabeth N. Agnew, *From Charity to Social Work: Mary E. Richmond and the Creation of the American Profession* (Urbana: University of Illinois Press, 2004); Muncy, *Creating a Female Dominion*; Katz, *In the Shadow of the Poorhouse*; Ellen Fitzpatrick, *Endless Crusade*; John H. Ehrenreich, *The Altruistic Imagination: A History of Social Work and Social Policy in the United States* (Ithaca, NY: Cornell University Press, 1985).

of legal aid quickly concluded that social workers should have little or no role in providing legal assistance. Yet social workers and their often female lawyer allies contested the project to masculinize legal aid and situate it in the professional world of lawyers. They asserted their own authority over providing legal aid, especially with the development of specialized juvenile and domestic relations courts, which were often staffed by female social workers and lay lawyers.[9] New schools of social work began to teach law to their predominately female students, with the idea that these students would provide legal services to the poor.

By the early 1920s, male leaders in legal aid panicked over legal aid's relationship to social work, their concerns linked to issues of gender, authority, expertise, and professionalization. The resulting controversy raised questions about what constituted the practice law, what the rule of law meant, what was a legal problem, what types of services legal aid should provide, and which clients legal aid should serve. Central to these issues was a fundamental question: Was legal aid meant to offer a process-based form of justice by allowing access to an attorney, or was it intended to create substantive justice? Although scholars of legal aid have long pointed to its conservative nature, social workers presented an alternative, more expansive version of legal aid based on ideas of social justice. In exploring these issues, *Women and Justice for the Poor* demonstrates how law and social work were in contest with each other, and how each helped to define the other in that opposition. It thus refuses to see law and social work as distinct disciplines – one largely male and the other largely female.[10]

---

[9] On these specialized courts, see David Tanenhaus, *Juvenile Justice in the Making* (New York: Oxford University Press, 2004); Michael Willrich, *City of Courts: Socializing Justice in Progressive-Era Chicago* (New York: Oxford University Press, 2003); Mae C. Quinn, "Feminist Legal Realism," *Harvard Journal of Law and Gender* 35 (2012): 1–54.

[10] A recent work that elegantly puts social workers and medical professionals in dialogue is Eileen Boris and Jennifer Klein, *Caring for America*. Similarly, Susan D. Carle unearths and examines how African American lawyers, sociologists, and members of women's clubs engaged together in civil rights work, in *Defining the Struggle: National Organizing for Racial Justice* (Oxford: Oxford University Press, 2013). Karen Tani looks at debates between lawyers and social workers during the New Deal in "Securing a Right to Welfare: Public Assistance and the Rule of Law, 1935–1965," PhD diss., University of Pennsylvania, 2011. Other works that explore interdisciplinary approaches to law in historical context include Christopher Tomlins, "Framing the Field of Law's Disciplinary Encounters: A Historical Narrative," *Law and Society Review* 34 (2000): 911; Laura Kalman, *Legal Realism at Yale, 1927–1960* (Chapel Hill: University of North Carolina Press, 1986).

Placing women, as both legal aid providers and clients, at the center of this history forces us to reexamine some of our fundamental assumptions about the development of the American legal profession and the relationship and boundaries between "professional" lawyers and "lay lawyers." Specifically, this book questions what it means to "practice law" and blurs the conventional division between lawyer and nonlawyer.[11] Although traditionally we have believed that, from the late nineteenth century onward, bar associations actively policed the practice of law, for decades bar associations knew but did nothing about the fact that women lay lawyers and social workers were engaged in a wide variety of legal activities.[12] The neat conventional narrative of the legal profession's steady monopolization of legal services looks messier when we acknowledge the roles that social workers played in legal aid organizations. Likewise, the book's geography or locus of inquiry is not spectacular courtroom trials but office practice, the provision of everyday legal advice, and the mediation of legal claims.[13] Similarly it is not about legal doctrine; rather, it provides a new way of thinking about the legal profession and the practice of law. From such different perspectives, the practice of law was more democratic and heterogeneous – and less male – than we understood it to have been.

How legal aid developed reflected larger societal tensions and contradictions involving the role of women and how gender functioned in society.[14] In the nineteenth and twentieth centuries, gender served as both a practice and a discourse through which people articulated, constructed, and defined rights and obligations. As a relational construct, it symbolized, mobilized, and even subverted power.[15] This book examines how historical actors spoke and wrote about manhood and womanhood and

[11] W. Wesley Pue and David Sugarman have written that the category of lawyers might actually include a wide variety of subgroups, and the demarcations between lawyers and nonlawyers are often historically contingent. See "Introduction: Towards a Cultural History of Lawyers," in *Lawyers and Vampires: Cultural Histories of Legal Professions*, ed. Pue and Sugarman (Oxford: Hart Publishing, 2003), 9.

[12] For a classic account of the historical development of bar associations, see Michael Powell, *From Patrician to Professional Elite: The Transformation of the New York City Bar Association* (New York: Russell Sage Foundation, 1988); Auerbach, *Unequal Justice*; Terrence C. Halliday, *Beyond Monopoly: Lawyers, State Crises, and Professional Empowerment* (Chicago: University of Chicago Press, 1987).

[13] See Kenneth W. Mack, *Representing the Race: The Creation of the Civil Rights Lawyer* (Cambridge, MA: Harvard University Press, 2012).

[14] Joan Scott, "Feminism's History," *Journal of Women's History* 16 (2004): 10–29, 20.

[15] There is a vast literature on gender and history; see, e.g., Joan Scott, "Gender: A Useful Category of Historical Analysis," *American Historical Review* 91 (December 1986):

what they claimed in connection with those ideas – and it also articulates how gender systems had real material consequences. The very terms *social work*, *charity*, and *profession* are gendered, insofar as they carry connotations of men's and women's appropriate roles and social and professional hierarchies.[16] Gender even defined whose labor was valued and visible and whose labor was not – or whose could not be recognized without subverting dominant gender constructs.[17]

This study also engages with an expanding and important literature on the history of women lawyers. Scholars have documented the story of the miniscule number of women who began seeking admission to the bar in the 1870s after having read law. Other women in the 1880s and 1890s began applying for entrance into law schools. These women pioneers fought with law schools for admission, and battled courts and legislatures to permit women to sit for bar examinations and then be admitted into a state's bar.[18] State and federal courts found that the

---

1053; Linda K. Kerber, *No Constitutional Rights to Be Ladies: Women and the Obligation of Citizenship* (New York: Hill and Wang, 1998); Barbara Young Welke, *Recasting American Liberty: Gender, Race, Law, and the Railroad Revolution* (Cambridge: Cambridge University Press, 2001); Kevin Murphy, *Political Manhood: Red Bloods, Mollycoddles, and the Politics of Progressive-Era Reform* (New York: Columbia University Press, 2008); Christopher Dummitt, *The Manly Modern: Masculinity in Postwar Canada* (Vancouver: University of British Columbia Press, 2007); Joanne Meyerwitz, "A History of 'Gender,'" *American Historical Review* 113 (December 2008): 1346–56; Tracy A. Thomas and Tracey Jean Boisseau, eds., *Feminist Legal History: Essays on Women and the Law* (New York: New York University Press, 2011).

[16] See, e.g., Mary Ryan, *Women in Public: Between Banners and Ballots, 1825–1880* (Baltimore: Johns Hopkins University Press, 1990); Rebecca Edwards, *Angels in the Machinery: Gender in American Party Politics from the Civil War to the Progressive Era* (New York: Oxford University Press, 1997); Laura Edwards, *Gendered Strife and Confusion: The Political Culture of Reconstruction* (Urbana: University of Illinois Press, 1997).

[17] See, e.g., Elizabeth Faue, "Reimagining Labor: Gender and New Directions in Labor and Working-Class History," in *Continuum Companion to United States Labor History*, ed. Donna Haverty-Stacke and Daniel J. Walkowitz (New York: Continuum International Publishers, 2010); Eileen Boris and Rachel Salazar Parreñas, eds., *Intimate Labors: Care, Sex, and Domestic Work* (Stanford, CA: Stanford University Press, 2010).

[18] See Jill Norgren, *Rebels at the Bar: The Fascinating, Forgotten Stories of America's First Women Lawyers* (New York: New York University Press, 2013); Barbara Babcock, *Woman Lawyer: The Trials of Clara Foltz* (Stanford, CA: Stanford University Press, 2011); Jill Norgren, *Belva Lockwood: The Woman Who Would Be President* (New York: New York University Press, 2007); Mary Jane Mossman, *The First Women Lawyers: A Comparative Study of Gender, Law, and the Legal Profession* (Oxford: Hart Publishing, 2006); Virginia Drachman, *Women Lawyers and the Origins of Professional Identity in America* (Ann Arbor: University of Michigan Press, 1993); Karen M. Tani, "Portia's Deal," *Chicago-Kent Law Review* 87 (2012): 549–70; Gwen Jordan, "Engendering the History of Race and International Relations: The Career of Edith Sampson,

Fourteenth Amendment did not require states to admit women to the bar, just as it did not give them the right of suffrage.[19] Those opposed to women lawyers reasoned that if a woman lawyer was permitted to represent others, why couldn't she represent herself and therefore vote, be a juror, or hold public office? Women's entry to the legal profession was thus a slippery slope to full citizenship. But even as legal barriers dropped, female lawyers well into the twentieth century found scarce employment opportunities; some found work by joining legal aid organizations or establishing solo practices that represented the poor.

Although groundbreaking, the literature on women lawyers prioritizes their professional status in shaping our understanding of what it meant for women to practice law, and in the process it leaves unexplored a much larger field of women's legal activities. When we look only at professional women attorneys, the history of women in the law appears to be one of slow but steady progress from the late nineteenth and into the twentieth century. In contrast, when we include women lay lawyers and, later, social workers in the analysis, the conventional story of progress over time becomes less linear and more complicated, revealing periods of declension that bring the narrative of progress into question.

Likewise, scholars have recently begun to study the role of race in the provision of legal assistance.[20] Superficially, all the legal aid organizations examined in this book claimed to accept cases without regard to race, religion, or creed. Such pronouncements were important to these organizations, as they confirmed that justice was available to all. Yet in decades' worth of legal aid material, there is little discussion of African Americans either as clients or legal aid providers. In fact, among women's organizations the very claim to legal authority was partly based on their members' whiteness. The providers of legal aid, whether lay lawyers or professionals, were primarily white, creating a complicated nexus of race, ethnicity, gender, and class.

African Americans, however, certainly used the services of legal aid organizations. The Legal Aid Society of Chicago employed publicity

---

1927–1978," *Chicago-Kent Law Review* 87 (2012): 521–48; Phyllis Eckhaus, "Restless Women: The Pioneering Alumnae of New York University School of Law," *New York University Law Review* 66 (1991): 1996–2013.

[19] See Bradwell v. Illinois, 83 U.S. 130 (1873); Minor v. Happersett, 88 U.S. 162 (1875).

[20] Shaun Ossei-Owusu, *Law's Underbelly: Legal Aid from Slavery to Mass Incarceration*, PhD diss., University of California, Berkeley, 2014; Kris Shepard, *Rationing Justice: Poverty Lawyers and Poor People in the Deep South* (Baton Rouge: Louisiana University Press, 2007); Carle, *Defining the Struggle*; Mack, *Representing the Race*.

photographs that clearly depicted African American clients. Yet, as we shall see, other organizations adopted supposedly neutral eligibility policies that had the effect of limiting the number of African American clients. Most blatantly, legal aid was slow to grow in the South, where it was feared that even the smallest claims of African Americans against whites would subvert white supremacy. Whether in the North or the South, none of the legal aid organizations examined here saw the dismantling of racial discrimination as being within their purview. Across decades, legal aid organizations studiously separated the everyday provision of legal aid from cases that overtly challenged white supremacy.

This book examines only organizations that specifically understood and identified themselves as providing free, organized, civil legal aid to the poor on a continual basis. Undoubtedly, many individual lawyers provided such assistance on occasion, and organizations such as mutual aid societies, churches, labor unions, settlement houses, and a vast array of social service agencies provided some legal assistance. For instance, male African American lawyers held high positions in black fraternal orders; it is certainly possible that such orders provided legal assistance to members.[21] The poor, especially immigrants who were not from Western Europe, and racial minorities may have looked first to this wide array of other organizations before turning to established legal aid organizations. Although this book at times points to those alternative institutions, it leaves to others the important work of uncovering the full range and mix of legal assistance.

The provision of free legal aid to the poor was not unique to the United States, but it flourished in America.[22] Paralleling John Fabian Witt's conclusions regarding insurance and personal injury cases in the late nineteenth century, it is clear that the growth of legal aid was propelled indirectly by the lack of powerful unions (especially for women) and the absence of strong state regulation or a robust administrative bureaucracy.[23] Issues of small and great consequence depended on bringing or at least threatening to bring individual lawsuits. The largest

---

[21] Theda Skocpol, Ariane Liazos, and Marshall Ganz, *What a Mighty Power We Can Be: African American Fraternal Groups and the Struggle for Racial Equality* (Princeton, NJ: Princeton University Press, 2006).

[22] See Henning Grunwald, *Courtroom to Revolutionary Stage: Performance and Ideology in Weimar Political Trials* (Oxford: Oxford University Press, 2012).

[23] John Fabian Witt, *The Accidental Republic: Crippled Workingmen, Destitute Widows, and the Remaking of American Law* (Cambridge, MA: Harvard University Press, 2004). See also Theda Skocpol, *Protecting Soldiers and Mothers: The Political Origins of Social Policy in the United States* (Cambridge, MA: Belknap Press of Harvard University Press,

category of legal aid claims in the nineteenth and early twentieth centuries involved employees' wages; the second largest involved domestic relations. Yet the weak state does not fully explain the phenomenon of legal aid, because the later development of the administrative state and even the "semi-welfare state" of the 1960s did not retard the growth or use of legal aid organizations.[24]

From one perspective, legal aid stood at the margins of the legal profession because it ministered to the poor and least empowered. Some studies imply that legal aid organizations were moribund until the 1960s, when federal funds began to flow to legal aid and an energetic cadre of young lawyers aligned with the New Left worked to revamp it.[25] But long before the 1960s, legal aid organizations provided services to an enormous number of people: from the 1870s up until 1938, such organizations handled more than five million cases.[26] Throughout the twentieth century, the demand for legal aid consistently outpaced the capacity of legal aid organizations. As legal aid offices opened, people flocked to them.

Studying legal aid is not only important because of the vast number of clients served but also because it brought together men and women of all classes, from the poorest of the poor to some of the most elite lawyers in America. Well-known women's reform organizations, such as Boston's Women's Educational and Industrial Union and the Chicago Women's Club, and some of the most prestigious bar associations, including the Association of the Bar of the City of New York (which long prohibited women lawyers from membership) appear here because legal aid brought them into (often confrontational) contact. Such legal luminaries as Roscoe Pound, Charles Evans Hughes, and Sophonisba Breckinridge were forced to reckon with one another's ideas of what constituted justice.

Legal aid could have transformative possibilities. It could permit lawyers to stand momentarily outside the market and allow upper- and middle-class women to function as lawyers; a desperately poor person

1995); Susan J. Pearson, *The Rights of the Defenseless: Protecting Animals and Children in Gilded-Age America* (Chicago: University of Chicago Press, 2011).

[24] Michael Katz uses this term in *In the Shadow of the Poorhouse*, 242.

[25] See, e.g., Johnson; *Justice and Reform*; Alan Houseman, "Political Lessons: Legal Services for the Poor – A Commentary," *Georgetown Law Journal* 83 (April 1995): 1669.

[26] National Association of Legal Aid Organizations, *Reports of Committee, 1938–1939* (Rochester, 1939), 29. In 1939 NALAO stopped estimating the aggregate number of cases handled, understanding that such numbers were probably inaccurate because they did not include the work of many organizations and because of disagreement regarding what counted as a case.

could become a rights-bearing individual; an abused wife could find new stability. Legal aid also could be conservative: legal aid organizations often disciplined workers to fit into a capitalist, wage-based economy, and some of them put tremendous pressure on men to become steady breadwinners. Additionally, many organizations refused to handle divorce cases and failed to see wife beating as a serious problem. Instead, they worked to uphold the prerogatives of husbands. Such organizations were also hesitant to take the claims of domestic servants, thereby shielding the labor practices of elites. At moments, legal aid providers openly expressed a profound dislike for and distrust of their clients. They might deplore urban poverty, but few organizations before the 1960s used the law to promote structural reforms that might eliminate either poverty or white supremacy. Instead, legal aid organizations were often founded in response to poor people's political and labor activities and represented an attempt to placate workers and elide class conflict. Where possible, this study draws on the voices of those seeking legal assistance, but for the most part it makes use of the documents of legal aid organizations, which were written, of course, by the providers of legal aid.

Finally, although *Women and Justice for the Poor* is a work of history, it speaks to the present as well. Legal aid is in crisis in the early twenty-first century, as government funding shrinks and poverty expands. Some controversial proposals to reinvigorate legal aid call for increasing the use of nonlawyers.[27] Some advocates claim that the presence of lawyers may actually hinder the productive resolution of poor clients' legal problems because attorneys escalate disputes and create delays.[28] Under the new model, legal services would focus more on mediating disputes and providing social services to clients, and less on the adversarial process and formal law. One of the leading voices in the access-to-justice community, Jeanne Charn, argues for a "functionalist, pragmatic approach" that would use lawyers only when specialized legal expertise is necessary.[29] She claims that low-income people prefer readily available, informal advice from nonlawyers over formal advice from lawyers. The

---

[27] Rhode, *Access to Justice*; Gillian Hadfield, "Summary of Testimony: Task Force to Expand Access to Civil Legal Services in New York, Chief Judge's Hearings, October 1, 2012," http://richardzorza.files.wordpress.com/2012/10/hadfield-testimony-october-2012-final-2.pdf.

[28] Rebecca Aviel, "Why Civil *Gideon* Won't Fix Family Law," *Yale Law Journal* 22 (June 2013): 2106–24, 2118–19.

[29] Jeanne Charn, "Celebrating the 'Null' Finding: Evidence-Based Strategies for Improving Access to Legal Services," *Yale Law Journal* 22 (June 2013): 2206–34, 2213.

adversarial attorney-based model of law would be replaced by negotiation and problem solving.[30] Likewise, scholars are beginning to question whether the legal profession should have a monopoly over law and how social workers and others might deliver legal assistance in a wide range of areas.[31]

There is a long, hidden history of nonlawyers providing legal assistance along with social services.[32] And there is no evidence that, historically, the work of nonlawyers was inferior to that of lawyers. Given this, we should ask why lawyers believe that they alone should handle the legal needs of the poor. *Women and Justice for the Poor* establishes a very different, more capacious view of legal aid grounded in women's history and legal history.

---

[30] Ibid.

[31] See, e.g., Deborah L. Rhode and Lucy Buford Ricca, "Protecting the Profession or the Public? Rethinking Unauthorized-Practice Enforcement," *Fordham Law Review* 82 (2014): 2587–610; Jack Sahl, "Cracks in the Profession's Monopoly Armor," *Fordham Law Review* 82 (2014): 2635–63.

[32] For an important older work that argues against such an approach while demonstrating the long history of mediation and arbitration in the United States, see Jerold S. Auerbach, *Justice without Law* (New York: Oxford University Press, 1983).

PART I

A FEMALE DOMINION OF LEGAL AID, 1863–1910

I

The Origins of Legal Aid

Organized legal aid began with the founding of the Working Women's Protective Union in New York City in 1863.[1] In part, it was an attempt to quell working women's own protests regarding their low pay and poor employment conditions. Instead of labor organizing, the union devoted itself to providing legal services to impoverished and working-class women who had wage claims against their employers. Although the union long presented its legal work as being carried out by male lawyers, the reality was that its full-time staff of women lay lawyers conducted most of the work, including its legal work. Much like the history of legal aid in general, such women's work was hidden. Recognizing their work would have called into question not only the altruism of the male bar but also what constituted the practice of law and whether it was appropriate for women to be lawyers.

During the Civil War, New York City suffered from significant wartime inflation – as did much of the nation – and segments of the working class responded with outbursts of collective action, including strikes.

---

[1] A number of works mention the Working Women's Protective Union (WWPU) but do not fully explore how it functioned as a legal aid organization. See Alice Kessler-Harris, *Out to Work: A History of Wage-Earning Women in the United States* (New York: Oxford University Press, 1982), 91–92; Lori Ginzberg, *Women and the Work of Benevolence: Morality, Politics, and Class in the Nineteenth-Century United States* (New Haven, CT: Yale University Press, 1990), 182; Catherine Clinton, *The Other Civil War: American Women in the Nineteenth Century* (New York: Hill and Wang, 1999), 173; Wendy Gamber, *The Female Economy: The Millinery and Dressmaking Trades, 1860–1930* (Champaign: University of Illinois Press, 1997), 86 n. 76; Martha Minow, "'Forming Underneath Everything That Grows': Toward a History of Family Law," *Wisconsin Law Review* 1985 (1985): 819–98, n. 227.

Prices had risen dramatically on everyday goods, but workers' wages stagnated. Machinists and other skilled male workers, who earned about $2.00 a day, complained that they could no longer live on such wages. By contrast, in the sewing trades, an industry employing large numbers of white and immigrant women both in factories and at home, women earned about $2.50 a week.[2] As one newspaper reported, "[Women's wages] have been so depreciated that it is scarcely possible to realize how anyone could live from the proceeds of such work."[3]

In the fall of 1863, male skilled workers called for a citywide strike by all laborers; women workers, in the sewing and notions trades, soon began engaging in their own labor agitation.[4] Sympathetic newspapers published letters from women complaining about the unfair practices of employers, low wages, long hours, and dehumanizing treatment.[5] This nascent labor movement attracted hundreds of women, who attended citywide meetings.[6] These working women, along with a number of male allies, formed the Working Women's Union, which was open to all working women.[7] The union was unique because it was composed of and led by women at a time when many Americans believed that women workers were incapable of collective labor action and when male labor leaders were often hostile to women workers.[8]

The early history of the Working Women's Union is shrouded in mystery, but we do know that the union's initial male supporters defected, charging that working women had exaggerated their struggles and that they were not self-supporting breadwinners. One newspaper reported that the women who crowded the hall at the union's first large meeting appeared well fed and that there was no indication among them of "starvation" or "consumption (except for food)."[9] Further, some women "bragged" of their high wages, and others had "free support" because

[2] "Strike among the Females," *New York Herald*, November 13, 1863, 4.
[3] "The Working Women," *New York Herald*, November 14, 1863, 3.
[4] See Kessler-Harris, *Out to Work*, 76–77.
[5] "Sad Story of a Poor Girl – A Communication," *New York Sun*, November 17, 1863, 1. See also "Another Working Girl's Experience," *New York Sun*, November 18, 1863, 1.
[6] "Another Great Meeting of Working Women," *New York Sun*, November 19, 1863, 1.
[7] "Meeting of the Sewing Girls Last Evening," *New York Herald*, November 19, 1863, 10.
[8] See, e.g., Ellen Carol Dubois, *The Emergence of an Independent Women's Movement in America, 1848–1869* (Ithaca, NY: Cornell University Press, 1999); Christine Stansell, *City of Women: Sex and Class in New York, 1789–1860* (Urbana: University of Illinois Press, 1987).
[9] "Meeting of Workwomen," *New York Daily Tribune*, November 19, 1863, 1.

they lived with parents.[10] Male leaders found working women unruly, and complained that they were so ignorant of how to conduct a labor meeting that they refused to elect delegates.[11] Highlighting the potentially subversive undertones of working women's collective action, a number of newspaper articles claimed that the abolitionist and suffragist Susan B. Anthony had appeared at the meeting, in the company of a "colored girl."[12] According to one reporter, the union's male president asked her to leave, stating that she would "only confuse the meeting" and "lead it from the business at hand."[13] These and other complaints suggest that men wanted to control the union and keep it focused solely and narrowly on what they considered appropriate labor issues, rather than on abolition or women's rights.[14]

The Working Women's Union's death knell came when male strikers went back to work, having negotiated higher wages for themselves. With women's labor agitation no longer considered useful to male labor activists, an anonymous group of men held a series of meetings, formed a committee, drafted a constitution for the Working Women's Union, and issued a report explaining why men had to control the union, claiming that "the difficulties in the way of organizing and carrying on an association to be managed and controlled among yourselves, were so great as would seriously impair the usefulness of the Union."[15] A later report explained:

The [union's] earlier efforts were directed to the establishment of an organization among the working-women themselves for their own mutual protection. But their want of experience in the management of business affairs and some already evident machinations among the evil-disposed of their own sex, proved obstacles not easily surmounted. Thus the gentlemen . . . felt impelled to assume the entire control.[16]

Tellingly, the new committee changed the name of the Working Women's Union to the Working Women's Protective Union of the City of New

[10] Ibid.
[11] Ibid.
[12] "Meeting of the Sewing Girls," *New York Herald*, November 19, 1863, 10.
[13] "Meeting of Workwomen," *New York Daily Tribune*, November 19, 1863, 1.
[14] On the extraordinary difficulty and opposition faced by women's rights leaders in trying to account for issues of gender, race, and class, see Dubois, *The Emergence of an Independent Women's Movement*.
[15] "The Working Women," *New York Sun*, December 17, 1863, 1.
[16] WWPU, *Fifth Annual Report* (New York: John A. Gray and Green Printers, 1868), 6.

York, and limited membership to those who contributed at least twenty-five dollars.[17] Virtually no working-class woman could afford such a sum.

The Working Women's Protective Union

The new male leaders of the Working Women's Protective Union were the publisher of the *New York Sun*, Moses S. Beach; the labor activist Daniel Walford; and attorneys George Matsell, William MacKellar, and William Roberts. They redefined the Protective Union's mission as providing "working women with legal protection from the frauds and impositions of unscrupulous employers."[18] The reorganized Protective Union would not support strikes, and it admonished working women to behave in a manner "worthy of respect and esteem."[19]

Fear of radicalism, especially women's radicalism, may have been especially pronounced after New York City's Draft Riots, which occurred in July 1863, only months before the founding of the Working Women's Union. Working-class crowds had rampaged through the city protesting the drafting of men to fight in the Civil War and the ability of the wealthy to buy their way out of military service. The rioters inflicted violence on African Americans, destroyed their property, and damaged the property of certain wealthy New Yorkers. Some accounts of the riots pointed to women's vitriolic and visible participation.[20] The riots challenged the city's elite and posed the dilemma of how the Civil War could be waged in the face of widespread social unrest and working-class anger. At least some among New York City's middle-class and elite sought to placate the hostile white working class.[21]

Given the riots and women's participation in them, the coup that wrested control of the Working Women's Union out of women's hands may have been an attempt to funnel working women's grievances into orderly legal channels controlled by professional men. As some prominent Republicans engaged in efforts to raise money to aid African Americans

---

[17] "The Working Women," *New York Sun*, December 17, 1863, 1.
[18] Ibid.
[19] "Working Womens' [*sic*] Protective Union," *New York Sun*, March 24, 1864.
[20] Mary P. Ryan, *Women in Public: Between Banners and Ballots, 1825–1880* (Baltimore: John Hopkins University Press, 1990), 148–52.
[21] See Sven Beckert, *The Monied Metropolis: New York City and the Consolidation of the Bourgeoisie* (Cambridge: Cambridge University Press, 2001), 137–41.

who were injured or had lost property in the riots, the Working Women's Protective Union provided assistance to poor white women. The Protective Union attracted the support of Democrats and Republicans alike, including such leading members of the bar as James Brady, Charles Daly, William Roberts, and Peter Cooper.[22] Charles Daly, an anti-Tammany Democrat and one of New York City's most respected judges, soon became an officer of and an ardent advocate for the Protective Union, and he enlisted the support of other New York judges and lawyers.[23]

Contrasting the material reality of working women's lives with the ideology of gender and the liberal political economy may explain why legal aid was first provided to women who worked in industry. Poor women with children but no male breadwinner had always existed, but the war made them particularly visible, numerous, and sympathetic. Popular narratives explained that women who worked in the garment trades faced the danger of starvation and would turn to prostitution out of necessity.[24] If part of the distinction between slave labor and wage labor rested on the payment of wages and the noncommodification of white women's sexuality, the argument ran, women whose employers failed to pay them were unfairly denied the benefit of this bargain. Their dire choice between

[22] "The Working Womens' [sic] Protective Union," *New York Sun*, March 24, 1864.

[23] Throughout his life, Charles Daly was one of the WWPU's staunchest supporters. Born in 1816 of Irish immigrant parents, he was a ubiquitous presence in nineteenth-century New York City. In 1844 he became a judge in the Court of Common Pleas and then chief justice of the New York State Supreme Court, a post that he held until 1885. At various periods of his life he worked on tenement reform, was president of the American Geological Society, spent a brief time in the New York State legislature, and wrote on a wide range of topics. Although Daly was a Democrat, he was widely respected outside the party. In 1856 he married Maria Lydig, the daughter of a wealthy merchant. Mrs. Daly is best known for the publication of her Civil War diary. See Maria Lydig Daly, *Diary of a Union Lady, 1861–1865*, ed. Harold Earl Hammond (1962; repr., Lincoln: University of Nebraska Press, 2000); Harold Earl Hammond, *A Commoner's Judge: The Life and Times of Charles Patrick Daly* (Boston: Christopher Publishing House, 1954). On Daly, the Geological Society, and masculinity, see Karen Morin, "Charles P. Daly's Gendered Geography, 1860–1890," *Annals of the Association of American Geographers* 98 (2008): 897–919. Morin writes, "Through his many reform activities Daly fostered a patrician relationship to New York Irish immigrants, yet assiduously aligned himself against the stereotype of physically rough and primitive Irish manliness. In this patrician capacity Daly seems to have united himself with other men in dutiful service to the unmanly or dependent" (912).

[24] See, e.g., "Sad Story of a Poor Girl," *New York Sun*, November 17, 1863, 1; "Another Working Girl's Experience," *New York Sun*, November 18, 1863, 1; "Working Womens' [sic] Protective Union," *New York Sun*, March 24, 1864.

starving and prostitution made such women resemble slaves too closely, challenging the central premise of free wage labor.[25]

For the Protective Union, the constructs of gender and wage labor functioned in tandem, allowing male lawyers to uphold the contractual paradigm of wage labor while invoking the cliché that women were helpless and worthy of aid when a male breadwinner was absent. Women, with limited employment opportunities and unequal bargaining power, needed male support to be contractual actors fully integrated into a wage-labor economy. This conceptualization of women workers stood in contrast to the equally popular understanding of male workers as self-sufficient and robust contractual actors needing no such aid. Women workers thus teetered between dependence and independence.

All of the Protective Union's cases involved women's employment, but for the union the most salient feature of a case was a woman's familial relationship, not her identity as a worker. How an organization creates categories for recordkeeping is laden with meaning, reflecting larger values regarding what the organization or its administrators consider important.[26] The Protective Union did not record the race or ethnicity of its clients, categories that later legal aid providers would find of central importance. Rather, the Protective Union recorded whether a client was married, widowed, orphaned, half-orphaned, living with parents, a soldier's wife, or a soldier's widow. These categories treated familial relationships as the defining element of women's lives, even when such information was unrelated to their legal claims.[27] It demonstrated that the women the union aided were otherwise without male breadwinners.

By far the largest number of cases that the Protective Union handled involved women in the sewing trades. Employers withheld or reduced wages for a multitude of reasons, such as allegedly substandard work, paying at a lower rate than the worker was promised or simply claiming a lack of funds. Other common practices included hiring women to do unpaid "trial" sewing for an extended period and then terminating

[25] See Amy Dru Stanley, *From Bondage to Contract: Wage Labor, Marriage, and the Market in the Age of Slave Emancipation* (Cambridge: Cambridge University Press, 1998); Eric Foner, *Free Soil, Free Labor, Free Men: The Ideology of the Republican Party before the Civil War* (Oxford: Oxford University Press, 1978); Eileen Boris, *Home to Work: Motherhood and the Politics of Industrial Homework in the United States* (New York: Cambridge University Press, 1994).

[26] See, e.g., Morin, "Daly's Gendered Geography," 897–919; Dorothy Ross, *The Making of American Social Science* (New York: Cambridge University Press, 1991).

[27] See, e.g., WWPU, *Fifth Annual Report*, 36; WWPU, *Seventh Annual Report* (New York, 1870), 10.

them without payment. Some employers required workers to pay security deposits for materials such as needles, thread, and fabrics, which employers then refused to return, claiming some sort of damage or that the deposit was nonrefundable. Women working in the sewing industry also tended to remain with an employer for a relatively short interval, always searching for better-paid work; when women left to work elsewhere, employers sometimes refused to pay the full amount they had already earned, on the grounds that the worker had breached her contract by quitting before the end of its term.[28] The Protective Union took cases valued as low as twenty-five cents and as high as $300.[29]

From its inception, the Working Women's Protective Union refused to provide legal services to domestic workers, claiming that because board and bed were provided, they did not face the privations endured by other poor working women.[30] Such exclusions insulated the benefactors of the union who, as employers of household servants, might have had their own practices scrutinized. This policy also meant that many Irish immigrant women and African American women, who filled the ranks of domestic servants, were excluded from receiving aid.[31] The Protective Union understood the racial and ethnic dimensions of its policy. Its superintendent testified to a U.S. Senate committee that although the union did not discriminate on the basis of race, few African American women sought its assistance. "Colored women are more exclusively engaged in house-service. There are not so many of them [working as] seamstresses."[32] Thus, while the union could claim that it did not discriminate against African Americans, whiteness was part of what made poor women worthy of legal aid.

The union's policy of excluding domestic workers confined the problem of working women to the industrial sphere, thereby maintaining an

---

[28] On women in the sewing trades, see Gamber, *The Female Economy*; Nancy L. Green, *Ready-to-Wear: A Century of Industry and Immigrants in Paris and New York* (Durham, NC: Duke University Press, 1997).

[29] See, e.g., WWPU, *Fifth Annual Report*, 36; WWPU, *Seventh Annual Report*, 10; WWPU, *The Work Done and Doing by the Working Women's Protective Union* (New York, 1879); U.S. Education and Labor Committee, *Senate Report upon the Relations between Capital and Labor*, vol. 5 (Washington, DC: Government Printing Office, 1885), 642 (hereinafter *Senate Report*).

[30] *Senate Report*, 638.

[31] See Faye E. Dudden, *Serving Women: Household Service in Nineteenth-Century America* (Middletown, CT: Wesleyan University Press, 1983), 60–71. In 1855 in New York City, 25 percent of Irish immigrant women and 50 percent of African American women worked as domestics. Kessler-Harris, *Out to Work*, 55.

[32] *Senate Report*, 641.

understanding that traditional domestic work stood outside the market economy and wage labor. Finally, throughout the nineteenth century in New York, the middle and upper classes believed that a domestic labor crisis existed and that domestic help generally was unreliable and unruly.[33]

In its early years, the Protective Union did not limit its advocacy to legal cases. Its fundraising benefits in the 1860s displayed the garments women produced, and workers explained the amount of sewing time and the little employers paid. One woman spoke of a pair of drawers that required 1,800 stitches and needed to be finished with buckles, button-holes, and straps. She worked from 7:00 A.M. to 9:00 P.M. and could finish four garments a day. She received only sixteen cents a pair.[34] Such exhibitions gave working women the opportunity to voice their complaints, demonstrate their skills, and educate their audiences about the economy in which they labored. As Judge Charles Daly proclaimed, these women revealed the "eloquence of facts."[35]

The Protective Union situated actual breach of contract claims on a continuum with refusals to pay a living wage. In 1868 it represented female employees of a parasol factory who actively sought out the union's assistance. Although no legal claim was involved and the women did not allege that the employer withheld wages, the union took their demands seriously. It began negotiations with the employer and asked him to imagine that his own daughters had to live on the small wages he paid.[36] Cases such as this documented the benefits won by the Protective Union while playing on men's sympathy and paternalistic concern for women.

The Protective Union also sought to create new fields of employment for women.[37] It recognized that the few jobs available to women created an oversupply of labor that drove wages down and undermined women's bargaining power. In conjunction with this effort the union operated an employment bureau, but it did not succeed in finding alternative fields of

---

[33] For discussions of domestic labor in New York City, see Maureen E. Montgomery, *Displaying Women: Spectacles of Leisure in Edith Wharton's New York* (New York: Routledge, 1998), 82–86; Hasia Diner, *Erin's Daughters in America: Irish Immigrant Women in the Nineteenth Century* (Baltimore: Johns Hopkins University Press, 1983); Dudden, *Serving Women*; Vanessa H. May, *Unprotected Labor: Household Workers, Politics, and Middle-Class Reform in New York City, 1870–1940* (Chapel Hill: University of North Carolina Press, 2011).

[34] "Working Women's Protective Union," *New York Times*, March 22, 1864, 5.

[35] WWPU, *Fifth Annual Report*, 14.

[36] Ibid., 11.

[37] Ibid., 14.

work for women. It thus placed women primarily in sewing and notions jobs. Given the importance of sewing jobs to poor women, the union sold used sewing machines to them at discounted rates, keeping the machines out of the hands of those who sold them on installment plans with exorbitant interest rates.[38]

By the mid-1880s the Protective Union's agenda became more constricted. It adopted the slogan, "Oh, if we could always get paid for our work, we could get along."[39] This phrase narrowly defined the abuses and inequities that working women experienced. It implied that if working women could just collect their wages, they could "get along" in their lives – pay their rent and buy food for themselves and their families. The motto concretized a new stance for the Protective Union: the wages women received *were* living wages. It thus rejected the claims of labor reformers and feminists that the wages employers paid women in the sewing trades were so meager that women had to supplement their incomes with prostitution.[40] In the past, the Protective Union had helped women workers negotiate for higher wages; the new slogan proclaimed that the only conflict between women workers and employers was the actual payment of wages. This reworked position justified and underwrote the existing system of wage labor, implying that it was not the system that needed reform. Instead, the problem was the behavior of individual, unreliable employers who refused to be bound by their contractual obligations. The shift in the union's mission coincided with increasingly visible and often violent conflicts between labor and capital nationwide.[41] As worker unrest grew, so did the Protective Union's stance regarding the fairness of the status quo.

Increasingly, the Protective Union portrayed working women as embodying female passivity and helplessness. These very vulnerabilities now made them worthy of legal aid. What stands out about the organization's

---

[38] WWPU, *The Work Done and Doing*, 22.

[39] WWPU, *Twenty-Five Years' History* (New York, 1888), 16–17. The WWPU claimed that the phrase was used by a working woman in 1863.

[40] For a discussion of reformers' claims that sewing women could not survive on what they were paid and had to turn to prostitution, see Stanley, *From Bondage to Contract*, 232–35.

[41] See, e.g., Michael Bellesiles, *1877: America's Year of Living Violently* (New York: New York University Press, 2010); John B. Jentz and Richard Schneirove, *Chicago in the Age of Capital: Class, Politics, and Democracy during the Civil War Reconstruction* (Urbana: University of Illinois Press, 2012); James Green, *Death in the Haymarket: A Story of Chicago, the First Labor Movement, and the Bombing that Divided Gilded-Age America* (New York: Pantheon, 2006).

depiction of the poor, helpless, working woman is not its innovation but, rather, its widespread roots in antebellum literature.[42] The union cultivated this view, describing working women as helpless, downtrodden, and defenseless. Judge Noah Davis remarked: "In this union we see a corporation created for the noblest purposes – the protection of oppressed and helpless womanhood. Its motive was the idea of pure chivalry.... Outside of infancy, there is no object so helpless as a poor girl."[43] Such language emphasized the distance between the lawyer and the female worker and substituted protection for legal rights. Moreover all women workers, no matter their age or status as family breadwinners, became helpless girls.

The Protective Union's literature stressed that only with its support could working women confront employers. One lawyer stated at a union benefit that a woman without male protection will "shrink from [her employer's] cruelty without a word, and lie down and suffer without a murmur."[44] What empowered working women were male lawyers who used the law on their behalf. The more the Protective Union highlighted the helpless working woman, the greater its power, gallantry, and masculinity appeared. A typical case involved a woman who sewed sheets for two and a half cents each. When she sought to collect her wages, the company sent her from one person to another, each claiming that he was not responsible for the payment. The union proclaimed, "Finally Catherine gave up in despair, and called on the Hercules of the UNION for help."[45] In the union's depiction of itself, it became godlike. Lawyer Fredric Coudert called the men of the WWPU "knights" who used not the sword but the law to seek redress.[46] As with a command of "Open, Sesame," the union provided justice to working women.[47] Many of New York City's elite lawyers worked at desk jobs for corporations, and their association with the union allowed them to display a "protective chivalry" that bridged the gap between the reality of lawyers' everyday lives and their fantasies of their better selves.[48]

---

[42] See Stansell, *City of Women*, 151. For a discussion of sympathy as a means to emphasize a subject's inequality, see Susan J. Pearson, *The Rights of the Defenseless: Protecting Animals and Children in Gilded-Age America* (Chicago: University of Chicago Press, 2011), 130-1.

[43] "Protection of Working Women," *New York Times*, December 9, 1879, 2.

[44] WWPU, *Twenty-Five Years' History*, 20.

[45] Ibid., 8.

[46] Ibid., 20.

[47] Ibid., 20-21.

[48] Pearson, *The Rights of the Defenseless*, 151; Robert Gordon, "'The Ideal and the Actual in Law': Fantasies and Practices of New York City Lawyers, 1870-1910," in *The New*

The Protective Union's delicate balance of female helplessness and male capacity was unstable, however. In contrast to its descriptions, women workers did not stand idle when their wages went unpaid. Rather, they constantly harassed their employers. Some even camped out at employers' homes, refusing to leave until their wages were paid. At least one woman filed suit against her employer on her own and only later came to the union for assistance.[49] Although the union never admitted it, legal redress was just one of the tools working women used, often after self-help failed.

The Protective Union was a popular charity that drew support from many of New York's elite lawyers and judges, but in contrast to its outward image, it was women who did much of the actual work.[50] The union's female superintendent and her all-female staff performed the day-to-day work of the union, including much of its legal work. Many nineteenth-century institutions that assisted women had a female superintendent on staff, to be sure, but a number of elements were unique to the superintendent's work at the Protective Union.[51]

At a time when women were not admitted to the New York State Bar, the superintendent and her female staff functioned as lay lawyers.[52] They met with each woman seeking aid and listened to her story to determine whether a colorable legal claim existed. If it did, the superintendent sent a demand letter to the employer and attempted to settle the case.[53] Only if the case did not settle and a lawsuit was imminent would the supervisor call in the Protective Union's male part-time attorney.[54] The one thing

High Priests: Lawyers in Post–Civil War America, ed. Gerard W. Gawalt (Westport, CT: Greenwood Press, 1984); Christopher Tomlins, "What Is Left of the Law and Society Paradigm after the Critique? Revisiting Gordon's 'Critical Legal Histories,'" *Law and Social Inquiry* 37 (Winter 2012): 155–66.

[49] See, e.g., WWPU, *The Work Done and Doing*, 20.

[50] See, e.g., WWPU, *Working Women's Protective Union: Third Annual Report* (New York, 1867); WWPU, *Twenty-Five Years' History*; "Protection of Working Women," *New York Times*, December 9, 1879.

[51] See, e.g., Anne M. Boylan, *The Origins of Women's Activism: New York and Boston, 1797–1840* (Chapel Hill: University of North Carolina Press, 2002).

[52] Women were not admitted to the New York State Bar until 1886. See Melissa L. Breger and Mary A. Lynch, "From Kate Stoneman to Kate Stoneman Chair, Katheryn D. Katz: Feminist Waves and the First Domestic Violence Course at a United States Law School," *Albany Law Review* 77, no. 2 (2014): 444–71.

[53] WWPU, *Seventh Annual Report*, 4–5; "Protection for Working Women," *New York Times*, November 10, 1885, 8.

[54] Ibid. By contrast, when the Legal Aid Society of New York sent a demand notice, it was written and signed by an attorney. One of its chroniclers wrote, "The demand notes would lose effect if based upon exaggerated or fraudulent claims. And here again the Legal Aid attorney's constant experience stood him in good stead. He could swiftly detect

distinguishing the supervisor's duties from those of the attorney was that she did not appear in court. By 1881, the Protective Union had formally represented more than 20,000 women.[55] The superintendent or her staff would have met with each one of them.

Yet for many years the Protective Union obscured the legal work of its female employees. Despite their service, these women were almost invisible in the union's writings; little mention of them appears in newspaper articles about the union, and they did not speak at any of its benefits. The first superintendent, Mrs. C. Brooks, did not even want her name publicly announced at the Protective Union's first annual meeting.[56] From 1868 (when the position became salaried) to 1888, Superintendent Martha W. Ferrer left scarcely a trace in the organization's public documents.

An exception was the year of Martha Ferrer's death, 1888, which also marked the WWPU's twenty-fifth anniversary. During the celebration a union officer briefly eulogized Ferrer, praising her "tender care" and "love" for the working women who came to the union's offices.[57] His description, however, eclipsed Ferrer's legal work from view. Perhaps he chose the words he did because the union did not want to publicize the fact that women lay lawyers actually did most of the organization's work, especially when a popular debate was raging over whether women should be admitted to law schools and state bars. Advocates of allowing women to practice law often were linked with the woman's rights movement and women's suffrage.[58] Such connections to those progressive reforms could have alienated supporters of the union.

The Protective Union regularly reproduced an illustration depicting "complaint day" at its office (Plate 1). The most active, prominent, and authoritative figure in the illustration is the union's male attorney, who is shown standing and berating an employer. Seated adjacent to the attorney is a female employee, and seated next to her, in the foreground, is the union's superintendent, differentiated from the client by her more

---

either the imposter or the innocently mistaken claimant." John MacArthur Maguire, *The Lance of Justice: A Semi-Centennial History of the Legal Aid Society, 1876–1926* (Cambridge, MA: Harvard University Press, 1928), 28–29. See also Chapter 3 for a full discussion of the work of the Legal Aid Society of New York.

55 WWPU, *Seventeenth Annual Report and Anniversary of the Working Women's Protective Union* (New York, 1881), 3.

56 "Local News," *The Sun*, December 14, 1864, 1.

57 WWPU, *Twenty-Five Years' History*, 28–29.

58 See Barbara Babcock, *Woman Lawyer: The Trials of Clara Foltz* (Stanford, CA: Stanford University Press, 2011); Virginia Drachman, *Women Lawyers and the Origins of Professional Identity in America* (Ann Arbor: University of Michigan Press, 1993).

elaborate dress. Although only the male attorney is portrayed as speaking, the superintendent is not passive: she sits forward in her chair, glaring at the employer. Yet in this iconic illustration, the male attorney dominates the scene. The superintendent's role is more ambiguous and less active. She is as much an audience member watching the attorney's performance as an active participant.

A later image created by Georgina Davis, a pioneering female illustrator, presents a more powerful image of the superintendent and her staff (Plate 2). The assistant superintendent sits at a desk, surrounded by women in need of the Protective Union's services. She actively engages with a woman seeking assistance, and the union's supervisor stands at the door, ready to summon the next client. The Protective Union's women employees fully command the office. Yet the union did not reproduce this illustration, as it would have undermined its image of male attorneys in control and actively engaged in its work. The union's leadership recognized that it was more palatable for society to believe that it was male lawyers who tended to the legal needs of poor women.

As the union highlighted the gallantry of male lawyers, it also used domestic imagery to portray itself, its attorneys, workers, and the women who received legal aid. This emphasis on domestic matters shifted its working-women clients from the industrial sphere of the workplace into a familial atmosphere – a protected place where women naturally belonged.[59] The day after the Protective Union's offices opened in 1864, it proclaimed, "Before the present year closes, we feel confident that hundreds of homeless working girls will look upon the headquarters of the Union, as a home, and upon the lady in charge, as a mother."[60] Here, the union's female workers became substitute mothers, and its office a domestic refuge. In 1870, the union described itself as "a home where the story of fraud could be told."[61]

The image in Plate 1 is steeped in domesticity, even though it features the union's male lawyer. Viewed out of context, it could represent

---

[59] There is a vast literature on nineteenth-century gender ideology, domesticity, and separate spheres; see, e.g., Barbara Welter, "The Cult of True Womanhood, 1820–1860," *American Quarterly* 18 (1966): 151; Katherine Kish Sklar, *Florence Kelley and the Nation's Work: The Rise of Women's Political Culture, 1830–1900* (New Haven, CT: Yale University Press, 1995); Ryan, *Women in Public*; Barbara Young Welke, *Recasting American Liberty: Gender, Law, and the Railroad Revolution, 1865–1920* (Cambridge: Cambridge University Press, 2001).

[60] "The Working Women's Protective Union," *New York Sun*, February 16, 1864.

[61] WWPU, *Seventh Annual Report*, 4.

a middle-class family at home, with the lawyer a kind and protective father and the superintendent a concerned mother, both challenging the man threatening their daughter. A later illustration in *Harper's Monthly* carried the home and family metaphor further by portraying the union's attorney and a working woman comfortably seated in front of an ornate, blazing fireplace.[62] Such imagery supported the union's claim that it provided a place that, like home, was built on benevolence, altruism, and morality – a refuge from the harsh world of the labor market, where fraud occurred. Such depictions also situated the working woman as a daughter rather than as an exploited worker.

The Protective Union's writings embraced what Michael Grossberg calls, "responsible manhood." During the antebellum period, he writes, "[The] ideal lawyer carefully reasoned through problems, soberly addressed difficulties, courageously defended the dependent, and acted as an independent crusader."[63] Grossberg concludes that the post–Civil War period marked the demise of this model. The Protective Union, however, maintained and even strengthened such imagery throughout the late nineteenth century. As this older image of the lawyer increasingly conflicted with the everyday practice of law, it may have been even more important for the men of the union to be able to see the practice of law as embodying such traditional ideals. Historian Robert W. Gordon has astutely pointed out that elite New York City lawyers in the late nineteenth century longed for a higher calling that could reconfirm the legitimacy of law and legal practice.[64] In the union they found such a place (however illusory).

The Protective Union continually emphasized that it cared about justice in the individual case, not whether a case made economic sense. Antebellum charity was based on sentiments of giving, humanity, and sympathy; postwar charity rested on scientific efficiency and a "tough-minded dollar-and-cents approach."[65] The union used gender to override this new harsher understanding. It emphasized that it joyfully and freely

[62] William Rideing, "Working Women in New York," *Harper's New Monthly Magazine* 61 (1880): 25.

[63] Michael Grossberg, "Institutionalizing Masculinity: The Law as a Male Profession," in *Meanings for Manhood: Constructions of Masculinity in Victorian America*, ed. Mark C. Carnes and Clyde Griffen (Chicago: University of Chicago Press, 1990), 138.

[64] Gordon, "'The Ideal and the Actual in Law.'"

[65] George M. Fredrickson, *The Inner Civil War: Northern Intellectuals and the Crisis of the Union* (Urbana: University of Illinois Press, 1965), 104; Ginzberg, *Women and the Work of Benevolence*; Pearson, *The Rights of the Defenseless*.

gave money to needy women, took cases that cost more money to pursue than a claim was worth, and even purchased women's legal claims at par value. Just as they did not control the home, the rules of the market did not control the union. If benevolent organizations needed to prove their professional status in a world increasingly dominated by corporations, attorneys faced the opposite problem – they needed to demonstrate that they were not captured by corporations and that they possessed hearts and souls.

In 1880 the union's treasurer told the story of a client collecting money from a judgment won by the union:

"Here is your money – seven dollars and sixty-one cents," was the Matron's greeting to the next comer. [The woman] was expressing her thanks hesitantly when she suddenly asked, "How much am I to give you out of this?..." The reply came instantly and cheerfully, "Not one cent, my good woman; it is all yours." "But you spent some money to get it; You had Jane come all the way from New Hampshire to be a witness for me. I ought to pay you for that." "Yes, I know, we paid over nine dollars for Jane's fare and nearly fifteen dollars for other expenses, but that is part of our duty."[66]

By celebrating its market *inefficiency*, the Protective Union sought to re-habilitate the image of lawyers. One union speaker told his audience, "Lawyers are not a class...which are supposed by the community to do much for nothing, and yet they do more than any other."[67] The Protective Union's documents are replete with nineteenth-century lawyer jokes, typically focused on the high fees attorneys charged.[68] The men of the union viewed their support for working women as a visible refutation of that reputation. The union declared its legal advice was "without price."[69]

The Protective Union constantly reminded its audiences that what appeared to be small sums of money actually constituted significant amounts for the working women seeking to claim them. It pointed to cases in which a dollar represented the difference between eating or starving for a poor woman and her children. Thus the benefits provided, it said, could not be measured objectively in mere dollars and cents, for the

---

[66] WWPU, *Protection for the Working Women of New York: A Report of the Sixteenth Anniversary* (New York, 1880), 3.

[67] WWPU, *Twenty-Five Years' History*, 31.

[68] See WWPU, *Plain Facts about the Working Women of New York* (New York, 1879), 13.

[69] WWPU, *Seventh Annual Report*, 5.

good it provided to individual women was larger and more significant than that.[70]

Yet sometimes the Protective Union exhibited a certain discomfort with its own embrace of market inefficiency. On occasion it claimed that its true mission was to deter employers from engaging in fraud. Therefore, its real value needed to be measured by the (unprovable) number of employers who did *not* engage in fraud because of their fear of the union. It described itself as a policeman who patrolled industry, preventing the worst abuses by employers whose "polluting waters are restrained only by constant vigilance."[71]

As the Protective Union sought to remove itself from a world driven by arm's-length bargaining, it also sought to remove its clients' claims from the paradigm of contract. The union continually described women's claims for unpaid wages as involving fraud rather than contractual breach. Yet most of the claims that the union handled were for breach of contract. This seeming contradiction sorts itself out, however, when seen in the light of the union's portrayal of the working women whose claims it sought to vindicate; they were victims rather than free contractual agents. For the union, the breach of a poor woman's contract was fraud; it smacked of immorality.

The very idea of women making contracts was steeped in the politics and recent changes in the law of coverture. This common-law doctrine held that a married woman's legal identity merged into her husband's, and that she could not own property or enter into contracts in her individual capacity.[72] Although technically applying solely to married women, coverture cast a wide net, branding all women as noncontractual actors.[73] In 1860 the New York legislature dealt a significant blow to coverture by passing the New York Earnings Act, providing that the wages earned by a married woman were her property; it also gave women enhanced

---

[70] Ibid. In a much simplified form, the union's emphasis on the subjective value of a dollar and its greater utility for a poor person reflected a larger debate among economists on the issue, led in part by Alfred Marshall. See Herbert Hovenkamp, "The Marginalist Revolution in Legal Thought," *Vanderbilt Law Review* 46 (1993): 305–59.

[71] WWPU, *Seventh Annual Report*, 5.

[72] In 1848 the New York legislature had passed a statute that allowed married women to keep separate property gained from inheritance or as a gift; however, it did not provide married women with the right to contract in their own name or the right to their wages. Norma Basch, *In the Eyes of the Law: Women, Marriage, and Property in Nineteenth-Century New York* (Ithaca, NY: Cornell University Press, 1982), 136–61.

[73] See, e.g., Ariela Dubler, "In the Shadow of Marriage: Single Women and the Legal Construction of the Family and the State," *Yale Law Journal* 112 (May 2003): 1634–1715.

contractual power over their separate property. For the first time in New York, the law (at least on paper) recognized married women as full contractual actors. The New York Earnings Act laid the groundwork for women to enter and participate in the liberal political economy.

The independent, emancipated, contracting woman of the Earnings Act stood in sharp contrast to the poor, agency-less victim championed by the Protective Union.[74] The Protective Union's stress on fraud rather than contract pointed to the cultural and legal residue of coverture.[75] In practice, coverture lingered past the end of the century, as decisions from the New York courts undermined the Earnings Act.[76] The union's use of the paradigm of fraud, therefore, may have been in part strategic: by describing such claims as arising from fraud, the union could rise above the controversy over women's contracts.

The Protective Union was unable to fully comprehend women who did not conform to the passive model it had constructed for them. Although it labeled the wronged working woman a victim of fraud, it recognized another group of women as thieves, unworthy of its protection. Its reports are replete with descriptions of "fraudulent" claims made by working women, who, unlike the good women who were victims of fraud, stood out for their brazenness, foreignness, and agency. The focus of one such

---

[74] Amy Dru Stanley writes, "The image of the contracting subject was an 'isolated man' implying that the sentimental realm where contract did not prevail was woman's sphere." Stanley, *From Bondage to Contract*, 2. Lawrence M. Friedman surmises that the nineteenth-century doctrine of contract law revolved around abstract relationships. "Pure contract doctrine is blind to details of subject matter and person. It does not ask who buys, who sells, and what is bought and sold.... [I]t is a deliberate renunciation of the particular, a deliberate relinquishment of the temptation to restrict untrammeled individual autonomy." Lawrence M. Friedman, *Contract Law in America: A Social and Economic Case Study* (Madison: University of Wisconsin Press, 1965), 20–22. Grant Gilmore approvingly cites Friedman and argues that late nineteenth- and early twentieth-century contract law drew a sharp distinction between contract and tort. Grant Gilmore, *The Death of Contract* (Columbus: Ohio State University Press, 1974), 6–7, 87–88.

[75] Norma Basch has demonstrated that the New York judiciary often eviscerated the intent of the Earnings Act and continued to apply the common law rules of coverture. Basch, *In the Eyes of the Law*, 200–213. See also Hendrik Hartog, *Man and Wife in America: A History* (Cambridge, MA: Harvard University Press, 2000); Nancy Cott, *Public Vows: A History of Marriage and the Nation* (Cambridge, MA: Harvard University Press, 2000); Norma Basch, *Framing American Divorce: From the Revolutionary Generation to the Victorians* (Berkeley: University of California Press, 1999); Stanley, *From Bondage to Contract*, 206–17.

[76] See Reva B. Siegel, "The Modernization of Marital Status Law: Adjudicating Wives' Rights to Earnings, 1860–1930," *Georgetown Law Journal* 82 (1994): 2127, 2156–58; Birkbeck v. Ackroyd, 74 N.Y. 356 (1878); Reynolds v. Robinson, 64 N.Y. 589 (1876); Porter v. Dunn, 30 N.E. 122 (N.Y. 1892).

case was a woman named Bridgette, who complained to the union that she had made a dozen vests and her employer failed to pay her. Upon investigation, the union learned that she had completed only two vests but demanded that her employer pay for all twelve. Confronted by the union, Bridgette is described as responding, "Why shouldn't I make sure of me money? Hasen't he plinty of it, Id like to know? Ye're chaits yourself, that's what ye are." The union immediately obtained a warrant allowing it to seize the vests and materials that Bridgette had refused to relinquish to the employer.[77] In this story, the union made certain that its readers recognized the Irishness of the dishonest Bridgette. By highlighting such stories, the union assured that it was an advocate not just for working women but for the larger contractual regime.

One of the most striking contradictions afflicting the Protective Union's view of working women was the role played by women employers. The union usually depicted its adversaries as male, yet it also took cases involving female employers. These women, commonly dressmakers, point to the type of businesses the union often confronted – they were owners of small establishments teetering at the edge of solvency. As an indication of their financial straits, some women employers had to pay even very small amounts due to employees in multiple installments.[78]

The Protective Union found that bringing claims against women was particularly vexing. Such female entrepreneurs often were judgment-proof and repeat offenders. Although New York abolished imprisonment for debt in 1837, in the mid-1860s the union lobbied for and the New York legislature passed a law that gave judges discretion to imprison a man who failed to satisfy a judgment related to the payment of a woman's wage. The law provided solely for the imprisonment of men, and only when they failed to pay a woman's wages. Women workers required protection only from male employers, the law implied, and male laborers did not require such drastic state action for their protection. Yet by the late 1860s, the union lamented that there was no such punishment for female employers.[79]

[77] WWPU, *Report of the Sixteenth Anniversary*, 3.

[78] See, e.g., WWPU, *Twenty-Five Years' History*, 11.

[79] WWPU, *Fifth Annual Report*, 29. See also, *Senate Report*, 641. The New York legislature did not extend the law to cover male employees with wage claims until 1902. Female employers were not subject to arrest until 1915. Maguire, *The Lance of Justice*, 117–18. Beginning in the 1890s, various state committees debated extending the law to encompass female employees; see "Women Employers Are Unjust," *New York Times*, June 16, 1895, 5.

The Protective Union often found itself at a loss to explain the behavior of women employers who violated so consistently the reigning ideal of how women were supposed to behave. In 1880 the union's superintendent discussed with a benefactor the case of an art dealer who refused to pay for paintings sold on consignment. She commented, "But sir, the worst part of the whole story is that this dealer is a woman! It is a woman who thus seeks... to swindle one of her own sex!... [A]ccustomed as I am to *men's* swindles, these, by women, make me burn with intense indignation!"[80] The union understood female employers' failure to pay wages and the "cruelty" that they exhibited toward their workers as worse than men's treatment of women. One speaker explained, "It is one of those anomalies that I have never been able to account for that women are more cruel to each other than men are to them."[81]

The union also chastised middle-class and elite women's behavior as consumers, pointing out that they willingly wore the products that working women produced at starvation wages. "There is many a ball at Delmonico's to which the lady comes in a dress which is the jealousy and agony of all her sisters,... and yet this dress is sown [*sic*] with tears and fraud."[82] Well-to-do women, the speaker lamented, often spent money beyond their "allowance and the easiest person to cheat or put off is the seamstress."[83] Although there may well have been some truth in these claims, the union did not similarly chide male consumers.

One Protective Union case featured Catherine, a dressmaker, and her customer Mrs. Stewart. When Catherine asked for her wages, Mrs. Stewart claimed that she could not pay until after Christmas, even though Catherine was at that time quite ill. She told Catherine, "I have no more than enough money for my Christmas presents now."[84] The union approached Mrs. Stewart's husband with the claim, "which he immediately paid."[85] Its actions and words implied that even middle-class women

---

[80] WWPU, *Report of the Sixteenth Anniversary*, 5 (emphasis in original).

[81] Ibid., 9. See also, *Senate Report*, 644. Here the WWPU superintendent testified that male and female employers were equally at fault in refusing to pay wages.

[82] WWPU, Protection for the Working Women of New York: Eighteenth Annual Report and Anniversary (New York, 1882), 9.

[83] Ibid. For a discussion of the fashion practices and pressures that elite New York women faced, see Montgomery, *Displaying Women*.

[84] WWPU, *Twenty-Five Years' History*, 12.

[85] Ibid. In another case, a woman hired a seamstress to sew two dresses but refused to pay her fifteen dollars upon their completion. Although the woman's husband told the seamstress that he was not responsible for his wife's debts, when the union threatened to sue, he paid the debt. WWPU, *Working Women's Protective Union Thirty-First Year* (New York, 1894), 6.

were not entirely reliable contractual actors. Rather, they had to be disciplined by husbands, attorneys, and courts into complying with a contractual regime.

Despite the Protective Union's ambiguous stance regarding the visibility of its own female employees' legal labor, the organization linked women as recipients and providers of legal aid. It also successfully provided legal aid to tens of thousands of women. The union established a model for how a legal aid organization could be structured using non-lawyers. Elite and middle-class women in other parts of the country learned of and were inspired by it. Using the Working Women's Protective Union as a model for their own work, they further developed the role of women lay lawyers.

Boston's Women's Educational and Industrial Union

A number of women's organizations in the 1880s began to showcase the legal labor of their members, further building a female dominion of legal aid. Boston's Women's Educational and Industrial Union was the first women's organization to create a legal aid committee, and it was no mere copy of the Working Women's Protective Union. Where the Protective Union situated itself, its workers, and its clients outside the market in the framework of domestic space, the Women's Educational and Industrial Union brought the marketplace into the domestic sphere, specializing in the wage claims of domestic workers. Just as important, it saw legal assistance as a way to heal growing class rifts between the poor and wealthier classes.

By the 1870s, women's clubs were forming in American cities, spurred by the increasing role of women in philanthropy during the Civil War, by the expanding acceptance of education for women, and by the influence of a small but growing women's movement. These clubs were generally composed of elite and middle-class women; to varying degrees, they combined elements of self-education, civic reform, and the provision of charitable and educational services to poor and working-class women. Beginning in the late nineteenth century and continuing into the early twentieth century, these clubs expanded enormously – in terms of membership and in the types of activities in which they were involved.[86]

---

[86] There is a vast literature on women's changing roles following the Civil War and the growth of women's organizations. See, e.g., Christine Stansell, *The Feminist Promise: 1792 to the Present* (New York: Modern Library, 2011); Ruth Borden, *Frances Willard: A Biography* (Chapel Hill: University of North Carolina Press, 2001); Sklar, *Florence Kelley and the Nation's Work*; Nancy Cott, *The Grounding of Modern Feminism*

Boston's Women's Educational and Industrial Union became one of the nation's most important Progressive Era organizations, devoted to a wide range of reform activities, especially women's employment. Harriet Clisby, a pioneering woman physician, founded the organization in Boston in 1877 with Julia Ward Howe and a number of other prominent women.[87] Although the Educational and Industrial Union was created and controlled by elite and middle-class women, its vision was to forge cross-class alliances. The use of *union* in its name symbolized the gathering of all women together in social intercourse and mutual uplift. One of its early presidents declared, "The Payment of one dollar, annually, constitutes membership, with no limitations, as the aim of the society is, to help those who are most in need, whatever the necessity and above all to form a Union."[88]

Unlike the case of the Working Women's Protective Union, the Boston union was propelled by a strong sense of Christian fellowship, community, and social action. The leaders of the Educational and Industrial Union saw women – innately moral – as uniquely situated for spreading and enacting what it called the Social Gospel, which it interpreted broadly to include women's rights.[89] Speaking of the need for women's economic, social, political, and spiritual equality, its president exclaimed, "Will there never be an uprising of the slaves, a declaration of independence? Never, until she stands on equal ground with man, equally free to decide questions of duty, equally bound to develop all the powers of her being."[90] This comparison of women's inequality to slavery, a strong theme in antebellum feminism, also reflected the abolitionist roots of many of the Boston union's officers.[91]

(New Haven, CT: Yale University Press, 1989); Theda Skocpol, *Protecting Soldiers and Mothers: The Political Origins of Social Policy in the United States* (Cambridge, MA: Belknap Press of Harvard University Press, 1995); Karen J. Blair, *The Clubwoman as Feminist: True Womanhood Redefined, 1868–1914* (Teaneck, NJ: Holmes and Meier Publishers, 1980).

[87] Sarah Deutsch, *Woman and the City*, 144.

[88] Women's Educational and Industrial Union (WEIU), *Report of the Women's Educational and Industrial Union for the Year ending May 7, 1879* (Boston, 1879), 13, Women's Educational and Industrial Union, Schlesinger Library, Radcliffe Institute, Harvard University (hereinafter WEIU Papers).

[89] See, e.g., WEIU, *Report of the Women's Educational and Industrial Union for the Year ending May 1, 1884* (Boston, 1884), 13–15, WEIU Papers. Wendy J. Deichmann Edwards and Carolyn De Swarte Gifford, eds., *Gender and the Social Gospel* (Urbana: University of Illinois Press, 2003).

[90] WEIU, *Report for 1884*, 13.

[91] On abolitionism and feminism, see Cott, *The Roots of Modern Feminism*; Kathryn Kish Sklar, *Women's Rights Emerges within the Anti-Slavery Movement, 1830–1870*

In 1878, consciously emulating the Working Women's Protective Union, the Educational and Industrial Union created a Protective Committee to provide free legal advice to poor and working-class women. The union's board explained that it had long contemplated establishing such a committee, but doing so at first seemed "too weighty a matter" and required substantial "strength," language that indicated the seriousness with which the board approached the idea of the committee, as well as its hesitancy to expand into areas not considered to be within a woman's domain.[92] Although the Boston union publicized and celebrated the creation of the committee, it cautioned that ensuring women's legal rights was no more or less important than the other work that the organization performed.[93] Legal assistance was part of its larger agenda, which included everything from creating a reading room for working women to vocational training and a wide array of reform activities.

Unlike the Working Women's Protective Union, which was managed by a full-time superintendent and her staff, volunteers conducted the work of the Protective Committee. The committee also enlisted the help of a number of Boston attorneys, including Samuel Sewall, the husband of Harriett Sewall, an active committee member. The Sewalls, part of a prominent Massachusetts family, had been vociferous abolitionists and were strong supporters of women's rights. Samuel Sewall had represented runaway slaves and the radical abolitionist John Brown. Thus, offering free legal counsel in connection with a larger cause was not new to either of the Sewalls. What was new was the union's belief that upper-class women could do such work themselves.

Volunteers staffed the Protective Committee's office two or three days a week for a couple of hours a day. They listened to complaints from women who visited the office (whom they called clients), investigated their claims, and made personal appeals to those who owed money to a client.[94] As the committee learned, providing such services required significant time, energy, and skill. The chairperson explained, "It means hours to be spent by these ladies over one case, and ever so many persons

(New York: Palgrave Macmillan, 2000); Kathryn Kish Sklar, *Women's Rights and Transatlantic Antislavery in the Era of Emancipation* (New Haven, CT: Yale University Press, 2007); Stanley, *From Bondage to Contract*.

[92] WEIU, *Report for 1879*, 12.

[93] Ibid., 13.

[94] See, e.g., WEIU, *Report for 1879*, 21–22; WEIU, *Report of the Women's Educational and Industrial Union for the Year Ending May 2, 1882* (Boston, 1882), 40; WEIU, *Report for 1884*, 44.

to be seen, and requires not only listening, but talking, which must be so circumspect, yet kind, that it is more fatiguing than when impulsive; and also an endless amount of walking about from one distant street to another, for people are never at home."[95]

Domestic workers, boardinghouse owners, washerwomen, and seamstresses sought the Protective Committee's aid in collecting unpaid wages or bills. In its first year, the committee handled the complaint of a washerwoman who claimed that a Harvard student owed her $7.00. Another woman claimed that her boarder owed her $12.00, and a sewing woman sought $5.83 owed to her by a dressmaker.[96] Some of the most pitiful cases involved boardinghouse operators who seized the possessions of boarders who had failed to pay rent. At times, these possessions might include the woman's only coat, a comb, or even a pair of stockings.[97] That legal disputes revolved around such meager possessions indicates the poverty of many of the committee's clients. Nonetheless, the committee treated such claims seriously, and its volunteers spent long hours working to have the items returned to their clients. Although the committee did not record the race of its clients, undoubtedly it accepted African American clients, because such women often worked as domestics and laundresses, the principal occupations of the committee's clients.

Year after year the committee took on hundreds of very small claims, and members often expressed frustration at their inability to collect even those payments from parties who were too poor to pay.[98] Cases handled by the Working Women's Protective Union and the Protective Committee of the Industrial and Educational Union both presented the familiar pattern of cascading financial problems. Dressmakers, clients commissioning dresses, or householders employing domestic labor would not pay their employees, who in turn would be unable to pay for the rooms where they boarded, and in response the boardinghouse operator would evict them and retain their possessions.[99]

By the 1880s, the Protective Committee's caseload had grown and involved even more impoverished women. Working women who

---

[95] WEIU, *Report of the Women's Educational and Industrial Union for the Year Ending May 8, 1880* (Boston, 1880), 36, WEIU Papers.

[96] WEIU, *Report for 1884*, 13.

[97] WEIU, *Report of the Women's Educational and Industrial Union for the Year Ending May 1, 1886* (Boston, 1886), 40, WEIU Papers.

[98] WEIU, *Report of the Women's Educational and Industrial Union for the Year Ending May 2, 1882* (Boston, 1882), 48, WEIU Papers.

[99] See, e.g., WEIU, *Report for 1880*, 38.

habitually went unpaid had learned "the art of starving yet living," the committee reported.[100] Like the Working Women's Protective Union, the committee spoke of justice rather than economic efficiency, and its members believed that even the smallest claims were worth pursuing: "In speaking of our purpose, we always emphasize the painful fact that, to a needy sick person, even a few cents due her acquire a magnitude that one beyond want can only realize through sympathy; and, for that reason, we shall always set ourselves earnestly to work for this practical body and spirit saving work."[101] The committee reasoned that, even when it could collect nothing, its clients were gratified to know that the committee took their claims seriously.[102] The committee even boasted that its relentless pursuit of wage cases so infuriated employers that some called it the "Society for the Protection of Injustice and Incompetency."[103] Employers and others undoubtedly believed that they were entitled to withhold payments from employees for reasons of unsatisfactory work and hinted at the committee's lack of legal knowledge. Although many of the parties whom the committee pursued were poor themselves, the committee also was critical of wealthier employers; even when honest employers paid employees their wages, it said, the sums did not entail a living wage.[104]

The Protective Committee was the first organization to offer legal services to domestic servants. Although it was widely believed by the upper classes that domestic workers were privileged, the reality was that women workers often viewed domestic labor as highly exploitative, as it paid less than factory work, required longer hours, and offered little unsupervised time.[105] Additionally, domestic servants often had difficulty collecting their wages. Some mistresses claimed that they did not have the funds to pay when wages were due; others deducted from wages for poorly performed work or for damage to household items. It was also

---

[100] See, e.g., WEIU, *Report of the Women's Educational and Industrial Union 1898–1899* (Boston, 1899), 51, WEIU Papers.

[101] WEIU, *Report for 1884*, 46.

[102] Ibid.

[103] Ibid.

[104] WEIU, *Report for 1880*, 34.

[105] See Vanessa May, *Unprotected Labor: Household Workers, Politics, and Middle-Class Reform in New York, 1870–1940* (Chapel Hill: University of North Carolina Press, 2011); Lara Vapnek, *Breadwinners: Working Women and Economic Independence, 1865–1920* (Urbana: University of Illinois Press, 2009); Deutsch, *Women and the City*, 61; David Katzman. *Seven Days a Week: Women and Domestic Service in Industrializing America* (New York: Oxford University Press, 1978); Daniel Sutherland, *Americans and Their Servants: Domestic Service in the United States from 1800 to 1920* (Baton Rouge: Louisiana State University Press, 1981); Dudden, *Serving Women*.

common practice to dismiss servants before their term of service was complete and then refuse to pay for the work performed.[106] Domestic workers' unions in Boston and Chicago were weak and short-lived, in part because the work confined servants to individual households and left them with little time to meet.[107]

The Protective Committee's position – that domestic employment was wage work and potentially exploitive – was unique. Its members were critical of other women of their own class and stature and brought cases even against "well-known persons."[108] As the number of cases involving domestic servants increased, the Protective Committee gently urged any mistress who experienced "domestic troubles" to recognize that "the imperfections of her household are due to herself."[109] Moreover, the committee pushed upper-class women to acknowledge their legal duties to domestic workers; as it explained:

wages are due for services rendered even if girls have behaved badly.... The relation between servants and employers is one of contract; the "reasonable service" the girl is expected to render, however variously interpreted, does *not* exonerate the housekeeper from fulfillment of her part of the contract. After wages have been paid, girls can be sued for chipped china, broken teapots, or slander.[110]

Virtually no other provider of legal aid was as willing to take such cases or to interpret so liberally when wages were owed to domestic workers.

The union's Protective Committee firmly situated domestic employment within the realm of contract. It insisted that domestic workers and employers enter into written agreements, setting forth clear terms regarding wages, duties, and duration of employment. Employment relationships based on mutual trust and unstated assumptions all too often led to disputes, the union maintained.[111] It further warned domestic workers to leave their employment immediately if employers either failed to pay wages when due or asked workers for loans or credit. The committee understood that treating domestic labor as subject to a contract would modernize the relationship, redefining it as another form of wage labor.

[106] Dudden, *Serving Women*, 87–93. WEIU, *Report for 1882*, 45.
[107] See Vapnek, *Breadwinners*.
[108] See, e.g., WEIU, *Report for 1881*, 40.
[109] WEIU, *Report of the Women's Educational and Industrial Union for the Year Ending May 1, 1888* (Boston, 1888), 36.
[110] WEIU, *Report for 1883*, 45.
[111] See, e.g., WEIU, *Report of the Women's Educational and Industrial Union for the Year Ending May 7, 1889* (Boston, 1889), 36–37, WEIU Papers.

Without the legal certainty and security of a contract, the Women's Educational and Industrial Union reported, domestics often felt like "slaves," and many mistresses treated their servants as "property."[112] Contracts thus were necessary to bring such labor clearly into the realm of dignified free wage labor.[113]

The committee also performed a disciplinary function in connection with domestic workers' performance. One of the Boston union's major projects was a school that trained young women properly as cooks and housekeepers. It also ran an employment agency.[114] The committee described some claims in which domestics were legally entitled to their wages but were not morally entitled to them, owing to "impertinence," "carelessness," "negligence," or "imprudence."[115] The committee might take on such morally dubious cases, but it also lectured those clients on appropriate work ethics and demeanor. In some cases, it barred such women from using the union's employment agency.[116]

Members of the Protective Committee understood that they were engaging in legal work, and they publicized and took pride in that fact. They stressed the need for women involved in philanthropic efforts to learn law, and they saw their own legal knowledge as enhancing their effectiveness and "opportunity for action."[117] As members of the committee gained more legal experience, they proudly relied less on their consulting attorneys. In 1881 the committee announced, "While none the less grateful to our counsel, we feel that our own success in obtaining payments is much more marked than it was last year, for fully one-half of the cases brought to us have we ourselves settled."[118] A year later another

---

[112] WEIU, *Trained and Supplementary Workers in Domestic Service*, 34–35, WEIU Papers, box 1, folder 5, cited in Deutsch, *Women and the City*, 150.

[113] On the complicated transition between slavery and wage labor and the role of the household, see Stanley, *From Bondage to Contract*; Peggie R. Smith, "Regulating Paid Housework: Class, Gender, Race, and Agendas of Reform," *American University Law Review* 48 (April 1999): 851–923.

[114] See Deutsch, *Women and the City*; Vapnek, *Breadwinners*.

[115] WEIU, *Report for 1883*, 45.

[116] Many women's organizations created employment agencies for domestic workers because upper-class women viewed many for-profit agencies as untrustworthy, given that they often took payment from domestic workers but failed to find them jobs. Likewise, employers often found the domestic workers placed by such agencies to be untrained and undisciplined. The first such effort by women occurred in 1825 in New York with the founding of the New York Society for the Encouragement of Faithful Domestic Servants. Dudden, *Serving Women*, 82–85.

[117] WEIU, *Report of the Women's Educational and Industrial Union for the Year Ending May 2, 1882* (Boston, 1882), 49, WEIU Papers.

[118] WEIU, *Report for 1881*, 39.

report boasted, "Mrs. Sewall and Mrs. Willey are the prosecuting agents of the department. They hear and investigate all complaints, and have already attained such legal skill that the Boston bar could properly call them *sisters-in-law*."[119]

The report imagined these women opening their own law firm and thus crossing the boundary between lay lawyer and professional lawyer: "In the future there may be a firm of Mesdames Sewall and Willey.... One should see the calm persistency.... They listen for hours of tales that could be told in ten minutes. They win the confidence and learn the secret grieves or zealous hatreds of their plaintiffs."[120] It concluded, "Their duty of lawyers completed, as kindly women they follow the struggling, faint-hearted, often hungry plaintiff to her attic, give her a dinner, find her work."[121] This account reflects a gendered dynamic in which women's sympathy, empathy, and patience were highly valued. These women worked first as lawyers, and then took up their maternal role of caring and providing for their clients' material needs. This resulted in a combination of "legal skill and womanly tact."[122]

The community called Sewall and Willey the "lady lawyers," and women went to the union to "inquire about many points of law."[123] As members of the committee gained legal knowledge and identified themselves as being akin to lawyers, they also explained that their work required special talent. A volunteer needed to possess dedication and legal knowledge. It explained, "Our work cannot be done by many. It must have special agents."[124]

Yet even with experience, the women of the committee recognized that they were dependent on male lawyers to bring cases to court. With ire and sarcasm, the Protective Committee members remarked that lawyers were necessary to administer "all that part of the law which is outside the pale of permitted feminine ability."[125] In 1888, those limits changed when Leila Robinson, a professionally trained lawyer and the first woman to become a member of the Massachusetts Bar, began volunteering for the

---

[119] WEIU, *Report for 1882*, 46 (emphasis in original).
[120] WEIU, *Report for 1884*, 43.
[121] Ibid., 44.
[122] WEIU, *Report for 1888*, 36.
[123] Ibid.; WEIU, *Report of the Women's Educational and Industrial Union for the Year Ending May 1, 1886* (Boston, 1886), 41, WEIU Papers.
[124] WEIU, *Report of the Women's Educational and Industrial Union for the Year Ending May 1, 1883* (Boston, 1883), 44, WEIU Papers.
[125] WEIU, *Report for 1882*, 46.

committee and acting as its attorney.[126] With the addition of Robinson, the committee curtailed its dependence on male lawyers and began to build a women's legal institution.[127]

At times, however, the committee sought to distinguish itself from the legal profession. A significant difference between women lay lawyers and male professional lawyers, one that would resonate and provoke controversy for decades, was the issue of fees. Women lay lawyers and their organizations refused to charge their clients fees or to take a percentage of any recovery. One of the Protective Committee's male legal advisers tried to convince the members to institute a fee, arguing that free legal advice was too much like charity and that paying fees would make those they aided "feel more independent."[128] The committee rejected the idea, adamant that its services should be free: "We are thus stringent that the women may not feel that justice procured on their behalf rebounds to any one's benefit."[129] A client could always make a donation "if thereby she will feel more independent."[130] The committee found it absurd to believe that a woman living on the brink of poverty, who labored day in and day out, would feel dependent if she received free legal aid to help her get the wages that already were justly hers.

The Protective Committee did not treat its clients simply as workers with legal problems. Adopting a philosophy that later women labor activists would call "bread and roses," the committee understood its work as integrated with the union's larger mission.[131] "We exist, to protect [women] in regard to payment of wages, that thus protected, they may live better in their homes, and living better, find more time and health for occasional enjoyment of a lecture or social evening."[132] Legal aid was about more than a monetary award or winning a case; it was part of the

---

[126] On Leila Robinson see Drachman, *Women Lawyers*.

[127] See Estelle Freedman, "Separatism as Strategy: Female Institution Building and American Feminism, 1870–1930," *Feminist Studies* 5 (Autumn 1979): 512–29.

[128] WEIU, Protective Committee Minutes, February 23, 1880, series 2, box 6, folder 106, WEIU Papers, quoted in Deutsch, *Woman and the City*, 150.

[129] Protective Committee Minutes, March 8, 1880, series 2, box 6, folder 106, WEIU Papers, quoted in Deutsch, *Woman and the City*, 150.

[130] WEIU, *Report for 1880*, 37.

[131] "Bread and roses" refers to the idea that a working-class woman needed decent wages which would allow her to live a full life, including access to education and cultural activities. On this concept, see, e.g., Annelise Orleck, *Common Sense and a Little Fire: Women and Working-Class Politics in the United States, 1900–1965* (Chapel Hill: University of North Carolina Press, 1995).

[132] WEIU, *Report for 1880*, 34.

larger goal of enabling working women to achieve self-sufficiency and enrichment.

At the same time, the Protective Committee avoided certain kinds of cases on the grounds that they were too controversial or required more time and legal acumen than the committee possessed. One example was the committee's refusal to take paternity cases.[133] It was one thing to pressure employers to pay wages due; it was another to threaten men with lawsuits for support of children sired out of wedlock. Likewise, the committee did not accept divorce cases or even cases in which women sought support payments from husbands.

By the turn of the century, the idea that women could provide legal aid to other women had become acceptable, and it quickly spread from Boston to other cities in the East, including Philadelphia, Rochester, Buffalo, Jersey City, and Washington, D.C.[134] These new organizations looked to the Working Women's Protective Union and the Women's Educational and Industrial Union's Protective Committee as models for how women could provide legal aid and as evidence of the immense, unmet need for such aid, especially in cases involving women's wages.

Yet the work of these new women's legal aid organizations was severely limited. Staffed entirely by volunteers, they did not have the capacity to

---

[133] WEIU, Protective Committee Minutes, April 28, 1879, series 2, carton 6, folder 106, WEIU Papers, quoted in Deutsch, *Women and the City*, 61.

[134] See, e.g., Rochester WEIU, *Year Book of the Woman's Educational and Industrial Union, Rochester, New York, 1896–1897* (Rochester: H. D. Bryan Printers); Buffalo WEIU, *First Annual Report of the Buffalo Women's Educational and Industrial Union for the Year Ending May 1st, 1885* (Buffalo: Courier Company, 1885); Barbara Petrick, *Mary Philbrook: Radical Feminist in New Jersey* (New Jersey: New Jersey Historical Society, 1981) (discussing establishment of a legal aid organization at Whittier Settlement House in New Jersey); Legal Aid Society of Philadelphia, *First Annual Report* (Philadelphia, 1903) (discussing predecessor organization, the Committee for the Legal Protection of Working Women, run by women). Letter from Arthur von Briesen to Carolina Cook, April 27, 1912, Arthur von Briesen Papers, Public Policy Papers, Department of Rare Books and Special Collections, Princeton University Library, box 5, folder 19 (discussing the early existence in Washington, D.C., of a women's legal aid organization). In addition, sometime between the 1870s and the 1890s, Rebecca Cole, the second African American graduate of a U.S. medical school and a public health expert, formed the Women's Directory, which provided free medical and legal advice to poor women. However, the lack of extant records makes it difficult to know who was providing legal services, who the clients were, and what types of cases were handled. See Darlene Clark Hine, "Co-Laborers in the Work of the Lord," in *The "Racial" Economy of Science: Toward a Democratic Future*, ed. Sandra Harding (Bloomington: Indiana University Press; 1993); Charlotte Abby, "Illegitimacy and Sex Perversion," in *A Child Welfare Symposium*, ed. William Henry Slingerland (New York: Russell Sage, 1915), 24.

handle more than a few hundred cases a year in each city. Even the simplest legal cases required significant time and energy and often were frustrating, as defendants at times turned out to be as poor as the plaintiffs. Moreover, legal aid was only a small part of the organizations' larger mission. New York's Working Women's Protective Union, in contrast, had the capacity to handle a large number of cases thanks to its full-time staff of women, but its board of directors (consisting overwhelmingly of male lawyers) never sought to expand the kinds of cases that it accepted. In Chicago, however, women's organized reform activities, and an agenda grounded in feminism – combined with a sophisticated critique of law and the legal system – produced an expansive dominion of women's legal aid.

2

The Chicago Experience

The Maturation of Women's Legal Aid

Women's dominion of legal aid came to full fruition with the founding of Chicago's Protective Agency for Women and Children (PAWC) in 1885. The agency provided legal and nonlegal services to poor and working-class women. Its leaders saw women's exploitation as arising from the distinct but connected realms of the home, the marketplace, and the state. Aiding poor women was crucial to the agency's mission, but a corollary was that its leaders often held poor, working-class, and immigrant men responsible for much of the harm that poor women experienced. They further understood that such male behavior called for intervention on the part of elite white women. Owing to their members' gender, class standing, and cultural capital, the agency was able to get its foot in the door of Chicago's municipal legal institutions. Over time, the agency's power grew as it accumulated substantial experience and legal knowledge. Many of its ideas and practices would be incorporated by later legal aid organizations and would be institutionally formalized when Chicago created its juvenile and domestic relations courts.

The Chicago Women's Club

The Protective Agency for Women and Children began without fanfare, growing out of the Chicago Women's Club (CWC). Caroline M. Brown, a wealthy woman and the mother of two children, founded the club in 1876 when she invited twenty-one women to meet in her living room to learn about and discuss the' pressing social, political, and cultural issues of the day. Brown was acutely aware of the limited sphere in which respectable women could maneuver and worried that some might take a dim view of the club. In the aftermath of the disastrous Chicago fire in 1872, however, the city was a particularly hospitable place for such a group. Women had created organizations to provide charity and relief to victims of the fire, thus starting the tradition of women's organizing in Chicago.[1] Without quite knowing it, Brown began articulating the rationale for what would come to be known as "municipal housekeeping," the idea that women's roles as mothers and housewives required them to be knowledgeable about and involved in issues affecting the home and children that, as the nineteenth century progressed, involved an ever-widening swath of activity.[2] Recalling the club's formation, Brown wrote, "Timid souls who feared that woman might get outside her sphere could surely not object to [her] serving in the interests of the home. Mothers all take a lively interest in education; all good church workers might lend a hand to philanthropy, and the unterrified would gravitate toward reform."[3]

The women of the CWC spent the first year engaging in a program of self-education, with the understanding that eventually they would "take up some of the live issues of this world."[4] The first overtly political activity that the club undertook was a campaign to appoint women to the Chicago Board of Education.[5] This issue appealed to women reformers of all types around the country, as it fit easily with the understanding that women were responsible for and knowledgeable about children. The club's efforts in this particular controversy failed, but it soon began holding large public meetings demanding the appointment of women to a variety of city public offices. As the CWC's demands became stronger and more public, its arguments expanded. Its leaders proclaimed, "The interest of the women of Chicago on all that pertain to education, whether

---

[1] See Maureen A. Flanagan, *Seeing with Their Hearts: Chicago Women and the Vision of the Good City, 1871–1933* (Princeton, NJ: Princeton University Press, 2002).

[2] On the idea and tropes of municipal housekeeping, see, e.g., Mary Ritter Beard, *Woman's Work in Municipalities* (1915; repr., New York: Arno Press, 1972); Seth Koven and Sonya Michael, eds., *Mothers of a New World: Maternalist Politics and the Origins of Welfare States* (New York: Routledge, 1993); Ruth Bordin, *Frances Willard: A Biography* (Chapel Hill: University of North Carolina Press, 1986); Kathryn Kish Sklar, *Florence Kelley and the Nation's Work: The Rise of Women's Political Culture, 1880–1900* (New Haven, CT: Yale University Press, 1995); Anne Meis Knupfer, *Toward a Tenderer Humanity and a Nobler Womanhood: African American Women's Clubs in Turn-of-the-Century Chicago* (New York: New York University Press, 1996).

[3] Henriette Greenbaum Frank and Amalie Hofer Jerome, *Annals of the Chicago Woman's Club for the First Forty Years of Its Organization: 1876–1916* (Chicago: Libby Company, 1916), 16. Contained in the *Annals* are many of the minutes from the CWC.

[4] Ibid., 16.

[5] Ibid., 28–29.

as mothers, teachers, or citizens, being as great as that of men, entitles them to a voice."[6] The club would use similar arguments to support women's suffrage. Club leaders understood their actions as radical and impinging on the borders of what society considered women's appropriate sphere. The club's history declared: "It seemed as advanced in '76 to belong to a Club in the eyes of many good house-mothers, as it would in this day to run for State Senators."[7]

Until the early 1880s, the club's work focused primarily on its members' own education and increasing elite and middle-class women's power in municipal government through appointments to office. The club's members also grappled with how to undertake a major and sustained project that involved "practical work," which meant hands-on work with the poor.[8] They found one way in 1881, when the club founded the Women's Physiological Institute of Chicago in cooperation with local women physicians. The institute's purpose was to educate working-class and poor mothers about infant hygiene and care. (In the late 1880s the institute was moved to Hull House.)[9]

The CWC's second project involved placing a female night matron in each of the city's police stations, by participating in hiring for the position and raising funds for the matron's salary. The club conducted this work in tandem with the Women's Christian Temperance Union, which already sponsored a day matron. Again, the issue of using women police matrons was one embraced by numerous women's organizations across the country because it involved the supervision of working-class and poor women under the rationale of protecting women's virtue from male prisoners as well as from policemen.[10] Its responsibility for the night matron gave CWC members cause to visit the jails as well as to follow imprisoned women's cases through court proceedings. They observed firsthand the treatment of poor women and girls in Chicago courts as defendants, witnesses, and victims.

The Protective Agency for Women and Children

These early experiences underlay the CWC's decision to create the Protective Agency for Women and Children in 1885. The Protective Agency

---

[6] Ibid., 70–71.
[7] Ibid., 9.
[8] Ibid., 40–41
[9] Ibid., 37.
[10] Ibid., 42, 76–77.

announced as its objective: "To secure justice for women and children, to give legal counsel free of charge, and to extend moral support to the wronged and helpless."[11] Sponsoring clubs included the Cook County Suffrage Association, the Women's Christian Temperance Union, the Woman's Homeopathic Society, the Illinois Women's Press Association, the Illinois State Industrial School for Girls, and a number of women's groups from community churches. The agency's founders, then, were the new women's professional and reform clubs, all of which contributed to Chicago's early progressive institutions. This network of clubs together covered the gamut of health, moral, social, political, and economic reform. They likewise reflected and nurtured an expanded public role for middle-class and elite women by highlighting the unique responsibility such women had to aid and care for poor and working-class women.[12]

The creation of the agency was also a response to developments in the larger world: labor unrest, the extraordinary growth of Chicago in the post–Civil War era, and the explosion in the number of female laborers, which had gone from negligible before the Civil War to 18 percent of the manufacturing workforce by 1870. Chicago was the railroad hub of the nation and was in the midst of a brutalizing level of industrialization, which created radical working-class leaders as well as reformers.[13] The women of the agency were witnessing historical change and sought to become active agents by specializing in law and the court system.

Caroline Brown became the agency's first president, and her new organization garnered the financial support and attention of the CWC's wealthy members. Brown described the agency's work one year after its founding:

[11] "To Protect Women and Children," *Chicago Daily Tribune*, March 7, 1885, 12.

[12] Discussing Frances Willard, the Chicago-based leader of the Women's Christian Temperance Union, her biographer writes that her brilliance lay in her ability to combine the antagonistic equal-rights feminism of Susan B. Anthony with the idea of a separate women's sphere that focused on women's special mission in society. Bordin, *Frances Willard*, 103. This also can be said of the Protective Agency, and certainly the Temperance Union influenced the agency, just as the agency influenced the Temperance Union.

[13] See, e.g., William Cronon, *Nature's Metropolis: Chicago and the Great West* (New York: Norton, 1992); Andrew Wender Cohen, *The Racketeer's Progress: Chicago and the Struggle for the Modern America Economy, 1900–1940* (Cambridge: Cambridge University Press, 2004); Elizabeth Dale, *The Chicago Trunk Show Murder: Law and Justice at the Turn of the Century* (De Kalb: Northern Illinois University Press, 2011); John B. Jentz and Richard Schneirove, *Chicago in the Age of Capital: Class, Politics, and Democracy during the Civil War Reconstruction* (Urbana: University of Illinois Press, 2012).

Its object is to protect helpless women and children by procuring enforcement of the laws, to punish those who injure and maltreat them, to procure alterations in the laws when they are unjust or inefficient, and, in general, to lend a helping hand where it is needed. This is done by advice, legal or friendly, collecting wages due, baffling the schemes of sewing machine sharpers and chattel mortgage usurers, looking up girls enticed away from home, defending wives and children against brutal husbands and fathers, releasing women condemned to false imprisonment under the pretext of debt or insanity, and, lastly by sending to the penitentiary those wretches whose crimes against women are not to be named.[14]

The breadth of the agency's work is striking. Equally significant is that its leaders did not make lawyerlike distinctions between civil and criminal cases, lobbying for new legislation, enforcing laws, or providing personal, legal, or other advice. All of these efforts were part of its mission to "protect" women.

Although the agency was one of the jewels in the Chicago Women Club's crown, by the 1890s the club was at the forefront of almost every progressive cause in the nation, including reform of psychiatric hospitals, lobbying for limited working hours for women, creating kindergartens, advocating compulsory education laws, supporting civil service reform, creating juvenile courts and juvenile and adult probation, building bathhouses, passing tenement house laws, instituting sex education in the schools, raising the age of consent, campaigning for women's suffrage, and advocating more generally for the equal political and legal treatment of women.[15] As one board member wrote,

The 19th century woman is outgrowing her old environment. She has burst the chrysalis of tradition and ignorance and is beginning to try her strength independently – to think and act for herself and to use her influence to form a more elevated public sentiment. And the Chicago Women's Club is one of the helpful instruments towards the attainment of a broader view and nobler womanhood.[16]

The club's relationship with the Protective Agency for Women and Children and its wide-ranging agenda prevented it from being isolated, and placed it in a thick network of Progressive Era reform organizations and projects. Senior officers of the CWC easily moved into the presidency

---

[14] Caroline M. Brown, *Report of the Association of the Advancement for Women*, Nineteenth Women's Congress, Grand Rapids, MI, 1891.

[15] See Frank and Jerome, *Annals of the Chicago Woman's Club*.

[16] Mary Spalding Brown, *Annual Report of the Chicago Women's Club for the Year Ending March 14, 1891*, Chicago Women's Club Records, Chicago History Museum, box 1, folder 12.

and vice presidency of the agency.[17] This would deeply influence the nature and structure of legal aid in Chicago and, later, the nation.

Gender and class shaped how members defined the agency's roles and duties and how they identified, and managed, its problems. Late-nineteenth-century understandings of differences between men and women positioned upper- and middle-class white women as potentially more moral and virtuous than men. Theoretically situated in an idealized domestic sphere, these women were supposedly above motives of self-interest, markets, and electoral politics. They also had the ability and the duty to minister to others, especially poor women, while remaining within their own sphere of activity, which in the post–Civil War period was expanding. Because of such differences between men and women, women reformers argued that only they could fully understand the problems that women faced and sculpt appropriate solutions.[18]

The Protective Agency proclaimed that it was now women's responsibility to work for the "world's redemption."[19] "We stand for justice," one report stated, continuing with the agency's belief that

the only way to lessen these crimes [against women] is to punish them; that without such punishment, Chicago will not be a safe place for an honest women to live; and we feel that every instinct of true womanhood should make us glad to help and protect other women less fortunate than ourselves . . . that public opinion should be educated up to the point of considering the virtue of poor women as well worthy the protection of the law as the purse of a rich man.[20]

Such change would not occur through a sentimental cry for women's helplessness but through the institutional changes that the agency championed.[21]

---

[17] The CWC carefully selected its members. A potential member needed to be sponsored by two other members, voted on by a committee, and then approved by the board. This selection process made sure that members were of the upper class. Another criterion for selection was that the prospective member showed enthusiasm and commitment for doing the work of the club. Ibid., 64–65. By the 1890s a handful of African American women and Jewish women had been selected for membership.

[18] Susan J. Pearson, *The Rights of the Defenseless: Protecting Animals and Children in Gilded-Age America* (Chicago: University of Chicago Press, 2011), 75–76; Lori Ginzberg, *Women and the Work of Benevolence: Morality, Politics, and Class in the Nineteenth-Century United States* (New Haven, CT: Yale University Press, 1990), 14, 24.

[19] PAWC, *Fourth Annual Report of the Protective Agency for Women and Children* (Chicago, 1890), 13.

[20] PAWC, *First Annual Report of the Protective Agency for Women and Children* (Chicago, 1887), 14.

[21] See, e.g., PAWC, *Fourth Annual Report*, 13.

In modern parlance, the Protective Agency's officers wanted power and a seat at the table, and they believed that they were entitled to both. At least part of what contributed to their confidence was the elite class standing of its founders and board members, who generally came from prominent East Coast families, were white Protestants, and were married to leading businessmen and professionals, some of whom were also involved in politics.[22] Over time, the board members became increasingly progressive in their politics, supporting women's suffrage, women in the professions, labor unions, and the eight-hour workday for women. The agency's most active members had learned through firsthand experience how law and the courts treated women, and they would play prominent roles in the creation of Chicago's juvenile and domestic relations courts. Although the agency's founders were generally a generation older than the famed reformer and founder of Hull House, Jane Addams, many would become her allies and supporters.[23] Some would also hold national leadership posts in the General Federation of Women's Clubs and the Women's Trade Union League.[24]

The Protective Agency became a stable, strong, and expanding organization, thanks to the time, energy, and resources (including funds and cultural capital) that its members contributed. Its chairman boasted, "The character of the women composing the Agency, as well as of the societies backing it, give it a weight and power to its action, which, of itself, often gains the day for justice.... We thus concentrate, in one small body, the power, wisdom, and dignity of a large number of estimable and influential women."[25] Such a self-identity helps explain the women's confidence in believing that they had the capacity to establish, manage, and work in an organization that trod so boldly into the domain of politics and the male legal profession.

The founders of the Protective Agency were well aware of New York's Working Women's Protective Union and the legal work of women lay

---

[22] See, e.g., PAWC, *Second Annual Report of the Protective Agency for Women and Children* (Chicago, 1888), 9.

[23] Frank and Jerome, *Annals*, 76.

[24] For discussions of some of the board members of the agency, including Ellen Martin Henrotin, Lucy Flower, and Mary Potter Crane, see Kathleen D. McCarthy, *Noblesse Oblige: Charity and Cultural Philanthropy in Chicago, 1849–1929* (Chicago: University of Chicago Press, 1982); Rima Lunin Schultz and Adele Hast, eds., *Women Building Chicago, 1790 1990: A Biographical Dictionary* (Bloomington: Indiana University Press, 2001).

[25] PAWC, *Second Annual Report*, 9.

lawyers in other cities.[26] Using them as starting points for Chicago, it soon pushed beyond their agendas, boasting that it was doing work that "has not been achieved or even attempted in any other city."[27] For one thing, the agency employed a paid supervisor and used volunteers. Its supervisor, Charlotte Holt, managed the office and interviewed women in need of aid. She and her assistants, board members, and volunteers would then investigate cases. Similar to women's organizations in other cities, a male attorney became involved only if a lawsuit was necessary. The agency's governing structure was large, filled with delegates from each one of the women's organizations that supported it, a structure that situated the agency firmly within the broader community of reform-minded organizations. This allowed for the cross-pollination of ideas, a broad understanding of women's needs, and a network that could mobilize quickly to lobby for new legislation.[28]

Each year, the number of agency clients grew exponentially. In its first year, 1886, the Protective Agency handled 156 cases, in its third year 1,145, and by 1905 it had more than 4,000.[29] This expansion did not occur in other cities that had protective committees run by volunteers. Such committees generally handled the intake of new cases for a couple of hours per week. In contrast, the Chicago agency's office stayed open for long hours five or six days a week. For growth to occur, a full-time, paid staff was crucial, something other women's organizations either could not afford or did not prioritize. Legal aid organizations of all types repeatedly found that providing legal assistance was labor intensive and expensive.

The Protective Agency's agenda combined ideas of traditional legal rights with equitable justice and sisterhood. Caroline Brown in her first annual report declared: "The bandage has fallen from the eyes of Justice, and she keeps a sharp lookout."[30] Blind justice did not necessarily provide women with real justice. To the agency's leaders, rights were not just formal legal rights, but also legal rights to protection from male sexuality, irresponsibility, and corruption. Such rights affirmatively included bodily

---

[26] PAWC, *First Annual Report*, 7.

[27] PAWC, *Seventh Annual Report of the Protective Agency for Women and Children* (Chicago, 1893), 7.

[28] See, e.g., PAWC, *Thirteenth Annual Report of the Protective Agency for Woman and Children* (Chicago, 1899), 11.

[29] PAWC, *First Annual Report*; PAWC, *Nineteenth Annual Report of the Protective Agency for Women and Children of Chicago* (Chicago, 1905).

[30] PAWC, *First Annual Report*, 7.

protection and security as well as property rights.[31] Agency leaders demanded "justice" for women "not mercy."[32]

Members of the agency saw poor and working-class women as primarily without power – economic, political, and social – and therefore deeply vulnerable. This vulnerability made it easy for men to gain their confidence and prey upon them sexually and financially. The women of the PAWC viewed poor women as having volition, but also as being easily overcome by male coercion and violence.[33] Although overdrawn, this view of poor and working-class women was not wrong. Given the realities of the wage-labor market for women, domestic violence, and women's lack of political and legal rights, women were often materially dependent on and vulnerable to men.[34] Yet this image of the vulnerable female victim stood in stark contrast to the actions of real radical women labor activists, such as the Chicago firebrand and anarchist Lucy Parsons, founder of the short-lived Chicago Working Women's Union, whose public protests regarding labor conditions took place within blocks of the agency's meetings.[35] The agency, however, was silent about working women's radical political behavior and the growing, visible, organized, and sometimes violent labor unrest in Chicago in which working

---

[31] See, e.g., PAWC, *First Annual Report*, 12; PAWC, *Seventh Annual Report*, 7–9.

[32] PAWC, *Fourth Annual Report*, 11.

[33] See, e.g., PAWC, *First Annual Report*, 12; PAWC, *Third Annual Report of the Protective Agency for Women and Children* (Chicago, 1889), 9–10, 14–16; PAWC, *Fifth Annual Report*, 12–14.

[34] Women's legal history has long shown how law systematically disabled women. This, of course, did not mean that women had no legal agency. See, e.g., Barbara Young Welke, *Law and the Borders of Belonging in the Long Nineteenth Century United States* (Cambridge: Cambridge University Press, 2010); Linda K. Kerber, *No Constitutional Rights to Be Ladies: Women and the Obligation of Citizenship* (New York: Hill and Wang, 1998); Joan Hoff, *Law, Gender, and Injustice: A Legal History of U.S. Women* (New York: New York University Press, 1991).

[35] Parsons was one of the organizers of the 1885 workers' march on the Chicago Board of Trade and was the widow of a Haymarket defendant. She is perhaps most famous for her essay "To Tramps," in which she called on the poor to learn to use explosives. Parsons identified herself as multiracial and claimed that her ancestors included African Americans, Mexicans, and Native Americans. Her radicalism, working-class background, and embrace of anarchism made her in many ways the complete antithesis of the women of the Protective Agency. See Gale Aherns, ed., *Lucy Parsons: Freedom, Equality, and Solidarity, Writings and Speeches 1878–1937* (Chicago: Charles Kerr Publishing, 2004); Robin D. G. Kelley, "Lucy Parsons," in *Black Women in America: An Historical Encyclopedia*, ed. Darlene Clark Hine (Brooklyn, NY: Carlson, 1993), 910.

women participated.[36] Like the Working Women's Protective Union, the PAWC realized it was much less controversial to present working women as being in need of protection. Such a perspective also allowed agency leaders to understand that a sisterhood (uninterrupted by class or racial differences) existed among women and that white upper-class women could speak in the name of women as a whole.[37]

The Protective Agency's leadership nurtured the hope of a slow revolution that would overturn existing gender hierarchies, even if it evidenced little desire to undermine structures of class or race. Members' understanding of the unity of women, their shared problems, and the duty of upper-class women to protect less privileged women was so encompassing that it linked elements of moral reform, social purity, municipal housekeeping, first-wave feminism, and progressivism to the provision of legal aid to individuals.

A part of the Protective Agency's primary mission was to oversee cases involving sexual violence and to protect women not just from sexual predators but also from a legal system that often further harmed the victim.[38] The agency complained that the courts dismissed charges in cases of rape and sexual assault; prosecutors charged defendants with only minor offenses; and judges and juries often found defendants innocent when there was overwhelming evidence of guilt.[39] Defendants' lawyers also endlessly delayed cases and inappropriately influenced judges and court clerks.[40] Even if a case progressed to trial, the defendant's lawyer humiliated the victim by attacking her character and chastity.[41]

---

[36] On labor unrest in Chicago in the 1870s and 1880s, see, e.g., Cohen, *The Racketeer's Progress*; James Green, *Death in the Haymarket: A Story of Chicago, the First Labor Movement, and the Bombing that Divided Gilded-Age America* (New York: Pantheon, 2006); Jentz and Schneirove, *Chicago in the Age of Capital*.

[37] Historian Gwen Jordan, however, argues that certain members of the Protective Agency and even its agent Charlotte Holt were involved in radical politics and anarchism. Whether or not this is correct, radical political activity, which focused on overturning rather than ameliorating class inequality, occurred outside of the purview of the Protective Agency as an organization. Gwen Jordan, "Radical Women and the Development of Legal Aid Societies in Chicago and Los Angeles, 1886–1914," *Journal of Gender, Race and Justice* (forthcoming).

[38] PAWC, *First Annual Report*, 11–12.

[39] See, e.g., PAWC, *Second Annual Report*, 19–20; PAWC, *Sixteenth Annual Report of the Protective Agency for Woman and Children* (Chicago, 1901), 12.

[40] See PAWC, *First Annual Report*, 12, describing how lawyers and others would arrange to have files "lost."

[41] PAWC, *Fourth Annual Report*, 11–12.

Although criticism of Chicago's unwieldy courts and their often ethnic judges was a theme among Chicago's male elites, the agency's women focused their critique on how the courts treated victims of sexual violence.[42] The agency leaders believed, with considerable reason, that Chicago's court system was corrupt.[43] The typical justice of the peace had little or no legal training, and he was paid with the fees collected from litigants – an easily abused system.[44] Chicago's lower courts were commonly referred to as "justice shops," inferring that justice was a commodity that could be purchased. By all accounts, lower-court judicial appointments were highly political and often controlled by ward bosses.[45] The Protective Agency early on admonished that these lower courts dispensed "injustice" rather than justice.[46] Continuing this refrain, as late as 1903 the agency announced that it would continue its activities until courts were "administered only by faithful and competent officers."[47]

Agency members cast themselves as more knowledgeable and virtuous than corrupt justices of the peace, police magistrates, and lawyers.[48] In 1887, agency officers wrote to state appellate judges about the lower courts: "We have had cases in which we believe political influences have governed the Justices. We have had cases in which sympathy with vice seemingly decided the question. We have had cases in which the attorney for the accused controlled the Justice, and it was deemed impossible to secure a fair hearing."[49] They further complained of discourteous treatment by court personnel, crowded courtrooms, magistrates' favoritism toward those with power or influence, and magistrates' and court officers' lack of sympathy with or concern for poor women:[50]

---

[42] On Chicago's morass of courts at this time and efforts to reform them, see Michael Willrich, *City of Courts: Socializing Justice in Progressive-Era Chicago* (New York: Oxford University Press, 2003), 3–28. On women's entry into traditionally male debates regarding political appointments and civil service reform, see Helene Silverberg, "A Government of Men: Gender, the City, and the New Science of Politics," in *Gender and American Social Science: The Formative Years*, ed. Helene Silverberg (Princeton, NJ: Princeton University Press, 1998).

[43] PAWC, *Seventh Annual Report*, 7–8; PAWC, *Eleventh Annual Report of the Protective Agency for Women and Children* (Chicago, 1897), 22–23; PAWC, *Sixteenth Annual Report of the Protective Agency for Woman and Children* (Chicago, 1902), 21.

[44] See, e.g., PAWC, *Fourth Annual Report*, 25.

[45] See, e.g., "Constable Errs: Court Surprised," *Chicago Daily Tribune*, April 14, 1902.

[46] PAWC, *First Annual Report*, 10.

[47] See, e.g., PAWC, *Fourth Annual Report*, 10–11.

[48] PAWC, *Seventh Annual Report*, 9.

[49] "Bettering the Justice Courts," *Chicago Daily Tribune*, March 1, 1887, 1.

[50] "Ibid.; see also PAWC, *First Annual Report*, 11–12.

Let us take cases of criminal assault or attempted criminal assault upon women and children. It is humiliation enough for an afflicted woman to appear in court to tell her story, but to tell it in the midst of the crowd ... with an attorney who is permitted by the Justices to use language abusive and full of vile insinuations, makes an ordeal for the prosecuting witness which practically amounts to intimidation.[51]

They urged the appellate judges to ensure that only the most qualified attorneys were appointed to judicial positions, and further offered a complete list of the corruption and problems that they had personally witnessed.[52] When court officials were not reappointed, they celebrated and claimed victory.[53] In contrast with the supposedly illegitimate power exercised by nonelite court officials, the members of the agency saw the power that they hoped to exercise as being earned, natural, and above reproach – used only to protect the virtue of other women.[54]

The Protective Agency was at times so distrustful of Chicago's legal system that it sought to substitute its own resources for those of the state. When the agency learned about a case of sexual violence, for example, it became involved in multiple ways, including conducting its own investigation, gathering evidence, and speaking with judges and attorneys.[55] The women of the agency created a role for themselves as victim advocates and legal reformers. At times agency members would pressure the state's attorney into allowing the agency's own attorney to prosecute cases.[56] Agency members would also act "the sister's part," by helping the victim to "obtain justice," "a home," and employment.[57]

One of the Protective Agency's best publicized and most visible tactics was to have members appear en masse in the courtroom when proceedings involved cases of sexual assault. In this way they functioned as judicial watchdogs whose presence was intended to shame court officials and lawyers into proper behavior.[58] As the women of the agency recognized, in cases involving sex, male lawyers, judges, jurors, and spectators created an intentionally rowdy, salacious, and intimidating atmosphere of male

---

[51] "Bettering the Justice Courts," *Chicago Daily Tribune*, March 1, 1887, 1.
[52] Ibid.
[53] See, e.g., PAWC, *First Annual Report*, 10; PAWC, *Fourth Annual Report*, 11–12.
[54] See, e.g., PAWC, *First Annual Report*, 14; PAWC, *Fourth Annual Report*, 11–12.
[55] PAWC, *First Annual Report*, 13. See also "Funds to Fight Dowie," *Chicago Daily Tribune*, June 8, 1900, 10.
[56] See, e.g., "The Justice Boggs Case," *Chicago Daily Tribune*, May 5, 1888, 8.
[57] PAWC, *First Annual Report*, 13.
[58] See, e.g., PAWC, *Fourth Annual Report* (Chicago, 1890), 11–12; PAWC, *Ninth Annual Report of the Protective Agency for Women and Children* (Chicago, 1895), 4.

camaraderie.[59] The agency's idea was that if upper-class ladies appeared in court, men would be forced to act as gentlemen. "The presence of a delegation of reputable women, women of social position and influence, changes the moral tone of Police court, and imparts courage to a timid girl, whose very innocence confuses her, in the presence of so many strange men."[60] Its tactics also served to "counteract" the "political influence" put on lower court judges to favor male defendants.[61]

Protective Agency members walked a fine line in assuming this role, as truly respectable women rarely appeared in court, which society recognized as a masculine space.[62] Chicago's police courts were rough-and-tumble places: crowded, noisy, filled with smoke, and teeming with defendants and "vile crowds" – hardly places where ladies appeared.[63] As historian Melisa Hayes writes, in cases involving sex, "attorneys not only prompted litigants and witnesses to indecorous discourse; they often initiated it. Scurrilous sexual humor sprung from the public realm of officialdom."[64] This was certainly true of Chicago's courts. Carole Brown, the PAWC's president, explained:

Even now, a woman so unfortunate as to get into court, whether through her own fault or that of someone else, was ostracized from the society of respectable people, and those who should befriend her passed by on the other side.... [W]e have long ceased to think it a matter of pride to say "we were never in a court-room in our lives." Courts, where women's interests' are at stake, are the objects of our especial care.[65]

---

[59] See Melissa A. Hayes, "Sex in the Witness Stand: Erotic Sensationalism, Voyeurism, Sexual Boasting, and Bawdy Humor in Nineteenth-Century Courts," *Law and History Review* 32 (February 2014): 149–202, 153.

[60] PAWC, *First Annual Report*, 14; See also PAWC, *Sixteenth Annual Report*, 10.

[61] PAWC, *Third Annual Report*, 11; PAWC, *Fifteenth Annual Report of the Protective Agency for Woman and Children* (Chicago, 1901), 19; PAWC, *Sixteenth Annual Report*, 12.

[62] On women's use of courtroom space to seek reforms during the same period, see Felice Batlan, "The Ladies' Health Protective Association: Lay Lawyers and Urban Cause Lawyering," *Akron Law Review* 41 (2008): 701. Otherwise, women primarily appeared in court in sensational divorce cases and as criminal defendants; see, e.g., Norma Basch, *Framing American Divorce: From the Revolutionary Generation to the Victorians* (Berkeley: University of California Press, 1999); Regina Morantz-Sanchez, *Conduct Unbecoming a Woman: Medicine on Trial in Turn-of-the-Century Brooklyn* (New York: Oxford University Press, 1999); Lisa Duggan, *Sapphic Slashers: Sex, Violence, and American Modernity* (Durham, NC: Duke University Press, 2000); Carol Haber, *The Trials of Laura Fair – Sex, Murder, and Insanity in the Victorian West* (Chapel Hill: University of North Carolina Press, 2013).

[63] PAWC, *Second Annual Report*, 11. See Willrich, *City of Courts*, 13–14.

[64] Hayes, "Sex in the Witness Stand," 194.

[65] PAWC, *Seventh Annual Report*, 8 (emphasis in original).

Some court officials declared that the courts, especially police courts, were not an appropriate place for respectable women.[66] Caroline Brown responded, "We are told that it does not become modest women to appear in court rooms, and listen to proofs of crime . . . that to go out in the highways and byways of life, and lift up those who are trodden under the feet of wicked men, is very dirty business. . . . [T]he shame and scandal of these crimes lies in the fact, not in the telling of it."[67] Believing that righteousness and justice were on their side, these elite women used such opinions and the chastisements of court officials and others to further justify their presence.

As Protective Agency members invaded the courtroom, they began to question substantive and evidentiary laws regarding sex crimes, divorce, and custody proceedings. They questioned why "criminal assaults upon little girls are generally dismissed with a trifling fine for 'disorderly conduct,' while larceny sends a man to the penitentiary."[68] Particularly galling to them was how defense lawyers raised issues of a victim's past sexual conduct to demonstrate consent in cases of sexual violence and seduction, as well as how judges used evidence of a women's moral character to deny her custody of children. For such women, the agency claimed, the courtroom became a "torture chamber."[69] "We have come to see that the point of attack was always the previous character of the complaining witness. Not, as is the case in prosecutions against men, the character for *truthfulness*, but for chastity."[70] In court cases involving sex, male defendants might even boast of their sexual conquests, which reconfirmed their masculinity, control, and virility. In contrast, evidence that a woman was unchaste went to the heart of her character.[71]

The agency asserted that the courts' unfair treatment of women in cases regarding sexual violence went beyond individual men's behavior. This treatment, they insisted, was engrained in law and required the enactment of new laws that would exclude evidence of a women's chastity or previous conduct. The agency explained, "Immorality should be no hindrance to legal rights in one sex more than the other."[72] But to

[66] PAWC, *First Annual Report*, 13. See also Hayes, "Sex in the Witness Stand," 169.
[67] Ibid., 14.
[68] Ibid., 12.
[69] PAWC, *Second Annual Report*, 11.
[70] PAWC, *Fourth Annual Report*, 11 (emphasis in original). See also PAWC, *First Annual Report*, 12; "Moral Support for Mrs. Rawson," *Chicago Daily Tribune*, July 28, 1888, 8.
[71] Hayes, "Sex in the Witness Stand," 190.
[72] PAWC, *Third Annual Report*, 9.

attack this double standard undermined the sexual and legal privileges of men.[73]

Along with other women's organizations, the agency campaigned to raise the legal age of consent, which at that time in Illinois was ten for a girl. Laws raising the age of consent went hand in hand with reforming evidentiary rules and burden-of-proof standards, as statutory rape made questions of consent and a girl's or woman's character and past sexual conduct moot.[74] The agency wanted new laws that would remove a judge's discretion to allow evidence of character; such laws would further rein in defense attorneys' behavior. Moving well beyond silent witnessing, by the 1890s the agency voiced claims that the protection of a woman's rights in court could not occur until women controlled the courtroom.[75] The members of the agency thus began to stake out their jurisdiction: elite and middle-class women needed to be in charge of legal issues involving other women.[76]

The women of the Protective Agency also claimed characteristics typically deemed to be male. One officer wrote, "Thus slowly arises in the world the new chivalry – the chivalry of strong, earnest, intelligent womanhood, girding itself for the defense and protection of all classes and conditions of women, . . . in the maintenance of their honor and sacred right."[77] As the men of the Working Women's Protective Union had figured themselves as "brave" and "courageous" knights, so, too, did the women of Chicago's Protective Agency.[78] Although those active in the agency viewed themselves as bestowing kindness and services on poor women, such poor women allowed these elite women the chance to mold themselves into sophisticated legal actors with a public role. Poor women's needs could thus transform respectable ladies, limited in their sphere of activity, into knights.

Although the Protective Agency's most dramatic and visible work focused on sexual violence, its officers, employees, and volunteers spent

[73] Estelle B. Freedman, *Redefining Rape: Sexual Violence in the Era of Suffrage and Segregation* (Cambridge, MA: Harvard University Press, 2013), 126.

[74] Ibid. On nineteenth-century seduction trials see, e.g., Jane E. Larsen, "'Even a Worm Will Turn at Last': Rape Reform in Late Nineteenth-Century America," *Yale Journal of Law and Humanities* 9 (Winter 1997): 1–72, 2; Brian Donovan, "Gender Inequality and Criminal Seduction: Prosecuting Sexual Coercion in the Early-20th Century," *Law and Social Inquiry* 30 (Winter 2005): 61–88; Hayes, "Sex in the Witness Stand."

[75] See, e.g., PAWC, *Fourth Annual Report*, 11.

[76] PAWC, *Second Annual Report*, 11. Willrich, *City of Courts*, 13–14.

[77] PAWC, *Third Annual Report*, 12.

[78] See, e.g., PAWC, *Third Annual Report*, 9; PAWC, *Fifth Annual Report*, 8–10; *Fourth Annual Report*, 13.

the bulk of their time meeting with and responding to the women who sought everyday legal help at their office. The agency had few rules regarding the kinds of cases that it would take; it functioned flexibly and often improvised, meeting needs as they arose. Unlike later legal aid societies, the agency did not have eligibility requirements and it was unconcerned that it might take cases away from attorneys. The agency's superintendent explained this pragmatic approach, "We do not make any rules, but judge of each case as it comes to us."[79] The agency did not keep track of its clients' race, ethnicity, age, or marital status, but it is likely that many of its clients were immigrants, and its records occasionally mention African American clients.

The Chicago Protective Agency accepted cases of wage claims as well as what we would now call domestic violence. It explained that it was well established that a lawsuit could be brought when a woman did not receive wages. Adequate laws, however, did not exist to protect a wife and children when her husband was an abusive drunk who failed to support the family.[80] This recognition of, and focus on, domestic violence was unusual for the period, although leaders of the agency primarily imagined that domestic violence occurred only in poor and working-class homes, rooted in lower-class men's depravity and lack of self-discipline.[81] In its early years, the agency handled wage claims, including those of servants, more than any other kind of case, but by the turn of the century domestic relations cases surpassed those of wage claims.[82]

The Protective Agency rarely initiated lawsuits. A lawsuit would require its male lawyer to become involved. Moreover, the agency had little faith in the courts. Instead the agent, other board members, and volunteers used their influence and persuasion through letters and personal visits to pressure employers to pay wages due. This form of conciliation was used so often that the agency dubbed it "whitemailing." "One frequently hears of blackmailing schemes; may there not be a *whitemailing*

---

[79] PAWC, *Second Annual Report*, 21.

[80] PAWC, *First Annual Report*, 8–9.

[81] Linda Gordon writes that societies for the protection of children often became involved in protecting poor women, although that was not their primary focus. Gordon also argues that these societies interpreted the problem of family violence as one affecting only the poor. Linda Gordon, *Heroes of Their Own Lives: The Politics and History of Family Violence* (New York: Penguin Books, 1988), 20.

[82] For instance, in 1889 the PAWC handled 462 wage claims and 181 complaints by "wives against husbands." PAWC, *Third Annual Report*, 16. Between 1904 and 1905, it handled 152 wage claims and 892 "domestic relations" claims. PAWC, *Nineteenth Annual Report*, 10.

method of getting money when justly due, by arraying on the side of justice the higher elements of society."[83] Engaging in these tactics was the "cheapest and easiest way" to resolve a claim.[84] The agency thus used its suasion and cultural capital, including the threat of exposure, to enforce its conception of justice for women.[85]

The Protective Agency also handled a continuing assortment of chattel mortgage cases, often involving a lender charging extraordinarily high interest rates combined with an errant husband who had brought the family to the brink of disaster.[86] One case involved Mrs. Sarah L., whose husband had mortgaged the family's furniture for thirty dollars and then deserted her and their ill child. Sarah managed to pay back twenty-seven dollars. The lender than informed her that she still owed forty-two dollars, and that it would repossess her furniture if she did not immediately pay. The agency reached an agreement whereby Sarah paid an additional three dollars in full settlement of the original debt. Sarah's case was typical of the chattel mortgage cases handled by the agency.[87] Likewise, the purchase of sewing machines on installment brought significant problems. Sales agents of the large sewing machine companies promised buyers that training on the machine would be provided, that the salesman would help the buyer obtain sewing work, and that payments would be small. The buyer would then unwittingly sign an agreement that omitted such promises, and that stated that up to half of the payments constituted rent for the machine, not payment on the interest or the principal. When the buyer missed a payment, the machine would be repossessed. The agency was involved in a number of such cases.[88] It continually lobbied for legislation that would require court action to repossess goods. Without such court action, the agency argued, repossession was really "*confiscation*."[89] In most of these cases, the agency bargained in the shadow of the law and negotiated settlements.

[83] PAWC *Second Annual Report*, 9 (emphasis in original); see also PAWC, *Ninth Annual Report*, 9.

[84] PAWC, *Second Annual Report*, 10.

[85] Historian Andrew Cohen describes tactics used by Chicago's craft unions at the turn of the century. Those groups refused to accept courts or the state as having a monopoly on power, and through boycotts and even physical violence they attempted to maintain and control a craft economy. Whitemailing might be understood as a similar practice. Cohen, *The Racketeer's Progress*, 128–9.

[86] PAWC, *First Annual Report*, 9; PAWC, *Second Annual Report*, 12.

[87] PAWC, *Eleventh Annual Report*, 19.

[88] PAWC, *Third Annual Report*, 18–19

[89] Ibid., 19 (emphasis in original).

The bulk of the Protective Agency's domestic relations cases raised issues of abandonment or nonsupport of wives by husbands. These cases went to the heart of the agency's belief in the absolute obligation of a husband to support his wife and children. In a typical case, a woman would visit the agency's office, claiming that her drunken husband had disappeared weeks before, leaving her penniless. Now the landlord was demanding rent and the furniture was being repossessed. Often the wife would have some sense of where the husband was staying and where he worked, so the agency would take the case, search for the husband, threaten him with a lawsuit for failure to support, and collect support payments for the wife. If the husband did not agree to pay, the employer might be convinced to pay wages directly to the agency for the benefit of the wife.[90] Actions such as these combined the threat of litigation with public humiliation by making visible a man's failure as a breadwinner. When these methods failed, the agency might file a lawsuit against the husband for nonsupport. Meanwhile, it would also negotiate with the landlord and the furniture dealer for lower or postponed payments.

The most contentious and controversial issue the agency faced was whether to accept divorce cases. This would remain a significant problem for legal aid providers well into the twentieth century. Publicly, the agency labeled itself "antidivorce," but it accepted divorce cases in what it deemed exceptional circumstances.[91] The agency's first report stated:

Perhaps the most embarrassing of all the questions which have come before us, has been that of divorce. We began with a firm determination in no case to counsel the breaking up of families; but in a few cases, notably one where a man who married a widow with two daughters seemed persistently determined to ruin these girls, we have felt that the welfare of children made absolute divorce the only course possible.[92]

The report continued, saying that where "cruelty and violence existed such marriages were not true marriages but rather were a cover for deliberate and persistent wickedness."[93] Such a home failed to provide care, love, and protection; instead it was a place of violence, rendering divorce

---

[90] PAWC, *Tenth Annual Report of the Protective Agency for Women and Children* (Chicago, 1896), 6; "To Protect Women and Children," *Chicago Daily Tribune*, May 7, 1895, 12.

[91] PAWC, *Second Annual Report*, 10. Regarding the checkered history of Americans acceptance of divorce, see Hendrik Hartog, *Man and Wife in America: A History* (Cambridge, MA: Harvard University Press, 2002); Basch, *Framing American Divorce*.

[92] PAWC, *First Annual Report*, 10.

[93] Ibid.

acceptable.[94] Charlotte Holt explained, "The home element was wholly lacking in them; they afforded no protection to women and children."[95] The agency's officers reasoned that if the PAWC it did not take these cases, women would be forced to hire "irresponsible legal practitioners."[96]

The agency's membership was divided over divorce cases. In its third year, the agency announced that it would limit the divorces cases it accepted to those raising issues of serious physical violence. Some members of the board thought this policy too restrictive, arguing that they were forced to reject "heartbreaking" cases.[97] Within a year, the policy again changed. Now the agency would evaluate each case on its own merit. The agency's leadership attacked those who criticized its decision to accept divorce cases, asserting their superior and direct knowledge of such cases. "Day by day, week by week, year by year, we go on doing in each instance what seems best at the time.... We can only live up to our light, and since that comes through our experience, what wonder that those outside with less experience, doubt our methods and deplore our mistakes!"[98]

These defensive statements reveal two fundamental characteristics of the agency. First, it adopted a constantly evolving pragmatist approach rather than concrete rules. Its goal was to provide equity particularized to each individual. Second, as time went on, the agency's members used their class position and gender, as well as their growing practical experience, to define and bolster their claim to expertise.[99]

Even with its experience of domestic problems, the agency accepted few divorce cases. Its attorney explained that in the cases that he filed, divorce released women "from the thralldom of continual misery for themselves and their children [which was caused] by the inhuman treatment of their husbands."[100] The agency did not accept a divorce case because a woman wanted to leave her husband – even when adultery or other legal grounds

94 Ibid.
95 PAWC, *Fifth Annual Report*, 14.
96 PAWC, *First Annual Report*, 10.
97 PAWC, *Third Annual Report*, 13.
98 PAWC, *Fourth Annual Report*, 13.
99 Some scholars have understood this combination of gender-based intuition with concrete personal and lived experience to be a hallmark of late-nineteenth-century women reformers' thought. See Dorothy Ross, "Gendered Social Knowledge: Domestic Discourse, Jane Addams, and the Possibilities of Social Science," in *Gender and American Social Science: The Formative Years*, ed. Helene Silverberg (Princeton, NJ: Princeton University Press, 1998).
100 Protective Agency for Women and Children, *Fourteenth Annual Report of the Protective Agency for Women and Children* (Chicago, 1900), 13.

for divorce existed.[101] Without some form of physical abuse or long-term abandonment, the best that a woman could hope for from the agency was a legal separation.

In contrast, the Protective Agency generously defended women whose husbands sued for divorce, claiming that its representation prevented immoral husbands from obtaining custody of children or being relieved of the duty to provide financial support for their families.[102] It further viewed the legal system itself as disadvantaging women. "Women's [*sic*] civil rights are seriously menaced if her opponent was wealthy and unscrupulous. In divorce cases it is of no infrequent occurrence that a man will 'procure' evidence against his wife's character for chastity in order to win *his* case and thus deprive [her] of all rights to *his* property (which often they had jointly earned) and the custody of her children. And this, too, when the man was known to be immoral and unprincipled."[103] Taking up the banner of women's rights activists, the agency demanded that men and women be subject to the same moral code and have the same legal rights to property and custody of children.[104]

Significantly, the agency did not distinguish its legal work from its other work, such as providing financial aid, locating lodgings, finding employment, and seeking medical services for its clients.[105] It would have made little sense to the women of the agency to treat legal assistance as separate from a concern with substantive justice or material well-being. Moreover, they claimed that the agency's clients gained a new sense of "self-respect" and "self-dependence" through their interactions with the Protective Agency.[106]

The women of the agency recognized that many women who sought aid did not have legally cognizable claims, but they believed that client narratives had value in and of themselves. They understood the importance of allowing clients to tell their stories slowly, which, they asserted, "busy lawyers would not bear."[107] "Many a tale of woe is told in our

---

[101] The agency's view incorporated a larger cultural understanding that preventing divorce was about putting the societal good above individual happiness. Nancy F. Cott, *Public Vows: A History of Marriage and the Nation* (Cambridge, MA: Harvard University Press, 2000).

[102] See e.g., PAWC, *Fifteenth Annual Report*, 18.

[103] PAWC, *Tenth Annual Report*, 66 (emphasis in original).

[104] See, e.g., PAWC, *Fourth Annual Report*, 11 (emphasis in original); PAWC, *First Annual Report*, 12; "Moral Support for Mrs. Rawson," *Chicago Daily Tribune*, July 28, 1888, 8.

[105] PAWC, *Eleventh Annual Report*, 12.

[106] PAWC, *Second Annual Report*, 17.

[107] PAWC, *Ninth Annual Report*, 7.

office, the mere listening to which by sympathetic and intelligent women is all the help possible. It is astonishing how grateful some of these women are for the opportunity of telling their trials to such listeners."[108] For a poor woman to tell her story to an upper class woman and to have her hear and validate it must have provided a sense of legitimacy. This mode of counseling would in the future disappear as legal aid was professionalized by lawyers.

Unlike the eventual practice of other legal aid societies composed of professional lawyers, the agency did not charge clients a fee, as they understood their work to be born of duty, love, and charity.[109] Charging a fee would have made the women of the agency less "self-sacrificing" and "noble" – traits on which they prided themselves.[110] Yet like attorneys, volunteers and employees of the agency treated conversations with clients as confidential, often refusing to write or speak about individual cases. Charlotte Holt explained, "Much of our work is of a confidential nature, and as our aim has always been to encourage women to come to us for advice and counsel, it has been one of the essential stimulants to them to be assured of the strictly private nature of all work that could be kept private."[111] Unlike the Working Women's Protective Union or later legal aid societies, the agency generally did not discuss its cases in any detail publicly, even in its fundraising materials.[112] In contrast to a variety of reform organizations, especially those related to women, the agency eschewed melodramatic stories of the seduction and betrayal of young women.[113] Their clients' stories and issues were so serious that they needed to stand outside popular narratives: they were not to be traded on and instead were to be treated as precious.

The agency's relationship to legal professionals was complicated because it looked askance at many lawyers, magistrates, and judges while

---

[108] Ibid. See also PAWC, *Sixteenth Annual Report*, 13.

[109] See, e.g., PAWC, *Fourth Annual Report*, 13.

[110] PAWC, *Fifteenth Annual Report*, 11–12.

[111] PAWC, *Seventh Annual Report*, 8.

[112] "Aid for Women," *Chicago Daily Tribune*, May 4, 1894, 28; "Protection for the Weak," *Chicago Tribune*, March 27, 1886, 9.

[113] As Mary E. Odem and a host of scholars have shown, turn-of-the-century moral reform organizations repeatedly told stories focusing on working women's sexual seduction. Some believe that these cultural narratives produced a type of hysteria regarding female sexuality. Mary E. Odem, *Delinquent Daughters: Protecting and Policing Adolescent Female Sexuality in the United States, 1885–1920* (Chapel Hill: University of North Carolina Press, 1995); Larson, "'Women Understand So Little They Call My Good Nature Deceit': A Feminist Rethinking of Seduction," *Columbia Law Review* 93 (1993): 395. Historian Melissa Hayes writes of how popular literature and tales of seduction influenced court cases. Hayes, "Sex in the Witness Stand," 171.

at the same time longing for their acceptance and basking in their compliments regarding its members' legal knowledge and expertise. When longtime board member Mary Potter Crane died, the agency boasted that "she had a judicial mind, and was always welcome at the State's Attorney's office, and her advice and counsel in difficult cases . . . were frequently sought by attorneys."[114] Likewise, one board member wrote that Charlotte Holt "has so won the respect and confidence of the courts that whatever case she presents is sure of respectful hearing."[115] A journalist, after spending time in the agency's office, wrote, "Everything pertaining to law comes up for discussion, involving a thorough knowledge of law on the part of the agency."[116] In the late 1890s, the agency received requests from judges to station a representative in every police court to manage cases involving women, an affirmation of the agency's importance and its members' legal and practical expertise.[117]

Even while the agency was becoming a widely accepted urban legal institution, it separated itself from and criticized nonelite lawyers. "We are given some annoyance by a certain class of lawyers, who are desirous of obtaining our influence . . . or are presumptuous enough to imagine that they are capable of deciding what kind of case we ought to take up."[118] Such attorneys, the agency implied, did not possess better knowledge, skill, or expertise than their own. In fact, the agency's officers labeled some lawyers "vampires."[119] Such lawyers, they claimed, preyed on the poor, were incompetent, failed to respond to client needs, and charged excessive fees. At times the agency advocated the disbarment of certain lawyers. Unlike later legal aid societies, it also accepted cases involving client complaints against attorneys, and it did not hesitate to replace a lawyer on a case, claiming he was overcharging, incompetent, or otherwise engaging in unethical conduct.[120]

One case involved an African American woman whose husband accused her of bigamy after he had long abandoned her. The husband's lawyer physically detained the woman at his offices until she agreed pay a certain sum of money. Eventually the woman contacted the agency,

---

[114] PAWC, *Sixteenth Annual Report*, 10.
[115] Mary Allen West, "Protective Agency for Women and Children," *Chautauquan* 13 (1891): 511.
[116] "To Protect Women and Children," *Chicago Daily Tribune*, March 7, 1895, 12.
[117] PAWC, *Thirteenth Annual Report*, 9.
[118] PAWC, *Second Annual Report*, 21
[119] "Bettering the Justice Courts," *Chicago Daily Tribune*, March 1, 1887, 1.
[120] See, e.g., PAWC, *Third Annual Report*, 18.

and its agent forced the attorney to return her money.[121] Another case concerned an attorney who refused to return a client's funds, claiming that he was broke. The agency unsuccessfully tried to convince the state's attorney to charge the lawyer with embezzlement.[122]

The agency, standing outside the professional bar, had significant leeway to wage a campaign against nonelite lawyers, even before bar associations attempted to close the legal profession to such lawyers.[123] Sharing an understanding that the elite bar would later express, the women of the agency concluded that nonelite lawyers lacked virtue, were bound by no moral code, were driven by self-interest, and, like vampires, lived off the sustenance they extorted from innocent women.[124] In fact, their dislike went so far that they represented and supported one woman who shot her husband's attorney. The agency asserted that its client had been driven crazy by a hostile legal system, and in particular by lawyers (including her victim), who besmirched her character and "engaged in a course of persecution well calculated to unsettle her reason."[125] The client, they reasoned, could have been any woman caught in the web of the legal system. Insanity and violence were rational responses by women confronted with defense attorneys' tactics.[126]

The work of the agency shaped other legal aid organizations and legal institutions. A number of the founders and leaders of the agency were

---

[121] PAWC, *Second Annual Report*, 23.

[122] Ibid.

[123] On campaigns by bar associations against nonelite lawyers, see, e.g., Jerold S. Auerbach, *Unequal Justice: Lawyers and Social Change in Modern America* (New York: Oxford University Press, 1977). Michael Willrich writes that elite lawyers' campaigns to rid the Chicago bar of immigrant attorneys were unsuccessful because of the proliferation of evening law schools and a steady stream of personal injury suits. Willrich also notes that, in the late nineteenth century, immigrant lawyers were the fastest growing element of the bar. Willrich, *City of Courts*, 19–20.

[124] For a discussion of Dracula as embodying conflicting ideas of the role of the attorney, see Anne McGillivray, "'He Would Have Made a Wonderful Solicitor': Law, Modernity, and Professionalism in Bram Stoker's *Dracula*," in *Lawyers and Vampires: Cultural Histories of Legal Professions*, ed. W. Wesley Pue and David Sugarman (Oxford: Hart Publishing, 2003). On turn-of-the-century manliness, see Gail Bederman, *Manliness and Civilization: A Cultural History of Gender and Race in the United States, 1880–1917* (Chicago: University of Chicago Press, 1996). On how tropes of manliness were used by women's organizations to convince legislators to raise the age of consent, see Larson, "Women Understand So Little They Call My Good Nature Deceit," 45.

[125] PAWC, *Third Annual Report*, 9.

[126] See, e.g., Frances E. Dolan, "Battered Women, Petty Traitors, and the Legacy of Coverture," *Feminist Studies* 29 (Summer 2003): 249–77.

involved in creating, building, and staffing Chicago's Juvenile Court, and they used the agency as a model.[127] Lucy Flower and Mary Potter Crane were devoted agency officers and leading juvenile court advocates. Through the agency they developed a sophisticated understanding of law and the legal process that they brought to building the court.[128] Likewise, they had learned how to work with male legislators, judges, and elite lawyers. Shortly after the juvenile court opened in 1899, the court appointed an agency employee as one of its first probation officer.[129] Her salary came not from the state but from the Chicago Women's Club.

The new juvenile court adopted much of the methodology, philosophy, and ideas of the agency. Before the juvenile court existed, the Protective Agency took on cases of children charged with petty crimes. It investigated the children's lives and living situations and sought leniency for them, often finding the child's behavior was linked to problems at home. At times, the agency functioned as a guardian or parole officer, keeping the children out of adult jails. It had also worked to remove children from homes where abuse occurred, and in some cases the child became the ward of the agency.[130]

Like the agency, the juvenile court rejected an adversarial model of law and minimized the role of lawyers. The court instead invested tremendous discretion in female probation officers (called "paid volunteers") as well as unpaid women volunteers, often middle-class women. The wording "paid volunteer" placed the probation officer outside the market and closer to the sphere of women's reform activities and their more altruistic bent, as the agency had done.[131] Paid probation officers were on a continuum with unpaid volunteers, and both were to fashion individual solutions for each case. Further mirroring the agency, the juvenile court was intended to be a flexible institution not bound by strict understandings of the rule of law. Probation officers investigated children and families and presented a "fact-based report" for the nonadversarial

[127] See, e.g., PAWC, *Fifteenth Annual Report*, 11.

[128] See Frank and Jerome, *Annals*, 176–7.

[129] See, e.g., ibid.

[130] See, e.g., PAWC, *Sixth Annual Report of the Protective Agency for Women and Children* (Chicago, 1893), 9.

[131] Historian Anne Meis Knupfer points out that the term "paid volunteer" emphasized the enormous amount of experience and knowledge that the women involved in the juvenile court already possessed. Anne Meis Knupfer, *Reform and Resistance: Gender Delinquency and America's First Juvenile Court* (Routledge: New York, 2001), 48.

proceedings. Law and legal process were secondary to what the probation officer and the court perceived as the needs of the child. Like the agency had done, women from the Chicago Women's Club attended juvenile court sessions and freely spoke with judges and probation officers.[132]

The agency's influence on the juvenile court had a ripple effect, as the juvenile court in turn influenced the development of new legal aid organizations. Joel Hunter, the head of the United Charities of Chicago, which would became one of the country's largest legal aid organizations, began his career as a probation officer in the Chicago courts. Likewise, Minnie Low, a Jewish social worker who served as a juvenile court probation officer shortly after the court opened, would later establish a legal aid bureau for poor Jews. Her legal aid bureau was modeled on both the agency and the juvenile court.[133]

The agency also influenced Chicago's domestic relations court, which opened in 1911. This new court dealt primarily with desertion cases, failure to support, bastardy, and abuse – the kinds of cases that the agency had long handled for women. The court was staffed by female social workers and one male judge, and it focused on forcing husbands to support wives. In an office decorated more like a home than a court, wives would recount their husband's failures to provide for the family. The social worker would investigate the case and attempt to resolve it without the male judge's involvement. To the extent that she could not achieve that goal, the judge might order support, probation, or, at times, imprisonment.[134] What is significant here is how the domestic relations court, institutionalized in the state court system, enacted long-standing practices of the agency. In keeping with the agency's logic that only a woman could understand cases involving other women, the first female judges in the United States would serve on these courts.

---

[132] Ibid., 49. On the development of Chicago's juvenile court see David Tanenhaus, *Juvenile Justice in the Making* (New York: Oxford University Press, 2004); Victoria Getis, *The Juvenile Court and the Progressives* (Urbana: University of Illinois Press, 2000); Elizabeth Clapp, *Mothers of All Children: Women Reformers and the Rise of Juvenile Courts in Progressive Era America* (University Park, PA: Penn State University Press, 1998); Carol Nackenoff and Kathleen S. Sullivan, "The House That Julia (and Friends) Built: Networking Chicago's Juvenile Court," in *Statebuilding from the Margins: Between Reconstruction and the New Deal*, ed. Carol Nackenoff and Julie Novkov (Philadelphia: University of Pennsylvania Press, 2014).

[133] Minnie Low, "The Russian Jew in Chicago," in *The Russian Jew in the United States*, ed. Charles Bernheimer (Philadelphia: John C. Winston, 1905); Minnie F. Low, "Legal Aid," *Proceedings of the Sixth National Conference on Jewish Charities* (1910), 189.

[134] Tanenhaus, *Juvenile Justice in the Making*; Willrich, *City of Courts*.

The Bureau of Justice

The Protective Agency for Women and Children often claimed that it was a unique organization, but just two years after its founding, Joseph Errant, the agency's first part-time lawyer, created Chicago's Bureau of Justice. The bureau's mission was to provide legal aid to men and women, and it had the support of Chicago's Society for Ethical Culture, an organization committed to seeking universal truths through reason, good works, and service to others.[135] Part athenaeum, part religious organization part reform entity, the group sponsored a popular lecture series, which in the 1880s featured such leading intellectuals and activists as Clarence Darrow and Jane Addams. The society also sought to bring together businessmen and laborers, as it believed in the need for reforms to prevent the exploitation of workers and abhorred class conflict and class violence of the kind that had occurred repeatedly in Chicago in the 1880s.[136]

The bureau was founded in 1888 after Errant delivered a speech to the Illinois Bar Association titled "Justice for the Friendless and Poor." In his speech Errant called for a critical examination of all institutions and for all men to have empathy for the poor. He asserted that the U.S. and Illinois constitutions required justice for all, although he did not define what justice meant or how it was to be achieved. Much of the remainder of Errant's talk focused on the lack of qualifications among justices of the peace and police magistrates. Errant argued that Chicago's lower-court judges and police magistrates were unqualified and should be replaced by appropriately educated lawyers.[137] Following the talk, Errant and two board members of the Society for Ethical Culture issued a call for a

---

[135] The Chicago organization was modeled on Rabbi Felix Adler's Society for Ethical Culture in New York. Part of the Social Gospel movement, the New York organization attracted a large number of Jews to its membership. Although Jewish men were active in the Chicago society, the organization's membership was not primarily Jewish.

[136] On strikes in Chicago in the 1880s, see James Green, *Death in the Haymarket: A Story of Chicago, the First Labor Movement, and the Bombing That Divided Gilded-Age America* (New York: Anchor Books, 2006); Timothy Messer-Kruse, *The Trial of the Haymarket Anarchists* (New York: Palgrave Macmillan, 2011). On ethical culture, see Benny Kraut, *From Reform Judaism to Ethical Culture: The Religious Evolution of Felix Adler* (Cincinnati, OH: Hebrew Union College Press, 1979); Howard B. Radest, *Toward Common Ground: The Story of the Ethical Societies in the United States* (New York: Fredrick Ungar Publishing, 1969).

[137] Joseph W. Errant, "Justice for the Friendless and the Poor: An Address," (Chicago, 1888), Ethical Humanist Society of Chicago Records, Special Collections, University of Illinois at Chicago, box 1, file 17; see also Willrich, *City of Courts*, 3–28.

public meeting to discuss forming a legal aid organization to be called the Bureau of Justice.

The bureau was focused on ameliorating growing class conflict. Errant's first address referred to class conflict and even class warfare: "The watchmen on the towers tell us of strife and conflict today; society is forming into hostile armies. O, that we might all strike the deep and far sounding chords of justice that they may pour forth a volume of harmony which shall drown out the discord of the day."[138] Justice, he continued, required the recognition of the brotherhood of man, direct contact with and knowledge of the poor and the conditions in which they lived and worked, and access to the courts. The press reported that the bureau would be devoted to battling large corporations, the wealthy, and the powerful on behalf of the poor.[139]

The Bureau of Justice's immediate and material goals tracked those of the Protective Agency for Women and Children and included providing legal advice and seeking legislation to protect the poor. Yet Errant made little mention of the agency or even that he had worked as its attorney. Instead, he tapped a number of the members of the Society for Ethical Culture to serve as directors of the bureau. Not surprisingly, the bureau's employees and its board were entirely male. The merchant Frank Tobey was a board member of the Society for Ethical Culture, an officer of the Bureau of Justice, and eventually the long-term president of the Chicago Legal Aid Society (formed in 1905). Although Tobey was professionally successful, the officers of the bureau could not claim the same social status as that of many agency directors.

The founders of the bureau structured and operated it in a manner different from women's legal aid organizations. Instead of using outside counsel and an internal supervisor, it had one male attorney who filled both positions. In addition, the bureau's board of directors was not involved in day-to-day management or with specific cases; its primary duty was fund-raising. In contrast, the Protective Agency's board stressed the importance of the board's day-to-day contact with clients and with managing cases. Such differences were gendered, as many men's organizations had neither a tradition of nor time for hands-on care for the poor. Situated in the realm of professional male lawyers and businessmen who were intimately tied to the market, the bureau charged its clients

[138] Errant, "Justice for the Friendless and the Poor," 12.
[139] See "A Bureau of Justice," *Chicago Daily Tribune*, February 11, 1888, 3.

10 percent of any amount that it collected. Free legal assistance in this case was thus not entirely free.

Officers of the Protective Agency and the bureau had different understandings of the fundamental nature of their callings. Whereas the members of the agency explicitly enunciated elite and middle-class women's special roles and duties to care for other women, the bureau drew liberally on the language and thoughts of the Social Gospel movement. Cornerstone tenets of the Social Gospel that resonated with the bureau's leadership emphasized brotherhood, some form of class equality (although generally not the actual redistribution of wealth), and the belief that a rejuvenated social order based on ethics could produce American ideals of justice.[140] A Bureau of Justice officer wrote, "We recognize the force of the obligation that we are our brother's keeper."[141] Another officer proclaimed that the provision of legal aid welcomed the client back into "the brotherhood of man."[142] The bureau's language of brotherhood was clearly addressed to other men. Women were an afterthought.

Concepts of brotherhood countered what the bureau called a "barbaric," "self-destructive" individualism, and the bureau rejected any idea that poverty was a natural or necessary component of society.[143] Rather, it recognized the connection between the salvation of society and that of the individual; that is, society as a whole could progress only when poverty and misery were eliminated – goals that would be achieved through the elimination of individual greed and the recognition of each person's humanity. Bureau president Charles Ham wrote, "As in a vision I see [the bureau's] work extending, until it shall embrace every city, . . . until

---

[140] Considerable historical debate exists regarding the Social Gospel movement's philosophy. Some consider it part of American evangelicalism and a response to urbanization, industrialization, and immigration, as well as a crucial component of American progressivism. See Ronald C. White Jr. and C. Howard Hopkins, *The Social Gospel: Religion and Reform in Changing America* (Philadelphia: Temple University Press, 1976); Janet Forsythe Fishburn, *The Fatherhood of God and the Victorian Family: The Social Gospel in America* (Philadelphia: Fortress Press, 1981); Wendy J. Deichmann Edwards and Carolyn De Swarte Gifford, eds., *Gender and the Social Gospel* (Urbana: University of Illinois Press, 2003), 3. Bureau of Justice (BoJ), *Fifth Annual Report of the Bureau of Justice of Chicago for the Year 1893* (Chicago, 1893), 6.

[141] BoJ, *Second Annual Report of the Bureau of Justice of Chicago for the Year 1890* (Chicago: Hornstein Bros. Printers, 1891), 6.

[142] Ibid., 4.

[143] BoJ, *Third Annual Report of the Bureau of Justice of Chicago for the Year 1891* (Chicago, 1891), 5.

the poor and unfortunate everywhere shall recognize it as the evangel of man's universal brotherhood."[144]

The men of the bureau optimistically believed that justice in the individual case had the ability to create a universal justice that would usher in a new world order. The writings of the officers of the bureau, especially Ham and Edward C. Wentworth, had a millenarian quality in which society, through the good works of men, was seen as slowly progressing to a kingdom of God on earth in which justice would prevail, poverty would cease, and all men would be equal. In 1890 Wentworth wrote, "The golden age of which bureaus of justice [are] destined to be such an important part, is yet remotely distant, but there can come, if we will, a morning on whose eastern sky is written, 'The Millennium Dawns.'"[145]

Preachers of the Social Gospel made distinctions between justice and charity. The Reverend Henry C. Potter, a labor activist and proponent of the Social Gospel, declared, "What the laborer wants from his employer is fair and fraternal dealings, not alms-giving, and a recognition of his manhood rather than a condescension to his inferiority."[146] Here Potter specifically saw manhood and charity as antithetical. This language became commonplace within the Social Gospel and labor movements. The bureau echoed this antithesis between manhood and charity and began to make it fundamental to legal aid. In its first annual report, the bureau defined "Charity" as producing "discord" and "Justice" as creating "harmony."[147] The need for charity arose only when there was injustice; if justice prevailed, charity was unnecessary. Rehearsing arguments that would become a mainstay of legal aid organizations, the bureau juxtaposed charity, which marked men in need as different and unequal from other men, with legal aid, which treated men as equals. "The leading object of the Bureau seems to be to substitute justice for charity. It seeks to procure for the poor their rights. Instead of debasing its beneficiaries by doling out disdainful charity it extends the right hand of fellowship and gives them justice to which they are entitled."[148] Ham continually

---

[144] BoJ, *Fifth Annual Report*, 6.

[145] BoJ, *Second Annual Report*, 9.

[146] Henry C. Potter, *The Treasury; a Magazine of Religious and Current Thought for Pastor and People*, 4 (1887): 187, 188. See also White and Hopkins, *The Social Gospel*, 64.

[147] BoJ, *First Annual Report of the Bureau of Justice of Chicago for the Year 1888–1889* (Chicago: Hornstein Bros. Printers, 1889), 3.

[148] "Annual Report, Bureau of Justice," *Chicago Daily Tribune*, April 20, 1890, 10.

warned against letting the bureau become a "charity," for the poor were "as worthy as the rich."[149]

The Bureau of Justice thus placed a tremendous amount of faith in the curative powers of law and legal aid. Soon it began to use the argument that the wronged man without access to law would become "an enemy of the social order."[150] In contrast, it claimed, the bureau's clients would "find a new confidence in the law and its administration."[151]

The Bureau of Justice's name showcased its purpose as providing justice, not just legal representation. Joseph Errant wrote, "I feel that it is important to see to it that no *innocent persons* shall suffer as it is to see to it that no guilty person shall escape punishment."[152] The bureau's president explained that if an employer in a wage-claim dispute offered to settle the dispute but honestly believed that he did not owe the sum, the bureau would not accept the offer, as it would further promote injustice.[153] Unlike the adversarial legal system, which produces one victor whose win may or may not correspond with the underlying truth and equity of the matter, the bureau strove to create a nonadversarial process that would produce an objective truth that corresponded with the substantive justice of the claim. In its view, lawyers were not to be zealous advocates of a client's claim but, rather, were to act as neutral parties. Ham explained, we never "seek to win for our clients by cunning or finesse; but solely by holding with even hand the scales of justice."[154] This understanding distinguished the bureau from the more general and negative reputation of lawyers in the popular mind – which held that the lawyer's job was to advocate for his client, irrespective of the underlying morality or honesty of his client's position. The bureau projected an image of itself and its lawyers as virtuous – seeking truth and effectuating the public good.[155]

---

[149] Ibid.

[150] BoJ, *Second Annual Report*, 4.

[151] Ibid., 21.

[152] BoJ, *First Annual Report*, 18 (emphasis in original).

[153] Ibid., 5.

[154] BoJ, *Third Annual Report*, 3.

[155] On the problems of lawyer's duties to clients versus more ethical ideas of lawyering, see Anthony Kronman, *The Lost Lawyer: Failing Ideas of the Legal Profession* (Cambridge, MA: Belknap Press of Harvard University Press, 1993). On the idea of "counsel for the situation" and the Progressive Era lawyer as representing the public good, see Clyde Spillenger, "Elusive Advocate: Reconsidering Brandeis as People's Lawyer," *Yale Law Journal* 105 (1996): 1445; and David W. Levy, "The Lawyer as Judge: Brandeis' View of the Legal Profession," *Oklahoma Law Review* 22 (1969): 374.

In conjunction with this idea of truth seeking, the bureau touted its ability to settle cases and emphasized its own impartiality. Errant explained, "The known fact that we investigate carefully and are always willing to hear the other side before we decide on our course of action, brings parties to us in answer to our notice or visit who are willing to submit the case to our judgment."[156] This focus on mediation dovetailed with the bureau's emphasis on creating a harmonious society in which justice prevailed and conflict easily could be resolved.

The large number of settlements and arbitrations that the Bureau of Justice (as well as nearly all legal aid organizations past and future) negotiated raises the question of why legal aid organizations had any authority in the eyes of claimants and potential defendants. Did parties to a dispute actually believe that the bureau provided impartial justice? Why were they so willing to submit to its self-constructed jurisdiction? Perhaps people trusted the bureau to arbitrate claims because of its position as simultaneously part of and apart from the community in which such claims arose. Despite statements that might indicate otherwise, the vast majority of claims handled by the bureau involved poor people making complaints against other poor people. The bureau functioned as an outsider with moral, class, and professional authority, while simultaneously representing itself as a community institution. The bureau also succeeded because it, like the Protective Agency, provided an alternative to the otherwise unruly magistrate courts. Like other providers of legal aid, the bureau did not impose its power single-handedly. Rather, the number of cases it handled grew each year, primarily through word of mouth, indicating that most clients must have felt some satisfaction with the process and the outcomes of their disputes.

Overwhelmingly the bureau's cases were small disputes, reflecting the everyday life of the poor – hundreds of small wage claims; mortgage foreclosures; loan defaults on beds, tools, sewing machines, furniture, and stoves; disputes pitting landlords who held tenants' goods against tenants challenging the landlords' right to do so; claims against lenders in which the borrower had assigned his wages, and pawnbrokers who refused to return goods such as a coat, shoes, a clock, a child's toy. This web of loans and credit defined the daily life of the urban poor, owing to the seasonality of their work, low wages, economic fluctuations, illness, death, desertion, and the beginning of a consumer economy. Although most of the claims were for very small sums, the amounts were crucial to those

[156] BoJ, *First Annual Report*, 18.

who had little or no savings or safety net on which they could rely. They represented the critical difference in people's lives – whether they ate or went hungry, had shelter or were homeless, had coal to burn in winter or froze, had a bed or slept on the floor, could secure medical treatment or had to suffer untreated.[157] The bureau recognized that predictable patterns for claims emerged: when employment was high, there were more wage claims; when employment was low, loan foreclosures dominated. Yet in significant contrast to the Protective Agency, the Bureau of Justice took few domestic relations claims and no divorce cases.[158]

In the various examples of cases that the bureau discussed, it did not emphasize law or legal process. One case involved a carpenter who had refused to pay a worker seven dollars in wages; when the bureau's lawyer accompanied the unpaid man on a visit to the carpenter, the carpenter paid the seven dollars. In connection with a case of an unpaid mortgage, the bureau contacted the lender, and the lender and borrower renegotiated the amount due, even though there was no valid legal claim. Many of the bureau's cases revolved around contracts, but it did not believe that all contracts should be enforced nor did it endorse an ideology of freedom to contract. Instead, the bureau viewed contracts through a paradigm of substantive justice. Even when a contract was valid, if it was one-sided, skirted the usury laws, or if the client claimed he had not understood the agreement, the bureau would often seek to modify it or push the lender to settle for what the borrower had already paid. These cases succeeded in part because lenders to the poor often sought to avoid the limelight, depended on a series of legal bluffs to pressure borrowers, and, when confronted with a sophisticated legal advocate, easily settled claims.[159] The point here is that, even when managed and supervised by a male lawyer, the everyday work of the bureau was quite similar to that of the various women's legal aid organizations. Most of it occurred outside of the courts, in the shadow of the law.

As was the case for other legal aid providers, more and more clients sought out the bureau's help, no matter how much it expanded, and with

---

[157] On the importance of credit and loans in the economy of the poor at the turn of the century, see Ann Fleming, "The Borrower's Tale: A History of Debtors in *Lochner*-Era New York City," *Law and History Review* 30 (November 2012): 1051–98; Louis Hyman, *Debtor Nation: The History of America in Red Ink* (Princeton, NJ: Princeton University Press, 2011).

[158] For example, in its first year, the bureau handled 328 wage claims and only 8 cases involving wives' domestic relations claims. BoJ, *First Annual Report*, 9.

[159] Fleming, "The Borrower's Tale," 1088–90.

more clients came rising costs. In the mid-1890s the bureau almost closed owing to a lack of funds, but it was saved by large contributions from two women – Dr. Julia Holmes Smith and Mrs. A. M. Rothschild, who then became the first two women appointed to the bureau's board of directors. Smith, a leader in the field of homeopathic medicine, had been president of the Chicago Women's Club and a longtime supporter of the Protective Agency. Her defection to the bureau probably stemmed from disagreements with other Women's Club officers over women's roles in the Chicago 1893 Columbian Exposition.[160] Eventually, Smith ran as a Democrat against Lucy Flower, another agency officer, in a local election. Rothschild was Jewish and the widow of a Chicago department store magnate. Although the agency did not prohibit Jewish women from its membership, it had none on its board. Both women, therefore, had reason to look outside the Protective Agency to pursue their philanthropic work in law.

With the appointment of these two women, the bureau for the first time began to emphasize the number of women that it counseled, boasting in 1895 that it "advised and aided 5,217 different persons, over two-fifths of whom were women."[161] It further proclaimed that it helped women seek support from husbands and handled women's wage claims.[162] Increasingly, the bureau's promotional materials featured and empha-sized women's wage cases. Despite this new visibility of women's cases, the bureau's board of directors soon returned to being all male, and the number of domestic relations cases it accepted remained small.[163]

By 1895 the bureau's finances were precarious, and it approached the Protective Agency regarding a potential merger of the two organizations,

---

[160] Chicago's World's Fair in 1893 was called the Columbian Exposition, and it was an enormous event for Chicago and the United States. Significant controversy surrounded the role of women in participating in building the fair, including who would be on the Lady's Board of Managers and whether women's exhibitions would be primar-ily grouped together in the Women's Building or spread throughout the fair. In the end, white male organizers of the fair primarily were unwilling to give women space throughout the fair, and the Women's Board of Mangers did not include African Ameri-can women or their accomplishments in the women's exhibits. Historian Gail Bederman claims that the fair served to reify white male civilization. Gail Bederman, *Manliness and Civilization: A Cultural History of Gender and Race in the United States, 1880–1917* (Chicago: University of Chicago Press, 1996), 34–40.

[161] BoJ, *Eighth Annual Report of the Bureau of Justice of Chicago for the Year 1895* (Chicago, 1895), 3.

[162] Ibid., 11.

[163] Unfortunately, I have been unable to find documentation explaining why Smith and Rothschild resigned.

a somewhat surprising development, since each organization had long ignored the other's existence. The agency's leaders explained that it would agree to a merger only if a board of women managers controlled all cases involving women and girls. They also required equal representation of women on any board of directors. In making such demands, the agency's officers recognized and feared a pattern of women's reform organizations allowing men to join in management only to suffer the ouster of women from positions of power.[164] The agency's demands further underscore how its leaders suspected men of being unable to understand and meet poor women's needs. Jurisdiction over such women needed to remain in the hands of women. The officers of the agency did not see the bureau as its equal. The agency was better managed, on firmer financial ground, and the unacknowledged "parent" from which the bureau had "borrowed" its idea.[165]

The agency's president pointed out other considerable differences:

When it is understood that the directors of the Protective Agency give their own time and their strength mental and physical to the cause, while those of the other Society are men immersed in the cares of their own business, who have not the time that we can give to this work, and so, by their own confession, it is left entirely to the Agents, you will see a good reason for our unwillingness to abandon our own conscientious and thorough methods.[166]

The board of the agency had little interest in just raising funds. Its board members saw their work as a labor of love; their method and self-identity required direct participation and interaction with clients, attorneys, and courts, and they believed that their experience gave them legal expertise, empathy, and a knowledge of the lives of poor women that a mere attorney, who possessed technical knowledge, did not and could not possess.

During ten slow years of negotiation, the bureau and the agency could not agree on terms. By 1904 both began to falter as they struggled to meet the needs of their ever-expanding caseloads. Moreover, the policy of directly involving agency directors and members in cases became more difficult as the Protective Agency's founders and its most active members aged, died, or turned to new reforms. Finally both groups agreed, as the president of the Protective Agency put it, to "meet together on

---

[164] A number of historians of women have also recognized and identified how women lost control of reform organizations to men. See Ginzberg, *Women and the Work of Benevolence*, 127–28; Suzanne Lebsock, *The Free Women of Petersburg: Status and Culture in a Southern Town, 1784–1860* (New York: Norton, 1984).

[165] PAWC, *Eleventh Annual Report*, 13.

[166] Ibid., 14.

equal terms."[167] The Bureau of Justice had accepted most of the agency's conditions. The agency's officers understood that the merger would bring change. Fannie Howe, the last president of the agency, wrote, "We have prided ourselves on the Women's work, which has been well done, now we are to join with our brothers and obtain the help and different outlook on life which is natural to men. Let us prove equal to the demand, and work with them as earnestly and loyally as we have worked with each other."[168]

The Legal Aid Society of Chicago

The Protective Agency for Women and Children and the Bureau of Justice merged to form the Legal Aid Society of Chicago (CLAS), and its new officers immediately engaged in a different kind of discourse. Society publications spoke of its "modern business equipment" and declared with pride that "the energies" of its workers had been "so systematized and co-ordinated as to secure the most effective results."[169] It likewise put in place new rules, including limiting eligibility of clients to those who were unable to afford a lawyer; imposing an initial fee of ten cents; and charging clients ten percent of amounts collected. The society claimed that it took only cases that other lawyers found unprofitable.[170] Such policies were intended to assure the legal bar that the Legal Aid Society was not in competition with it – an issue that had not concerned the Protective Agency.

Following the bureau's long-standing policy regarding divorce, the Legal Aid Society's public and official position was that it did not accept divorce cases. Attorneys reassured supporters that the "old policy of not taking up divorce matters is still maintained."[171] Despite such public statements, the society's Women's Committee did accept a small number of divorce cases and described its policy less categorically: "The Women's Committee is conservative on this question of divorce, but when a worthless man persists in annoying his family there is sometimes no other way to set the woman free."[172] Like the Protective Agency, the committee

---

[167] PAWC, *Tenth Annual Report*, 5.
[168] PAWC, *Nineteenth Annual Report of the Protective Agency for Women and Children of Chicago* (Chicago, 1905), 6.
[169] CLAS, *Quarterly Review* 2 (October 1905): 2.
[170] CLAS, *Third Annual Report: January 1908* (Chicago, 1908), 15.
[171] CLAS, *Sixth Annual Report: January 1911* (Chicago, 1911), 11.
[172] Ibid., 9.

insisted that it maintain some discretion over accepting divorce cases and that such decisions were a matter of judgment based on its members' years of experience. Nonetheless, the society was reticent about discussing divorces, and silence descended over the topic.

Women's influence within the Legal Aid Society, however, was still noticeable and notable. Women composed half of the board of directors and two-thirds of the society's clients. In addition, the Protective Agency's former superintendent, Maud Parcells Boyes, became the society's supervisor and was publicly lauded as an "expert" who had full control of the work of the new office.[173] Boyes and her female staff continued to serve as lay lawyers, interviewing clients, deciding how to handle cases, and resolving disputes. One early publication explained the daily work of Boyes's staff: Elizabeth Stokes specialized in wage claims. Boyes and her assistant supervisor, Mary Duffy, handled domestic relations cases, chattel mortgage cases, and those cases requiring further investigation.[174] Describing the everyday work of her assistants, Boyes explained,

Miss Moore sits all day long listening and mentally disentangling the stories of hundreds who come to the office.... This work requires patience and sympathy, for we try to keep the same standard which Mrs. Charlotte M. Holt set, which was, that even when nothing could be done for the applicant[,] his story be listened to with kindness and sympathy.[175]

The women employees of the society maintained and reaffirmed the Protective Agency's understanding of the importance of nonlegal services and the benefit for clients of narrating their stories. Yet they did much more than offer a friendly ear. Boyes continued,

During the year our staff of attorneys has changed and we have no one today who was with us a year ago.... It is always a source of gratification to the Superintendent that there are few changes made in the office staff, except among the attorneys; we expect that they will not stay with us long, but while they are here they bring all the enthusiasm of the beginner.[176]

Boyes's comment slyly reflects her position that the lay legal staff possessed knowledge, experience, and sustained devotion. The new, inexperienced lawyers primarily contributed an untutored "enthusiasm."

---

[173] CLAS, *Quarterly Review* (October 1905): 2.
[174] Ibid., 4.
[175] CLAS, *Fifth Annual Report: January, 1910* (Chicago, 1910), 10.
[176] CLAS, *Annual Report* (1917), 24–25, quoted in Jack Katz, *Poor People's Lawyers in Transition* (New Brunswick, NJ: Rutgers University Press, 1982), 47.

The Legal Aid Society was unique for its time as it strove to be sex integrated and to present itself as such. Women were well represented in each of its annual reports, with one entire section devoted to Boyes's report and another to the Women's Committee report. For years the cover of its annual report indicated that its predecessor organizations were the Protective Agency for Women and Children and the Bureau of Justice, and the society advertised itself as "A Free Law Office for men, women, and children."[177] Men and women were also visually present in the annual reports, which included portraits of the highest-ranking male and female directors. One illustration published by the society depicted Justice as a woman bent on one knee with arms outstretched to receive a frightened group of children fleeing a menacing, monstrous claw (Plate 3). Personally involved and deeply maternal, Justice perhaps represents the work of the Women's Committee.[178] Next to Justice lies her sword, with a banner that reads "Legislation." This refers to the many reforms that the Women's Committee and the society were involved in, including age-of-consent laws, juvenile justice, effective usury laws, the prohibition of wage assignments, and husbands' support obligations to their wives. Legal Aid Society photographs also document the racial diversity of its clients and emphasize the maternalism of both white and African American women. A photograph of the society's waiting room, (this book's cover photograph) featured on the front of a CLAS pamphlet, showed a roomful of clients – predominantly women, African American and white, some with babies and small children in their arms or on their laps.[179] Harkening back to illustrations used by New York's Working Women's Protective Union, this image also seems to depict an errant employer or other potential defendant, differentiated by his more formal dress and somewhat sinister look. He is otherwise surrounded by clients. Unusual for the time, African American women and white women appear united as mothers, and the photograph makes it clear that the society accepted the cases of African Americans.

The society also rehabilitated the image of poor and working-class men. Its more sympathetic view emphasized that, like his wealthier

[177] CLAS pamphlet, Legal Aid Society of Chicago, miscellaneous materials (no box or folder number, ca. 1905), Chicago History Museum.

[178] CLAS pamphlet cover, Legal Aid Society of Chicago, miscellaneous materials (no box or folder number, ca. 1905), photograph no. ICHi-68713, Chicago History Museum.

[179] CLAS, "Legal Aid Offices, c. 1905" (pamphlet), Legal Aid Society of Chicago, miscellaneous materials (no box or folder number, ca. 1909), photograph no. ICHi-36161, photographer Charles J. Bernauer, Chicago History Museum.

counterparts, even the poor working man was a breadwinner and father who supported, loved, and was intimately involved with his family. One elaborate illustration depicts a distraught husband and wife in their modest home (Plate 4). The husband reaches down to comfort his wife, who appears to be weeping or praying, while he stares at the nearby scene of his desperately ill, angelic daughter. The daughter lies on a makeshift bed, while a doctor observes her with grave concern. Above the illustration appears the text, "Regulate the Loan Sharks!" Across the bottom it reads, "Why Men Borrow Money and Pay 180% Interest Per Year!"[180] Before the merger, the Protective Agency often accused poor and working-class men of borrowing money for frivolous and selfish uses, and doing so without their wives' consent. Now, in this new scenario, the husband and father has borrowed money to save his ill daughter. This more domestic and certainly less brutish image of the poor man made him seem worthy of receiving legal aid.

The ability of professional men and women to work together at the Legal Aid Society, and for women to have substantive power, was unique to the Chicago society for a number of reasons. First, the Protective Agency's longevity and its connection, through its members and its relationship with the Chicago Women's Club, to a vast network of women's reform organizations gave women reformers gravitas and a power base. Second, in working together to create Chicago's juvenile and domestic relations courts, female reformers and male lawyers learned to cooperate and institutionalized a nonadversarial form of legal process.[181] Third, the Protective Agency was so well established and its leaders so well respected that in its negotiations with the Bureau of Justice they had contractually arranged to share power. Maud Parcells Boyes would remain with the Legal Aid Society for another decade, but she soon encountered a group of professional male lawyers outside of Chicago who would fail to recognize her experience and expertise.

---

[180] CLAS advertisement, "Regulate the Loan Sharks!" Legal Aid Society of Chicago, miscellaneous materials (no box or folder number, ca. 1905), photograph no. ICHi-36161, courtesy of the Chicago History Museum.

[181] On the women's network in Chicago and the building of the Juvenile Court, see Nackenoff and Sullivan, "The House that Julia (and Friends) Built."

PART II

THE PROFESSIONALIZATION OF LEGAL AID,
1890–1921

3

Of Immigrants, Sailors, and Servants

The Legal Aid Society of New York

The Legal Aid Society of New York (NYLAS) represented a significant departure from women's legal aid organizations and their focus on women's unique responsibilities and needs, as well as from the Bureau of Justice's emphasis on brotherhood. The New York society provided legal services to both men and women, it handled a wide range of legal cases, and male attorneys generally controlled it. It was also a secular organization in its approach, far removed from the Social Gospel and the sentimentality of earlier organizations. The Legal Aid Society of New York saw itself as part of the legal profession and viewed the mission of legal aid as Americanizing and disciplining new immigrants into the wage economy. Importantly, its leaders generally imagined the immigrants in need of legal services to be primarily male. This model for legal aid services spread from New York throughout urban areas in New England and to parts of the Midwest. Under its sway, legal aid organizations no longer saw themselves as charities, although they adopted some of the most punitive aspects of turn-of-the-century philanthropies.

In comparison to women's legal aid organizations, which were founded and managed primarily by native-born Protestant women, the precursor to the New York Legal Aid Society – Der Deutscher Rechts-Schutz Verein – was established by wealthy male German immigrants in 1876 to provide various forms of aid, including legal assistance, to German immigrants. Several of the founders of this organization were refugees from the 1848 revolution in Germany, in which ideas of constitutionalism and legal reform played large roles.[1] After establishing themselves in the

---

[1] Ann Goldberg, *Honor, Politics, and the Law in Imperial Germany, 1871–1914* (Cambridge: Cambridge University Press, 2010), 23–24.

United States, the founders generally became staunch Republicans, and a good number of them entered the legal profession.[2] They were committed to free labor, constitutionalism, and high German culture. In contrast, the founders of New York's Working Women's Protective Union, discussed in Chapter 1, tended to be Democrats and were often Irish American, and some had connections to the labor movement. There was little overlap between those who supported the Working Women's Protective Union and those who supported the New York society in its early years.

For a decade and a half, Der Deutscher Rechts-Schutz Verein remained insular. Only in the early 1890s, after a number of its founders had died, did it eliminate the requirement that those who sought aid had to be German. In 1896 it changed its name to the Legal Aid Society of New York.[3] These changes reflected its relatively new practice of taking clients of any nationality, as well as its goal of attracting a larger pool of financial contributors. Nevertheless, well into the 1890s, German immigrants or their first-generation children remained the largest group of clients served. Although some non-German lawyers were on its board of directors, the society's primary association was with the German immigrant community, not with the primarily Protestant and elite Association of the Bar of the City of New York.

Under the long leadership of Arthur von Briesen (1890–1915), the society expanded dramatically, eventually opening multiple offices across New York City. The seemingly tireless Briesen was obsessed with serving an increasing number of clients, while also continually claiming that the organization desperately needed funds. In Briesen's hands, the society's growth was remarkable: in 1890 it had 4,000 new cases; by 1905 it was handling more than 21,000 new cases.[4]

Similar to other legal aid organizations, wage claims were the society's single largest category of cases.[5] It is remarkable that, decade after

[2] Hasia R. Diner, *A Time for Gathering: The Second Migration, 1820–1880* (Baltimore: John Hopkins University Press, 1992), 164. Bertram Korn, "Jewish 48'ers in America," American Jewish Archives, http://americanjewisharchives.org/journal/PDF/1949_02_01_00_korn.pdf; I. B. Bailin, "Sigismund Kaufmann, Abolitionist," *Jewish Currents* (July–August 1961): 20–22.

[3] See John MacArthur Maguire, *The Lance of Justice: A Semi-Centennial History of the Legal Aid Society, 1876–1926* (Buffalo, NY: Wm. S. Hein Publishing, 1928), 16–17, 58.

[4] NYLAS, *Fifteenth Annual Report of the President, Treasurer, and Attorney of the German Legal Aid Society for the Year 1890* (New York: Evening Post Job Printing House, 1891), 4; NYLAS, *Thirtieth Annual Report of the President, Treasurer, and Attorneys of the Legal Aid Society for the Year 1905* (New York: Thomas Press, 1905), 5.

[5] See, e.g., NYLAS, *Twenty-Fifth Annual Report of the President, Treasurer, and Attorneys of the Legal Aid Society for the Year 1900* (New York: C. J. O'Brien, 1901), 24; *Legal Aid Review* 4 (October 1907): 28; *Legal Aid Review* 1 (January 1917): 16.

decade, wage claims predominated across organizations that provided legal aid to the poor. In legal aid literature, the unpaid worker transcended time and geography. The proliferation of such claims indicates the instability of employment for the poor, the marginality of those who employed them, and the absence of a state agency that could enforce the few wage laws that existed. Many immigrants at the turn of the century (and well beyond) worked in some form of manufacturing or in the building trades, which often involved layers of subcontractors who had little if any capital.[6] Subcontractors formed undercapitalized corporations and then abandoned them, leaving unpaid employees in their wake. Even honest and well-intentioned subcontractors depended for their pay on the contractor, who was dependent on the manufacturer, who depended on those who placed orders. A failure at any point in this chain left lower strata of subcontractors and employees unpaid.

One of the first major lobbying efforts undertaken by the society was to extend the law allowing for the arrest of a male employer who did not pay a woman's wage to apply to those who did not pay men's wages as well. The society explained,

It is to be assumed that a workingwoman generally supports herself alone; that a workingman, however, supports a wife and children. If the proviso of arrest is sound and works good results in cases of money due to women, it is evident that the same salutary provision . . . should be made in favor of him who supports and cares for women and children.[7]

The Legal Aid Society's rationale regarding the role of women wage earners was a tremendous departure from that of the Working Women's Protective Union, which had lobbied for the original law. The Protective Union had long recognized that many women were the breadwinners in their families, a fact seldom acknowledged by the society. As reflected in the society's comment, one of its basic tenets was that breadwinners were men, not women.

The New York society also differentiated itself from earlier legal aid providers in that it employed only full-time professional lawyers. It bestowed a backhanded compliment on New York's Working Women's

---

[6] See Diner, *A Time for Gathering*, 60–85; Gerald Sorin, *A Time for Building: The Third Migration, 1880–1920* (Baltimore: Johns Hopkins University Press, 1992), 69–105; Jared N. Day, *Urban Castles: Tenement Housing and Landlord Activism in New York City, 1890–1943* (New York: Columbia University Press, 2000). The failure of employers to pay employees remains a significant problem in America and around the globe. See Katherine Bobo, *Wage Theft in America* (New York: New Press, 2011).

[7] NYLAS, *Seventeenth Annual Report of the President, Treasurer, and Attorney of the German Legal Aid Society for the Year 1892* (New York: R. H. Plowman, 1893), 3.

Protective Union by describing it as our "one lovely sister" while pointing out how much more money the society collected for its clients and the union's lack of a full-time attorney.[8] By 1913, Briesen was convinced that the Protective Union no longer served a purpose and that it should merge with the society. The union was not interested.[9]

The claim that the Legal Aid Society employed only lawyers was also not quite true. In the 1890s, Albert Leuz, who held a law degree from a German university but was not a licensed attorney in New York, worked at the society. Its chief attorney explained, "Mr. Albert Leuz is . . . the hardest worked man in the office. He . . . takes the names of clients when they first apply . . . and hears their complaints. He also writes most of the demand notes, and sees many of the defendants, and acts as arbiter on many disputed questions."[10] Thus the vast majority of applicants and even clients of the society never saw a licensed attorney.[11] Most likely Leuz was the first man to perform what in women's legal aid organizations was the quintessential role of the female lay lawyer. By the second decade of the twentieth century, when professional lawyers carried out these functions at the society, it labeled them "Front Desk attorneys."[12]

Yet the society molded its identity as that of an organization of professional attorneys ensconced in the full-time practice of law. In fact, the society's leaders began to portray the very name "Legal Aid Society" as indicating that professionally trained attorneys provided all legal assistance.[13] This stood in contrast to those agencies that had "protective" in their name and employed female lay lawyers.

One of the differences between early legal aid providers and the New York Society's board and attorneys was how they envisioned their clients. Early women's legal aid organizations and the Chicago Bureau of Justice certainly provided assistance to immigrants and, at times, remarked on

---

[8] NYLAS, *Twenty-Second Annual Report of the President of the Legal Aid Society for the Year 1897* (New York: Albert B. King, 1898), 6.

[9] Arthur von Briesen to Starr J. Murphy, December 16, 1913, Arthur von Briesen Papers, Public Policy Papers, Department of Rare Books and Special Collections, Princeton University Library (hereinafter Briesen Papers), box 4, folder 3.

[10] NYLAS, *Eighteenth Annual Report of the President, Treasurer, and Attorney of the German Legal Aid Society for the Year 1893* (New York: R. H. Plowman, 1894), 20.

[11] NYLAS, *Nineteenth Annual Report of the President, Treasurer, and Attorney of the German Legal Aid Society for the Year 1894* (New York: R. H. Plowman, 1895), 27.

[12] See J. P. Schmitt, *History of the Legal Aid Society of New York, 1872–1912* (New York: Legal Aid Society of New York, 1912), 27.

[13] See Arthur von Briesen to Tharon G. Strong, September 28, 1910, Briesen Papers, box 4, folder 2.

the changing population that they served. But these organizations did not see their clients' ethnicity or nationality as defining them. Instead, women's legal aid organizations saw gender and poverty as the salient factors. Even with class separating early female aid providers from their clients, the providers imagined that gender united them – although it did not make them equals. In fact, class difference and shared gender had led upper-class women to become providers of legal assistance. Likewise, in the case of the Chicago Bureau of Justice, providers steeped in the Social Gospel identified themselves and their clients as sharing basic human qualities and, ideally, an underlying sense of brotherhood.

As immigration into the United States increased beginning in the 1890s, and as immigrants from places other than Germany became a larger portion of the New York Legal Aid Society's clientele, its board of directors and lawyers initially treated these new immigrants as different from and inferior to earlier German immigrants.[14] Neither sisterhood nor brotherhood united provider and client. According to the society, the new immigrants lacked character and intelligence, their emotions were overwrought, and they failed to appreciate the American legal system. They thought that this was especially true of Jewish immigrants from eastern Europe, who increasingly sought the services of the society.[15]

During the late 1890s and into the twentieth century, many cities experienced growth in their Jewish populations, but Ellis Island was the primary point of entry for European immigration, and many Jewish immigrants stayed and settled in New York City. Between 1881 and 1914, 2 million Jews (mostly from eastern Europe) arrived in the United States.[16] In 1870, New York City had a Jewish population of approximately 80,000; that number soared to 1.4 million in 1915, when Jews

---

[14] See, e.g., NYLAS, *Twenty-Eighth Annual Report of the President, Treasurer, and Attorneys of the Legal Aid Society for the Year 1903* (New York: Thomas Publishing Company, 1903).

[15] Around the turn of the century many Americans viewed Jews as not white, and doubted whether they were capable of assimilation and self-governance. See Mathew Frye Jacobson, *Whiteness of a Different Color: European Immigrants and the Alchemy of Race* (Cambridge, MA: Harvard University Press, 1998). See also Howard Markel, *Quarantine! East European Jewish Immigrants and the New York City Epidemics of 1892* (Baltimore: Johns Hopkins University Press, 1997); Sorin, *A Time for Building*; John Higham, *Stranger in the Land: Patterns of American Nativism, 1860–1925* (New Brunswick, NJ: Rutgers University Press, 2002).

[16] For an excellent account of why Jews immigrated and the difficult decisions that they made, see Jonathan D. Sarna, *American Judaism: A History* (New Haven, CT: Yale University Press, 2004). See also John Higham, *Send These to Me: Jews and Other Immigrants in America* (New York: Atheneum, 1975).

constituted almost 28 percent of the city's population.[17] More Jews lived in the lower part of New York City – Manhattan's Lower East Side – at the turn of the century than have lived in any other single place in America at any time before or since.[18] In reaction, the surge of Jewish immigrants produced a new and heightened anti-Semitism.[19] Moreover, German and central European Jews who had immigrated before the Civil War shared little with the large number of poor eastern European Jewish immigrants who arrived in New York City at the turn of the century.

These new immigrants affected how some Americans perceived all Jews.[20] As well, Jewish eastern European immigrants produced enormous tensions and strains within the New York Legal Aid Society, as it simultaneously sought out new immigrants as clients and was highly critical of and at certain times even repulsed by them. Some lawyers complained of the difficulty and unpleasantness they encountered when working with these new immigrants, explaining, "Russian and kindred immigrants are less in sympathy with the views of life and justice that prevail in the United States, . . . [b]eing frequently ignorant, suspicious and over charged with prejudices."[21] Whereas women's legal aid organizations emphasized the helplessness of the women they aided, the society viewed its eastern European Jewish clients as too aggressive and as calling too freely on its services.[22]

In the early 1890s the society's board of directors considered refusing services to eastern European Jewish immigrants altogether, claiming that they were too much of a burden and strained its resources. Eventually the society formed a committee – consisting of Oswald Ottendorfer, publisher and member of the board of directors of the German Society, Briesen, and the wealthy German-Jewish financier and philanthropist Jacob Schiff – to

[17] Sarna, *American Judaism*, 153.

[18] Hasia R. Diner, *Lower East Side Memories: A Jewish Place in America* (Princeton, NJ: Princeton University Press, 2000), 130. Diner also notes that in 1910 half a million Jews lived on the Lower East Side (131).

[19] Victoria Saker Woeste, *Henry Ford's War on Jews and the Legal Battle against Hate Speech* (Stanford, CA: Stanford University Press, 2012), 3. See also Leonard Dinner, *Anti-Semitism in America* (New York: Oxford University Press, 1994).

[20] Jacobson, *Whiteness of a Different Color*; Woeste, *Henry Ford's War on Jews*; Eric Goldstein, *The Price of Whiteness: Jews, Race, and American Identity* (Princeton, NJ: Princeton University Press, 2006); Markel, *Quarantine!*; Sorin, *A Time for Building*; Higham, *Stranger in the Land*.

[21] NYLAS, *Eighteenth Annual Report*, 2.

[22] Ibid.

determine how it might handle such immigrants. The committee, through Schiff, raised funds to hire a Jewish lawyer who spoke Yiddish.[23]

The Legal Aid Society opened its East Side Branch in 1900, first located in the University Settlement House on New York City's Lower East Side, to serve the influx of immigrant Jews.[24] Although the office regularly moved to larger quarters, it always stayed in the heart of the Lower East Side. One attorney estimated that fewer than 10 percent of the people who visited the branch spoke English.[25] Another chronicler of the society wrote, "The East Side Branch became in everything but name a Hebrew Legal Aid Society," claiming that 88 percent of its clients were "of that race."[26] As late as 1911, the society's chief attorney reported that the vast majority of clients of the East Side Branch were newly arrived Jews who were "exceedingly illiterate" and the poorest of any of its clients.[27]

The establishment of the East Side Branch did not prevent the society's lawyers and board members from complaining about the character

---

[23] NYLAS, *Eighteenth Annual Report*, 3–5. As historians have long pointed out, wealthy Jewish Americans, often German Jews who had immigrated earlier, built and donated heavily to philanthropies that provided services to eastern European Jews. They too often looked down on eastern European Jews as uncivilized, but their sense of obligation along with their fear that such immigrants would provoke anti-Semitism, thus endangering all Jews, led them to build and finance such philanthropic institutions in order to prevent Jewish immigrants from becoming public charges and to hasten immigrants' acculturation and Americanization. Diner, *A Time for Gathering*; Diner, *Lower East Side Memories*, 146; Anna Igra, *Wives without Husbands: Marriage, Desertion, and Welfare in New York, 1900–1935* (Chapel Hill: University of North Carolina Press, 2006); Benny Kraut, "Jewish Survival in Protestant America," in *Minority Faith and the American Protestant Mainstream*, ed. Jonathan D. Sarna (Urbana: University of Illinois Press, 1998); Sorin, *A Time for Building*.

[24] The branch was later moved to the corner of Orchard and Rivington Streets. University Settlement House was first opened in 1886. In contrast to many settlement houses, its workers and founders were male. Almost 40 percent of its founders were lawyers, and the settlement house had a long-standing interest in the Americanization of immigrants through law. See Felice Batlan, "Law and the Fabric of the Everyday: The Settlement Houses, Sociological Jurisprudence, and the Gendering of Urban Legal Culture," *Southern California Interdisciplinary Law Journal* 15 (2006): 235.

[25] NYLAS, *Twenty-Seventh Annual Report of the President, Treasurer, and Attorneys of the Legal Aid Society for the Year 1902* (New York: Evening Post Job Printing House, 1903), 32–33.

[26] Schmitt, *History of the Legal Aid Society of New York*, 26.

[27] NYLAS, *Thirty-Ninth Annual Report of the President, Treasurer, and Attorney of the Legal Aid Society for the Year 1914* (New York: Manger, Hughes and Manger, 1915), 35. See also NYLAS, *Thirty-Sixth Annual Report of the President, Treasurer, and Attorney-in-Chief of the Legal Aid Society for the Year 1911* (New York: Manger, Hughes and Manger, 1912), 32.

and litigiousness of eastern European Jews. One board member described them as "still living [in] the atmosphere of the middle ages" and as failing to possess a "proper respect for law," or "the sanctity" of contract.[28] Its lawyers also saw them as forever arguing over small issues.[29] Some lawyers attempted to discern whether quarrelsomeness and acrimony were inbred racial characteristics or a product of environment. One opined that eastern European Jews derived pleasure from litigation and conflict, and that it was the product of too much freedom in America.[30] Another thought that they were "naturally litigious."[31]

Accordingly, the society believed, such immigrants lacked the self-discipline necessary to be part of a democratic polity. They too frequently sought the assistance of legal aid. Pursuant to the society's paradoxical logic, *not* seeking legal assistance gauged an immigrant population's potential for assimilation and suitability for citizenship. That is, needing the society's assistance indicated that an immigrant was unable to solve his own problems and thus was civically immature. This was especially the case if an applicant brought a problem to the society that did not have a legal solution. One attorney complained that he often had to "disabuse [the eastern European applicant] of the impression of imaginary wrongs."[32]

The society's lawyers used the new immigrant's visit to its offices and his interaction with its employees as a lesson in citizenship and self-discipline. "Our interviews have been treated by us as so many opportunities of raising [immigrants] to truer manhood and better citizenship."[33] A society publication explained:

Very frequently an applicant [is]...indignant at the treatment he has received....It is then the duty of the attorney to point out...that the treatment he has received is not unjust, but...necessary to the social and political well-being of his community. The man...realizes...that everyone in a civilized state must give up certain privileges and advantages to which he feels himself entitled.[34]

---

[28] Louis Stoiber to Arthur von Breisen, April 19, 1905, Briesen Papers, box 4, folder 13.
[29] Daniel Bender, *Sweated Work, Weak Bodies: Anti-Sweatshop Campaigns and Languages of Labor* (New Brunswick, NJ: Rutgers University Press, 2004).
[30] NYLAS, *Twenty-Seventh Annual Report*, 32.
[31] NYLAS, *Twenty-Eighth Annual Report*, 31.
[32] Schmitt, *History of the Legal Aid Society of New York*, 19–20.
[33] NYLAS, *Nineteenth Annual Report*, 27.
[34] NYLAS, "Editorial," *Legal Aid Review* 1 (July 1903): 2.

Surprisingly, this process of transforming the immigrant into an American through legal aid did not include instructions about individual rights or concepts of liberty. Rather, its lesson was to inform immigrants that law held no solution.[35]

Lawyers also lectured these new immigrants about the cash nexus of law in a capitalist economy; first and foremost, a lawyer's time and services were valuable. The attorney for the East Side Branch elaborated on this theme: "This office continually dings into the ears of its clients the principle that suits are brought, not for the sake of inconveniencing the defendant but to gain something substantial for the plaintiff. Your Attorney also always brings home the fact that time is money."[36] The society rationed the legal services it dispensed, like the material relief that charities provided or withheld, to prevent the "vagrant giving of alimony or writs of *habeas corpus* or wage orders or divorces."[37] Legal aid was not to be freely given, but to be doled out carefully in those cases in which a "real wrong" and "real distress" existed.[38] Moreover, the society's services were not free; clients were charged twenty-five cents plus 10 percent of any money that they received, along with costs. The society also would not release money that it had received without first deducting its costs and fees. Some clients complained that this policy was unfair.[39]

In a drastic departure from the practices of earlier legal aid organizations, the society insisted that the only legitimate reason to pursue legal redress was to receive monetary damages – that anything else, even the pursuit of justice, was unmanly. This attitude was ironic, given that anti-Semitic imagery of Jewish men portrayed them as obsessed with money and profit. In contrast, the society viewed these immigrant clients as being driven by excess emotion. One attorney explained,

---

[35] On various understandings of what constituted the Americanization of immigrants, see Christina A. Ziegler-McPherson, *Americanization in the States: Immigrant Social Welfare Policy, Citizenship, and National Identity in the United States, 1908–1929* (Gainesville: University Press of Florida, 2009). For some early classic studies, see Edward George Hartmann, *The Movement to Americanize the Immigrant* (New York: Columbia University Press, 1948); Higham, *Stranger in the Land.*

[36] NYLAS, *Nineteenth Annual Report,* 17.

[37] William H. Allen (NYLAS), "How 'Relief Societies' May Profit from Studying Legal Relief," *Legal Aid Review* 1 (July 1903): 2.

[38] NYLAS, "Editorial Notes," *Legal Aid Review* 1 (October 1903): 1.

[39] See Arnold Kohn to Arthur von Briesen, November 22, 1911, Briesen to Kohn, November 23, 1911, Briesen Papers, box 4, folder 2.

We try to weed out those applicants who desire to begin litigation more out of spite than for any reason.... [E]ven after an action has been commenced [if] the plaintiff begins to show this desire of real persecution and informs us that "it is not the money I am after, but satisfaction,"... the action is discontinued and dropped by us.[40]

A lawsuit was thus warranted only to fulfill the market-based logic of the transfer of money from one party to another. Sentiments such as anger, spite, revenge, justice, and honor were inappropriate grounds for seeking legal assistance and represented the irrationality of the immigrant client. Such emotions were too associated with precapitalism and the feminine.[41]

The society thus offered lessons in the meaning of capitalist time, including the understanding that the lawyer's time was highly valuable and situated within the market. Following this logic, the society would not litigate a case if damages were less than five dollars. The society also refused to accept cases in which the client possessed any money, or if it was the type of case a private lawyer might take because of the potential for damages. New York's Working Women's Protective Union had prided itself on taking the smallest cases to court, claiming that justice outweighed time and money. Women's legal aid organizations also boasted of the time and labor they expended on even the smallest claims and were unconcerned about taking cases away from the private bar.

A Legal Aid Society lawyer, however, guarded his time, carrying out brusque exchanges with clients. One man wrote to Briesen: "[The lawyer] told me to be brief and impatiently stopped my first words as of no importance.... His attitude from the start was ... antagonistic, impatient, intolerant, and petulant."[42] The letter writer found the lawyer's behavior particularly galling because he had approached the lawyer with "courtesy" and the "attitude of a supplicant."[43] Briesen dismissively replied that it was standard practice to limit interviews to less than ten minutes.[44]

---

[40] NYLAS, *Thirtieth Annual Report*, 51.

[41] On honor and its relationship to capitalism, masculinity, and law, see Goldberg, *Honor, Politics, and the Law*; Christopher Dummit, *The Manly Modern: Masculinity in Postwar Canada* (Vancouver: University of British Columbia Press, 2007); Bertram Wyatt-Brown, *Honor and Violence in the Old South* (New York: Oxford University Press, 1986).

[42] William Champion Deming to Arthur von Briesen, February 21, 1911, Briesen Papers, box 4, folder 1.

[43] William Champion Deming to Arthur Von Briesen, February 25, 1911, Briesen Papers, box 4, folder 1.

[44] Arthur von Briesen to William Champion Deming, February 24, 1911, Briesen Papers, box 4, folder 1.

A worker who had a wage case complained that another society lawyer spoke "in such a offending manner as though I was the offending party."[45] Yet another applicant explained: "I was treated more like a criminal than anything else;" dissatisfied, she went to the Working Women's Protective Union instead.[46] Even Briesen chastised his chief attorney:

> Of late there has been an avalanche of complaints brought to me against the manner in which people are treated.... [S]ome of the men under you are liable to be unduly curt... loud in their commands, such as "Don't Speak but answer my questions." Some are turned away in tears, being told that no help can be extended to them, when perhaps a kindly direction would have accomplished a very different result.[47]

Historian Michael Katz's description of the conundrum of late-nineteenth-century charity organizations applies equally well to the New York society's understanding of legal aid. On the one hand, charity workers wanted clients to show deference and appreciation and to accept advice without argument. On the other hand, clients were expected to be independent of both charity and charity workers. A similar dynamic worked within the Legal Aid Society: if an immigrant expressed to an attorney that his claim was not adequately addressed, he was not appropriately deferential to lawyers and American law. His complaints and disappointment reflected his own lack of political, civic, and social progress. Yet the client who failed to seek the aid of the society when he suffered a legal wrong was also not an adequately independent man, as he was too meek to recognize and assert his rights.[48]

The society repeatedly announced that legal aid created better workers and servants and that it "antagonized the tendency towards communism."[49] One society report explained that 18,469 people received services from the society, costing it about one dollar per case.[50] This small expenditure, it said, satisfied "the craving for justice in the hearts of the poor and helpless" and diverted them away "from the band of the

---

[45] Wilhelmina Muller to Arthur Von Briesen, September 28, 1909, Briesen Papers, box 4, folder 5.

[46] Mary Cronin to Arthur von Briesen, n.d., Briesen Papers, box 4, folder 3.

[47] Arthur von Briesen to Leonard McGee, January 7, 1913, Briesen Papers, box 4, folder 10.

[48] Michael B. Katz, *In the Shadow of the Poorhouse: A Social History of Welfare in America* (New York: Basic Books, 1996), 68.

[49] German Legal Aid Society, *Seventeenth Annual Report of the German Legal Aid Society* (New York: B. H. Plowman, 1893), 5.

[50] NYLAS, *Twenty-Eighth Annual Report*.

dissatisfied," making them "good, loyal and enthusiastic citizens."[51]
Unlike the society, immigrants may have seen little connection between
legal aid, radicalism, and Americanization. They may have understood,
in a way that society lawyers did not, that legal aid was not an American phenomenon but also existed in western Europe, Germany, Russia,
and Poland.[52] Some immigrants even took offense at the idea that legal
aid provided lessons in American citizenship. The author of an article
in *Staats-Zeitung*, a German American newspaper, found the society's
Americanization arguments condescending and nativist, and he reversed
its rationale: immigrants already understood the meaning of law, justice,
and citizenship. Legal aid in the United States existed to protect "honest,
industrious men, accustomed to the safeguards of justice, against corrupt
and bad Americans."[53]

The treatment of eastern European Jews by the Legal Aid Society
was so troubling to some in the New York Jewish community that the
Educational Alliance, a large Jewish cultural and educational institution,
created its own legal aid bureau in 1903.[54] The bureau prided itself on
having evening and Sunday hours for clients in recognition of their long
workdays and in observation of the Saturday Sabbath. Its three part-time
male lawyers also spoke Yiddish. According to the philosophy of the
Educational Alliance's legal aid bureau, it was more effective to handle
as many small cases as possible, rather than taking a smaller number of
legally complicated cases.[55] Thus, it was willing to take cases that the
Legal Aid Society would not. In addition, the bureau long believed that it
gave its clients the type of "sympathetic treatment" the society did not.[56]

---

[51] Ibid., 6.

[52] See Henning Grunwald, *Courtroom to Revolutionary Stage: Performance and Ideology in Weimar Political Trials* (Oxford: Oxford University Press, 2012); Goldberg, *Honor, Politics, and the Law*; William Pomeranz, "Legal Assistance in Tsarist Russia: The St. Petersburg Consultation Bureaus," *Wisconsin International Law Journal* 14 (Summer 1996): 586.

[53] The *New York Times* reprinted parts of the article. "Hearts That Lie Overseas," *New York Times*, March 27, 1901, 8. See also Geoffrey Heeren, "Illegal Aid: Legal Assistance to Immigrants in the United States," *Cardozo Law Review* 33 (December 2011): 619–74, 631.

[54] "Helping the Poor to Right Their Wrongs Legally," *New York Times*, March 2, 1913. On the Educational Alliance, see Diner, *Lower East Side Memories*, 148–9.

[55] See Board of Directors Minutes for the Educational Alliance, December 19, 1927, Educational Alliance Records, reel 6, 842–843, YIVO Institute for Jewish Research, New York City (hereinafter Educational Alliance Records).

[56] Abram Glaser to Henry Fleischman, September 25, 1935, Educational Alliance Records, box 3, folder 59.

The New York Society's central message – that American law and access to legal process could produce some form of justice for the immigrant – often backfired. Even if it accepted a case, investigated it, went to trial, won, and obtained a judgment, clients were often left with nothing because many defendants simply had no assets. In 1900, the East Side Branch was able to collect only 15 percent of judgments awarded.[57] Unsatisfied judgments made plaintiffs angry at the legal system and convinced them of its lack of efficacy. At times, frustrated clients even accused the society of stealing money it collected from judgments.[58] Briesen was outraged: "One of the greatest difficulties with which the Society has to contend is the malice and ignorance of persons with uncollectable claims, who deem it their right and privilege to attack and insult the attorneys."[59] The society eventually decided that trying to obtain judgments in all cases was "useless" and that its lawyers would file suit only when there were "definite reasons for believing the defendant [was] financially responsible."[60] Such a policy underscored the poverty of most defendants but also burdened the applicant, who now had to prove that the defendant possessed adequate property to satisfy a judgment.

The society's relationship with its eastern European clients was, at best, conflicted. It simultaneously was drawn to such immigrants and resented providing legal services to them. But by locating its offices in areas populated by eastern European immigrants, and providing lawyers who spoke Yiddish, the society indicated it believed these men had some capacity to be Americanized. Immigrants from outside of Europe, in contrast, were seldom ever mentioned in the society's records. Even though Chinatown was just a few blocks from its offices, for example, society reports do not discuss providing services to Chinese immigrants.

Chinese immigrants did, however, have access to legal assistance at St. Bartholomew's Chinese Guild, which was part mission, part charity, part settlement house, part legal aid association. St. Bartholomew's was run by white Protestant missionaries in partnership with Chinese Christians.[61] The guild, which charged a small membership fee, was under the charge of

57 NYLAS, *Twenty-Fifth Annual Report of the President, Treasurer, and Attorneys of the Legal Aid Society for the Year 1900* (New York: C. J. O'Brien, 1901), 50.
58 J. W. H. Emmert to Arthur Von Briesen, October 22, 1908, Briesen Papers, box 4, folder 5.
59 Arthur von Briesen to Hon. St. Clair McKelway, n.d., Briesen Papers, box, 4, folder 5.
60 NYLAS, *Thirty-First Annual Report of the President, Treasurer, and Attorneys of the Legal Aid Society for the Year 1906* (New York: Thomas Press, 1907), 56.
61 See Mary Ting Li Lui's excellent account in *The Chinatown Trunk Mystery: Murder, Miscegenation, and Other Dangerous Encounters in Turn-of-the-Century New York*

Guy Maine (Yee Kai Man), who functioned as a lay lawyer. Maine helped Chinese victims of crimes to prosecute cases, aided Chinese immigrants who had been arrested, and helped guild members with quotidian legal problems – resolving landlord-tenant issues, drafting contracts, settling disputes, and functioning as an intermediary with the state by advocating on behalf of the Chinese community.[62] Maine's fluency in English, his Christian background, his unending energy, and his excellent reputation among city officials and reformers allowed him to function as a legal and cultural broker, and in fact he spent years as an official Chinese interpreter in the magistrates' court.[63]

Like St. Bartholomew's Chinese Guild, other mutual aid associations, fraternities, and associations provided a wide-range of legal assistance to different immigrant groups and racial minorities.[64] It is possible that those who received such services felt more welcomed, respected, and satisfied than those who sought aid from the New York Legal Aid Society.

Indeed, a series of contradictions stood at the heart of the New York society's mission. To the extent that its purpose and success were measured in money collected, it could not be effective: the poor were simply too poor and their claims too small. At the same time, it rejected any claims that potentially involved larger sums of money because a private lawyer might accept them. Legal aid thus needed a higher calling, which the society interpreted in part as a duty to shape its immigrant clients into appropriately masculine and well-disciplined citizens. Unconnected to larger reform efforts, however, this secular mission often left both clients and lawyers dissatisfied.

The Seaman's Branch

In contrast, the Legal Aid Society's Seaman's Branch celebrated the rough-hewn, working-class masculinity of the sailor, and this branch became the jewel in the society's crown. The Seaman's Branch, dedicated to providing legal services to sailors whose ships docked in New York, opened

---

City (Princeton, NJ: Princeton University Press, 2005), 124–5. Bruce Hall, *A Family Memoir of Chinatown* (New York: Free Press, 1998), 93–4.

[62] Lui, *The Chinatown Trunk Mystery*, 127–9.

[63] "Maine a Missionary Again," *New York Times*, February 13, 1916, 8.

[64] See, e.g., Theda Skocpol, Ariane Liazos, and Marshall Ganz, *What a Mighty Power We Can Be: African American Fraternal Groups and the Struggle for Racial Equality* (Princeton, NJ: Princeton University Press, 2006); Jerold S. Auerbach, *Justice without Law* (New York: Oxford University Press, 1983).

in 1900, in part through support from the Protestant Episcopal Church Missionary Society for Seamen and the American Seamen's Friend Society. The Legal Aid Society created different and more liberal policies for the legal assistance it provided to seamen, compared with the relatively limited legal services provided for immigrants at the East Side Branch. Lawyers and directors for the Seaman's Branch also engaged in significant lobbying and worked as advocates for sailors' interests in opposing what it called the "shipping interests."[65]

Unlike the other society branches, which were all supervised by a branch attorney who then reported to the society's chief attorney, the Seaman's Branch had both a branch attorney and a branch chairman. The chairman, J. Augustus Johnson, was also a member of the society's board of directors, and as such he advocated continually and effectively on behalf of the Seaman's Branch. Johnson had been the U.S. consul general to Syria in the 1860s and 1870s, where he occasionally had participated in resolving conflicts between American shipowners and their crews. Upon returning to the United States, Johnson, a member of New York's elite, engaged in wide-ranging reform activities and became a lay manager of the Church Missionary Society for Seamen.[66] Johnson explained that he sought the "divine" in even the roughest sailor.[67] He also believed that sailors needed a range of material assistance and services, and he had advocated for the opening of the Seaman's Branch.[68]

The Seaman's Branch harked back to earlier legal aid organizations: it provided an array of nonlegal services and, like Chicago's Bureau of Justice, was partially driven by a Christian understanding of brotherhood. Wrote Johnson, "[The sailor] has learned to regard the missions, the reading rooms, the pleasant entertainment, the care for his physical comfort and the legal aid offered him for the protection of his rights as having a direct bearing upon his present life, and as originating in an unselfish desire to serve the sailor as an individual."[69] Although the

---

[65] See, e.g., NYLAS, *Thirty-Seventh Annual Report of the President, Treasurer, and Attorneys of the Legal Aid Society for the Year 1912* (New York: Richardson Press, 1913), 20.

[66] J. Augustus Johnson, "For Justice and Protection to Sailors," in *Report of Addresses Delivered at a Meeting Held at Sherry's, New York, March 21, 1902* (New York: Protestant Episcopal Church Missionary Society for Seamen in the City and Port of New York, 1902), available at http://anglicanhistory.org/misc/seamen/johnson1902.html.

[67] Ibid., 12.

[68] J. Augustus Johnson, "What Can be Done for the Seamen?" *New York Times*, March 12, 1899, 9.

[69] Johnson, "For Justice and Protection to Sailors," 2.

Seaman's Branch saw applicants from around the world, it viewed sailors with significant sympathy and respect, not as inferior foreign "others."[70]

The development of the branch was part of a nineteenth-century campaign to protect, Christianize, and civilize sailors. By the turn of the century, Anglo-American regulation of the shipping industry had culminated in state and federal laws and international agreements governing the treatment of seamen, although the enforcement of such laws was weak.[71] Sailors received so much attention in the post–Civil War period in part because they straddled the boundary between slavery and wage work – captivity and freedom. In the long-standing practice known as "Shanghaing," shipmasters, often in cahoots with boardinghouse operators and others, conspired to abduct men and force them into work aboard ship. Even when physical force was not involved, intoxicated and drugged men might be tricked into signing on to a ship's crew. Reformers regularly decried such work contracts as involuntary and a mockery of "free labor."[72] In addition, sailors surrendered much of their freedom while aboard and were subject to physical discipline for a variety of infractions and even imprisonment in the case of desertion.

Popular culture often painted sailors as hypermasculine and even heroic but also boyish and at times courting trouble.[73] J. Augustus Johnson argued that the sailor's profession was dangerous, and that acts of strength, courage, brotherhood, and perseverance were necessary for his survival. Although many people looked down on the sailor's rough ways, he was, in fact, a hero charged with protecting countless lives, including the lives of the elite when wealthy passengers made ocean crossings. Johnson declared that such sailors possessed "innate nobility" and "chivalry"

---

[70] On the role of sailors in spreading radical political ideas in an earlier period, see Peter Linebaugh and Marcus Rediker, *The Many-Headed Hydra: Sailors, Slaves, Commoners, and the Hidden History of the Revolutionary Atlantic* (Boston: Beacon Press, 2001).

[71] Leon Fink, *Sweatshops at Sea: Merchant Seamen in the World's First Globalized Industry, from 1812 to the Present* (Chapel Hill: University of North Carolina Press, 2011).

[72] Ibid. On the long, uneven, and complex transition from slavery, indentured servitude, and more modern conceptions of free labor, see Robert L. Steinfeld, *The Invention of Free Labor: The Employment Relation in English and American Law and Culture, 1350–1870* (Chapel Hill: University of North Carolina Press, 1991); Christopher L. Tomlins, *Freedom Bound: Law, Labor, and Civic Identity in Colonizing English America, 1580–1865* (New York: Cambridge University Press, 2010).

[73] Fink, *Sweatshops at Sea*; Lisa Norling, *Captain Ahab Had a Wife: New England Women and the Whale Fishery, 1720–1870* (Chapel Hill: University of North Carolina Press, 2000).

that allowed them to "look death in the face."[74] Yet the sailor was also a solitary figure who roamed the globe, forever a stranger. In the public's imagination, sailors never became stable heads of households or bread-winners, even though, in reality, many of them supported wives and families. Imagined as cut off from women's civilizing and domesticating influence, the sailor remained in a perpetual state of uncivilized but coura-geous manhood, which was contrary to the cultivated self-discipline, rationality, and restraint of white middle-class men.[75]

As understood by society, the sailor in some ways remained a boy, too, continually in need of supervision and guidance, and whose mistakes and antics could thus be excused. Johnson accepted that the sailor "pre-ferred to have a good time in his own way during his brief residence on shore."[76] The Seaman's Branch thus took on the role of protecting sailors from danger and rescuing them from a variety of precarious situations.[77] One lawyer at the Seaman's Branch explained that "paternalism" was "fully justified" in the case of the seaman.[78] In his suspended state of boyish manhood, the sailor – according to the Seaman's Branch – was incapable of complete self-governance and needed the paternalistic aid of the branch's lawyers.[79]

The New York Legal Aid Society treated eastern European male immi-grants as ignorant foreigners with backward customs, but the Seaman's Branch saw its clients first and foremost as sailors, even though their clients came from across the globe and included men of different races.[80] Where the society continually chastened eastern European immigrants

---

74 Johnson, "For Justice and Protection to Sailors," 3.

75 Fink, *Sweatshops at Sea*, 57. See also Norling, *Captain Ahab Had a Wife*; Myra C. Glenn, "Troubled Manhood in the Early Republic: The Autobiography of Sailor Horace Lane," *Journal of the Early Republic* 26 (Spring 2006): 59–93; Dummit, *The Manly Modern*; James M. Lindgren, "Let Us Idealize Old Types of Manhood: The New Bedford Whaling Museum, 1903–1941," *New England Quarterly* 72 (June 1999): 163–206.

76 Johnson, "For Justice and Protection to Sailors," 2; see also "Seaman's Branch," *Legal Aid Review* 7 (April 1909): 12.

77 See "Legal Aid Society Meets," *New York Times*, February 29, 1902, 8; NYLAS, *Twenty-Sixth Annual Report of the President of the Legal Aid Society for the Year 1901* (New York: C. J. O'Brien, 1902), 27–31.

78 NYLAS, *Twenty-Ninth Annual Report of the President of the Legal Aid Society for the Year 1904* (New York: Thomas Press, 1905), 37.

79 Gail Bederman, *Manliness and Civilization: A Cultural History of Gender and Race in the United States, 1880–1917* (Chicago: University of Chicago Press, 1996); Dummit, *The Manly Modern*.

80 On the diversity of crews in the whaling industry, see Lindgren, "Let Us Idealize Old Types of Manhood," 163, 189–92.

for bringing in trivial claims and urged them to make an effort to solve their own disputes, the Seaman's Branch encouraged sailors to report all complaints to its staff.[81] It is tempting to argue that teaching discipline and citizenship was not a concern for the staff of the Seaman's Branch because sailors were only briefly in the United States. In reality, however, almost a quarter of its sailor-clients were from the United States, and many worked on domestic river barges and canal boats. Some of these American sailors must also have been immigrants, or African Americans, but the branch categorized them foremost as sailors.[82]

The legal problems of sailors were varied. They included the failure of shipmasters or agents to pay wages or provide sufficient food, and they involved boardinghouse operators and others who stole sailors' goods or money or charged exorbitant prices. Sailors also brought claims against shipowners for personal injuries. Not infrequently, sailors found themselves in criminal court owing to fighting, drinking, and other rowdiness, and the branch would represent them in those cases as well.[83]

Lawyers at the Seaman's Branch had an arsenal of advantageous procedural and substantive laws to work with, and they continually fought for more. Remarkably, a sailor could file a summary suit in libel for unpaid wages, which gave him a lien on the owner's vessel and prevented it from leaving port.[84] On more than one occasion the branch libeled ships worth hundreds of thousands of dollars for claims of unpaid wages that might total less than fifty dollars.[85] Ship captains quickly settled such claims to get ships released. In addition, shipmasters faced possible imprisonment for failure to pay wages, and in some cases an extra day's pay was assessed for each day that wages went unpaid.[86] On the other hand, a sailor who deserted his ship could face harsh punishment. In the United States, a sailor who deserted did not face imprisonment (as he did in some foreign ports), but he immediately forfeited his wages and, before 1904, any of his possessions left on board. The legal definition of desertion, however,

---

[81] See NYLAS, *Thirty-Second Annual Report of the President, Treasurer, and Attorneys of the Legal Aid Society for the Year 1907* (New York: Thomas Press, 1908), 40–41.

[82] See NYLAS, *Twenty-Seventh Annual Report*, 17.

[83] NYLAS, *Twenty-Ninth Annual Report*, 34–38; NYLAS, *Thirtieth Annual Report*, 10.

[84] NYLAS (Seamen's Branch), *The Sailor's Log* (New York, 1905), 8. George Lewis Canfield, George Walton Dalzell, and Jasper Yeates Brinton, *The Law of the Sea: A Manual of the Principles of Admiralty Law for Students, Mariners and Ship Operators* (New York: D. Appleton, 1921), 65.

[85] See NYLAS, *Twenty-Eighth Annual Report*, 35.

[86] NYLAS, *The Sailor's Log*, 8, 12–13.

required that the sailor permanently leave the vessel without cause, which gave attorneys significant room to mount a defense. The Seaman's Branch often defended sailors accused of desertion by seeking to prove they had left with cause or that they had planned to return.[87]

The Seaman's Branch positioned itself as an advocate for sailors as a class and brought what lawyers would now call test cases. Shipmasters had the ability to fine sailors for various violations, but the event had to be recorded in the ship's logbook and the sailor had to be given a chance to respond, which also had to be recorded. In one case, the shipmaster fined a sailor a large sum, which was deducted from his pay, but he was not given notice or a chance to respond to the charge. The Seaman's Branch, recognizing that this law was often ignored by shipmasters and hoping to set a favorable precedent, brought suit in federal court, where it won.[88] The branch also threatened to sue the federal government when sailors who had signed contracts to go to the Philippines were not paid according to the procedure set forth in their contract.[89] By lobbying for new legislation and bringing such test cases, the branch created advantageous procedural and substantive laws for seamen.

Adventurous Seaman's Branch lawyers protected sailors and policed the industry. Using small boats, they chased and boarded departing ships to ensure that captains were not kidnapping or abusing sailors.[90] The branch's lawyers emphasized the danger they faced in interacting with the shady characters that hung about the ports and did business with sailors. The branch's first attorney supposedly received so many threats that the society hired a police officer to protect him.[91] Branch attorneys also boasted that they were available day and night, because sailors could not miss a ship's departure time, wrongdoers could disappear, and ships that had sailed made the pursuit of libel suits difficult. Attorneys also collaborated with the U.S. Shipping Commission and foreign consuls, and they lobbied the U.S. Congress for enhanced regulation. Much like their sailor-clients, these lawyers functioned in a masculine world that episodically allowed them to flirt with danger and perform heroic acts. Furthermore, the masculinity of the sailor and the lawyer were in dialogue

---

[87] Ibid., 14–15.
[88] NYLAS, *Thirtieth Annual Report*, 38–41.
[89] Ibid., 42–43.
[90] NYLAS, *Twenty-Fifth Annual Report*, 14.
[91] NYLAS, *Twenty-Sixth Annual Report of the President, Treasurer, and Attorneys of the Legal Aid Society for the Year 1901* (New York: C. J. O'Brien, 1902), 17.

with each other; that is, working with sailors allowed the branch's middle-class, self-disciplined lawyers to enact their own fantasies of facing danger and adventures at sea.[92]

In 1905, the branch published and widely disseminated *The Sailor's Log*, a legal manual that explained a variety of laws that protected sailors. The *New York Times* opined that, with the manual, "every sailor may largely be his own lawyer."[93] The manual represented the first time that the Legal Aid Society attempted to educate laymen en masse. Throughout the manual, the society presented the sailor as a rights-bearing man, and it pledged that the Seaman's Branch would not just protect the sailor but would enable him to enforce rights that were robust and meaningful. It even requested that seamen report legal violations to the branch to assist it in policing the industry.[94] The manual ended with a list of organizations that provided material relief to sailors, seeing their need for such aid as both acceptable and unexceptional. *The Sailor's Log* was immensely popular and went into numerous printings. One Seaman's Branch attorney explained that some captains refused to allow the manual in their ship's library, believing that it taught the sailor too much law and claimed too many rights.[95]

Without doubt, the Seaman's Branch was the most masculine space of all the Legal Aid Society's branches and had the freest rein in determining its activities. Branch lawyers did not exhibit the disdain toward their clients that was typical of other society lawyers. In fact, the society made no secret of the uniqueness of the Seaman's Branch, publicly announcing that it "engaged in work altogether different from NYLAS's other branches" and that it handled all "cases concerning the rights of seaman on sea and shore."[96] Yet occasionally the branch also represented sailor's wives in suits for pensions or personal injuries in the case of a deceased husband. Even in this most masculine space, women were present.

Women and the Legal Aid Society

The Legal Aid Society of New York often behaved as though its clients and lawyers were all men. In reality, however, women always had been clients,

[92] For similar phenomena involving lawyers and explorers, see Karen Morin, "Charles P. Daly's Gendered Geography, 1860–1890," *Annals of the Association of American Geographers* 98 (2008): 897–919.

[93] "Legal Aid for Sailors," *New York Times*, January 6, 1904, 12.

[94] NYLAS, *The Sailor's Log*, 1–2.

[95] NYLAS, *Thirtieth Annual Report*, 39.

[96] NYLAS, *Thirty-Sixth Annual Report*, 30.

and by the turn of the century the society employed women lawyers. Its first female attorney, Rosalie Loew, was hired in 1897.[97] A graduate of New York University Law School, Loew was part of the second generation of professional women lawyers and did not experience the struggles the first generation faced in being admitted to law school and the bar. Nevertheless, as a legal aid attorney Loew garnered significant attention as one of the few women lawyers who regularly appeared in New York City trial courts. By all accounts she was an excellent attorney.[98] In 1901 she was appointed chief attorney, supervising a number of male lawyers and hiring other women attorneys. Although extant documents do not explain the society's decision to hire women, the role of female lay lawyers in women's legal aid organizations perhaps paved the way. In the first decade of the twentieth century, Mary Quackenbos, Annette Fisk, Josephine Stary, Sadie Frances Rothschild, Alice Dillingham, and Bertha Rembaugh all worked as Legal Aid Society attorneys, and Rembaugh served as head attorney at its West Side Branch.

Women also were increasingly visible as society patrons, a situation reflected in the invitation to the society's twenty-fifth anniversary celebration, which – signed by three women and two men – read, "You are invited by the *ladies and gentlemen* of the Legal Aid Society."[99] Another letter enticing patrons to attend the event explained, "The banquet is expected to be of more than usual interest because ladies as well as gentlemen will be seated at [the head] table."[100] Such a seating arrangement reflected the roles that women played as both patrons and lawyers. At the gala, Arthur von Briesen told the audience about women's work

---

[97] Loew's appointment was significant, for not only was she a woman but she was also Jewish and connected to the Jewish immigrant experience. Her parents emigrated from Hungary, where her grandfather had been an influential rabbi. Her father was a lawyer and her mother a milliner with whom Rosalie occasionally worked. Growing up in this milieu, Loew had learned to speak fluent German, Yiddish, and Hungarian. After graduating from New York University School of Law and passing the New York state Bar Examination, Loew worked in her father's law firm. See Rada Blumkin, "Rosalie Loew Whitney: The Early Years as Advocate for the Poor," Fall 2001, at http://wlh-static.law.stanford.edu/papers0203WhitneyR-Blumkino1.pdf. Barbara Babcock, *Woman Lawyer: The Trials of Clara Foltz* (Stanford, CA: Stanford University Press, 2011), 187–9.

[98] See, e.g., Julius Henry Cohen, *They Builded Better Than They Knew* (New York: Julian Messner, 1946).

[99] Invitation card from the Twenty-Fifth Anniversary Banquet Committee, 1901, Collection of Material Relating to Legal Aid, New York Historical Society (emphasis mine).

[100] Letter from the Twenty-Fifth Anniversary Banquet Committee, 1901, Collection of Material Relating to Legal Aid, New York Historical Society.

at the society: "I want you to understand that without them we could not have prospered.... Their energetic efforts on our behalf, their clear understanding of the duties which we have before us, has enabled [*sic*] us to increase not only our forte and our power for good."[101] Rosalie Loew wrote in her first annual report, "Your attorney believes that the interest of women has been of great assistance to the Legal Aid Society by spreading the knowledge of its benefits and its needs. It is perhaps gratifying... that a woman is in charge of the whole work, and another of one of its branches."[102]

Under Loew's tenure the society also opened the short-lived Women's Branch and staffed it entirely with women attorneys, expecting that female clients would use that branch.[103] The branch's location in the United Charities Building, where multiple philanthropic and reform organizations had offices, was intended to integrate the provision of legal advice with other social services. This proximity to and cooperation with social services was something that the society had previously avoided, seeking instead to be close to commerce, the courts, and other lawyers – places that were seen as male spaces. The society now announced that the abandoned wife who sought material aid from a social service agency could easily include a visit to the Women's Branch to seek advice about receiving support payments from her husband.[104]

The establishment of the Women's Branch also reflected a growing cultural understanding that women attorneys were better suited to represent women clients in certain types of cases, and that women clients would be more willing to speak honestly and openly to other women.[105] Simultaneously, the society hoped that the Women's Branch would reduce the number of women who sought aid, especially in domestic relations cases, at other branch offices.[106] In part, this expectation reflected an understanding that female clients in general were not the society's primary concern and that they distracted from the real work of the other branches.

---

[101] NYLAS, *Report of Speeches and Letters Delivered and Read at the Banquet of the Legal Aid Society on the Occasion of Its 25th Anniversary at the Waldorf-Astoria Hotel New York, Saturday, March 23, 1901* (New York: C. J. O'Brien, 1901), 34.

[102] NYLAS, *Twenty-Sixth Annual Report.*

[103] See, e.g., NYLAS, *Twenty-Fourth Annual Report of the President, Treasurer, and Attorneys of the Legal Aid Society for the Year 1899* (New York: C. J. O'Brien, 1900), 9–10, 35–37; NYLAS, *Twenty-Fifth Annual Report*, 1, 5, 53.

[104] See NYLAS, *Twenty-Fourth Annual Report*, 10.

[105] See NYLAS, *Twenty-Fifth Annual Report*, 12–13.

[106] Ibid., 1.

In contrast to the Seaman's Branch, the Woman's Branch almost from its founding was starved for attention and money, as all funding was supposed to be raised by the society's newly created Women's Committee. Unlike the other branches, and contrary to the society's stated policy of employing only full-time attorneys, the Women's Branch depended on the labor of women volunteers and part-time attorneys.[107]

Women clients used the new branch in connection with a range of domestic difficulties. Yet the branch attorneys struggled to advise abused women whose husbands, though violent, were nevertheless present and providing support. The branch's main legal strategies included seeking criminal charges, a separation, or a divorce, but all three options could leave a woman in a precarious financial position. Perhaps out of frustration, as well as disdain for poor women, the branch's attorneys sometimes blamed women for failing to perform adequately as wives. Josephine Stary, the head of the Women's Branch, wrote,

In dealing with these cases we must never disregard the fact that the woman who cannot manage her own affairs, who cannot maintain her dignity at the head of her home, though it be a lowly one, ought to have been taken in hand years ago ... and taught something of the responsibilities and duties of married life – of the virtues a woman must cultivate to maintain the respect of her husband.[108]

Although Stary admitted that many of these women had suffered "indignities," at times her only advice was to "pray."[109]

Women lay lawyers at Chicago's Protective Agency for Women and Children treated domestic relations claims differently from the professional lawyers at the New York society's Women's Branch. The Protective Agency stressed the importance of clients' stories above finding legally cognizable claims, and they believed that a client's lack of a legal claim was evidence of an unjust legal system, not a deficiency on the part of the client. For them, the situation crystallized the double victimization of poor women – by individual men and then by the law. In contrast, women lawyers at the society's Women's Branch became frustrated with such clients, reasoning that if a client had no legal claim, there was little that a lawyer could do. Listening to clients' stories became a waste of the lawyer's time; she needed to move on to the next client.

---

[107] Ibid., 13; NYLAS, *Twenty-Sixth Annual Report*, 18–19.

[108] NYLAS, *Twenty-Fourth Annual Report*, 35.

[109] Ibid., 36. At the turn of the century and for decades thereafter, it was common for reformers to blame wives' lack of domestic skills, failure to be submissive, and physical appearance for their husbands' desertion. Igra, *Wives without Husbands*, 59–61.

Unlike at the other branches, only one lawyer staffed the Women's Branch, and she had no permanent support staff. Stary, who did not take a salary, complained that she had to be in the office handling intake and meeting with clients, and she had to attend court or use the library. When she was out, the office had to be closed, frustrating applicants who had taken time off from work or left children untended in order to get there. Furthermore, the one-room space provided no privacy, so waiting applicants and clients could overhear confidential discussions.[110] For these reasons, Stary called for additional volunteers, claiming that at least fifty women in the city had law degrees that were "purely ornamental," as she put it.[111] Volunteering at the Women's Branch, she claimed, could make those women into real lawyers and put their legal education to use.[112] Her call, however, went primarily unheeded.

The Women's Branch served several thousand clients over the course of two years, but the society's Women's Committee was unable to raise sufficient funds to maintain it. Moreover, there were not enough women lawyers, especially those who would work as volunteers, to staff the branch, and clients also found the branch's location inconvenient, so they continued to use the society's other offices. To the surprise of Stary, and without any explanation, the society's board of directors decided to close the Women's Branch in 1903.[113] Its failure contrasted sharply with the success of the Seaman's Branch. In the metric of masculinity according to which some branches were privileged and supported above others, the Women's Branch ranked last.

Within a couple of years of the closure of the Women's Branch, Rosalie Loew resigned from the Legal Aid Society, and without any explanation the society drastically curtailed hiring women lawyers. There are, however, hints that the society's leaders were not satisfied with the performance of its women lawyers. When discussing the staffing of a new office, there seemed to be a general agreement among the society's male leadership that having women lawyers in positions of power had proved a failure.[114] Yet the women who had worked for the society went on to have significant careers. In 1919, Bertha Rembaugh became the first woman to run for municipal court judge in New York City. She also wrote *The Political Status of Women in the United States: A Digest of the Laws*

---

[110] NYLAS, *Twenty-Sixth Annual Report*, 45.

[111] Ibid.

[112] Ibid.

[113] See ibid., 44; McGuire, *The Lance of Justice*, 175–7.

[114] Leonard McGee to Arthur von Briesen, June 11, 1912, Briesen Papers, box 4, folder 10.

concerning Women in the Various States and Territories, and she was counsel for the Women's Trade Union League.[115] Rosalie Loew became a suffrage activist and held a number of government appointments, eventually becoming the first woman judge on New York's Domestic Relations Court. Mary Quackenbos opened the People's Law Firm, which handled the cases of poor people, and later she became the first female special assistant U.S. attorney. In that position she specialized in cases involving peonage and the exploitation of immigrants.[116]

In contrast to Chicago's Protective Agency for Women and Children, the New York Legal Aid Society's officers and attorneys expressed no outrage at domestic abuse. Rather, its lawyers were interested primarily in a husband's financial duty to support his wife and children. The central figure in one 1904 case was an elderly woman whose husband had beaten and starved her for twenty-six years. The husband earned eighty dollars a month as a city employee. The society boasted that it was able to obtain thirty dollars a month from the husband for the wife's support: "We even looked out for the husband's interests by suggesting to the judge not to file the papers and so make a record against the man. Since we desired only that he should do his duty and not lose his position."[117] Here the society's sole concern was that the husband supported his wife financially; there was no discussion about the wife's physical safety, the issue of wife beating, or the possibility of punishing the man. The only element that made this case unique was the husband's relatively large salary.

In fact, the society had a long-standing practice in domestic relations cases of dissuading wives from bringing cases against husbands. In the period between 1907 and 1909, the society commenced and completed only seventeen domestic relations cases – eight divorces, five separations, and four annulments.[118] The society considered divorce a "luxury" even

---

[115] Bertha Rembaugh, *The Political Status of Women in the United States: A Digest of the Laws concerning Women in the Various States and Territories* (New York: J. P. Putnam and Sons, Knickerbocker Press, 1911); see Janet Zandy, *Hands: Physical Labor, Class, and Cultural Work* (New Brunswick, NJ: Rutgers University Press, 2004), 132; Bertha Rembaugh, "The Triangle Fire: The Court's Decision," *Life and Labor* (April 1912): 117–19.

[116] "New Field of Legal Work among the Poor," *New York Times*, June 11, 1905; Jerrell Shofner, "Mary Grace Quackenbos: A Visitor Florida Did Not Want," *Florida Historical Quarterly* 58 (January 1980): 273–90; Randolph H. Boehm, "Mary Grace Quackenbos and the Federal Campaign against Peonage: The Case of Sunnyside Plantation," *Arkansas Historical Quarterly* 50 (Spring 1991): 40–59.

[117] NYLAS, "Specimen Cases," *Legal Aid Review* 2 (1904): 3, 5.

[118] Merrill Gates to the editor of *Legal Aid Review*, November 22, 1909, Briesen Papers, box 4, folder 5.

for women of "fine character" whose husbands had long ago abandoned and ceased supporting them. Such women, the society claimed, wanted to be "free," but as no concrete material benefit inured, the society would not accept their cases.[119] As the society stated, divorce and even legal separation were to be reserved for women with children, whose husbands were exceptionally cruel and created "impossible conditions."[120]

In many instances, instead of bringing suit, the society's attorneys sought to convince wives that they could do little for them, since men who had abandoned their wives and children generally either could not afford to make support payments or could not be found. In other cases, women hoping to increase support payments were told by the society that their husbands could not afford it. In one case, the society explained to a woman seeking support from her husband that the time entailed in going to court would result only in *her* further "neglecting" her "half-starved children."[121] The society may not have been incorrect about the issue of wasting time, as attending court and even meeting with a lawyer often required clients to miss work, which in most industries meant sacrificing wages, expending money on transportation, and leaving children untended.[122] But the society's attorney, not the client, made this decision about whether to pursue litigation against an erring or delinquent husband, and the society told such stories with little apparent emotion. Moreover, even for the most destitute women it did not pay court fees, forcing impoverished women to pay the fees themselves.[123]

Wives seeking assistance from the society also encountered pressure from lawyers to reconcile with husbands. One case, for example, involved a married woman and her child who had gone to visit friends. While she was away, her husband removed all of the furniture from their apartment and moved to another apartment with his mistress. The society agreed to pursue a separation with support for the wife, but later the husband decided that he wished to be reconciled with his wife. The wife's attorney argued that reconciliation would be best for the "child's

[119] NYLAS, "Introduction," *Legal Aid Review* 2 (1904): 4, 1.

[120] NYLAS, *Thirty-Fourth Annual Report of the President, Treasurer, and Attorneys of the Legal Aid Society for the Year 1909* (New York: Thomas Press, 1910), 7.

[121] Phillip J. McCook, "The Judicial Aspects of the Work of the Legal Aid Society," *Legal Aid Review* 5 (July 1907): 3, 17–19. McCook had been an attorney in the East Side Branch, and at the time he wrote the article he was a director of the NYLAS.

[122] Igra, *Wives without Husbands*, 71.

[123] Merrill Gates to the editor of *Legal Aid Review*, November 22, 1909, Briesen Papers, box 4, folder 5.

sake" and successfully pressured the very reluctant wife to return to her husband.[124]

After New York City's domestic relations court opened in 1910, the society sent women with domestic cases directly to an office of the court, which determined eligibility for claims and sought court orders.[125] Many reformers criticized the new court for its limited jurisdiction and its complicated forms and procedures, but the society saw its representation of such women as no longer necessary.[126] The Chicago Legal Aid Society, in contrast, continued to represent women seeking support even after Chicago's domestic relations court was established. The society also stopped accepting women's claims for mothers' pensions, which New York began to provide in 1915, and which many society applicants sought.[127] Such pensions were available to widows with children under the age of sixteen. To qualify, a woman had to have two years' residency in the city or county; she had to be mentally, morally, and physically fit to care for her children; and she had to show that her deceased husband had been a U.S. citizen and a resident of New York State.[128] The claimant had to collect many documents, go through multiple interviews, and explain her eligibility for the pension. When widows' pensions first became available, the New York society assisted some of the many women who began applying for them, but within a couple of months it ceased such work because it believed the Board of Child Welfare, which administered such claims, was responsible for assisting applicants. The society emphasized that the acceptance or rejection of a claim for a widow's pension was a

[124] Rosalie Loew Whitney (NYLAS), "The Legal Aid Society and Its Child Clients," *Legal Aid Review* 4 (January 1911): 2.

[125] On the New York domestic relations courts, see Sidney Entman, "The Origins and Development of a Family Court – Family Division, New York City," *Social Forces* 21 (October 1942–May 1943): 58–65. The domestic relations court grew out of a report by the Page Commission documenting the terrible state of the magistrate courts. The domestic relations court heard only cases of support.

[126] *General Municipal Laws of New York*, 1915, chap. 228; NYLAS, *Fortieth Annual Report of the President, Treasurer, and Attorney of the Legal Aid Society for the Year 1915* (New York: Manger, Hughes and Manger, 1916), 16–20; U.S. Department of Labor, Children's Bureau, *Laws Relating to "Mothers' Pensions."*

[127] NYLAS, *Fortieth Annual Report*, 16–20; U.S. Department of Labor, Children's Bureau, *Laws Relating to "Mothers' Pensions"*; Joanne Goodwin, *Gender and the Politics of Welfare Reform: Mothers' Pensions in Chicago, 1911–1929* (Chicago: University of Chicago Press, 1997); Linda Gordon, *Pitied but Not Entitled* (Cambridge, MA: Harvard University Press, 1998).

[128] 1915, N.Y. Laws 690, ch. 228.

matter purely for the board's discretion and thus women did not require representation.[129]

In these cases and in others, the society rejected the kinds of claims that women brought by interpreting them as not requiring legal assistance. Such decisions were not preordained but were, rather, choices deliberately made by the society, as demonstrated by its treatment of analogous claims involving men. The Seaman's Branch represented claims for sailor's pensions even though a separate bureaucratic process existed that did not require representation. So, too, when New York enacted workmen's compensation, the society represented claims before the Workmen's Compensation Board.[130] These various boards and agencies had been designed so that claimants did not need formal legal representation, but the society recognized the advantages for a claimant of an attorney's presence.

Indeed, a photograph of the Legal Aid Society's waiting room is telling in its absence of women (Plate 5). The visual center of the photograph is a white woman, perhaps an applicant or a client, but she is isolated in a roomful of men. She sits, self-contained and seemingly unconnected to her surroundings or even to the lawyer with whom she is conferring.[131] This photograph is extraordinarily different from the domestic images used earlier by the Working Women's Protective Union and the maternal illustrations employed by the Chicago Legal Aid Society. Not only are other women, children, and African Americans absent from the scene, but so is any sense of sympathy or empathy. Instead the austere photograph conveys a cold professionalism.

Domestic Servants

An examination of the Legal Aid Society's treatment of domestic servants provides even starker evidence of how it devalued women's claims while privileging other kinds of legal cases. Belatedly following the practice of women's legal aid organizations, the society made the representation of women domestic workers one of its specialties.[132] The society boasted

[129] NYLAS, *Fortieth Annual Report*, 18–19.

[130] On workmen's compensation, see John Witt, *The Accidental Republic: Crippled Workmen, Destitute Widows, and the Remaking of American Law* (Cambridge, MA: Harvard University Press, 2004).

[131] The photograph appeared in the program for Smentana's opera *The Bartered Bride*, presented for the benefit of the Legal Aid Society on April 29, 1909; New York Public Library, 1694532 SHO p.v. 3, no. 19.

[132] See Chapter 1 for a discussion of Boston's Women's Educational and Industrial Union and domestic servants.

about bringing such cases even when its own patrons were targeted by servants' complaints.[133] Yet the reality of its position was much more complicated. The society's interest went beyond representing servants, as it also sought to educate employers and their mostly female maids, cooks, and servants. In so doing, however, the society often favored employers and depicted servants as undisciplined, pampered, and irresponsible employees who had bargaining power equal to if not greater than that of their employers.

The society's publication *Domestic Employment* purported to set forth the law governing domestic work. It was intended for a female audience of domestic workers, just as the *Sailor's Log* functioned for its audience of male sailors.[134] The manual explained that there was no predefined category of law specifically governing domestic employment.[135] Instead, lawyers drew from contract law and the law of master and servant. The authors' view that the law of master and servant did not fully apply to domestic servants placed domestic employment outside even the minimum legal protections provided in cases of ordinary labor.[136]

In contrast to *The Sailor's Log*, which constructed the sailor as a rights-bearing man and worker who fully earned his pay and entitlements, *Domestic Employment* was full of internal tensions about the rights and responsibilities of domestic servants and their employers. The Boston Women's Educational and Industrial Union had long recognized the existence of strife between mistresses and servants, but the society sentimentalized the home and privileged domestic work over women's industrial work. The manual's introduction, written by Briesen, declared: "A good mistress, circumspect and kindly in disposition, will never give cause for complaint as to the manner in which servants are treated." Instead, the good mistress accepted the servant as "practically a member of the family."[137] Thus the relationship between mistress and servant

---

[133] NYLAS, "The Judicial Aspect of the Work of the Legal Aid Society," *Legal Aid Review* 5 (July 1907): 1.

[134] NYLAS, *Domestic Employment: A Handbook* (New York: Legal Aid Society of New York, 1908), 5. One of the manual's authors was Helen Arthur, who had a law degree from NYU and was involved in numerous reform activities. See Clare Coss, ed., *Lillian D. Wald: Progressive Activist* (New York: Feminist Press at City University of New York, 1993).

[135] NYLAS, *Domestic Employment*, 5.

[136] See Jean Christian Vinel, *The Employee: A Political History* (Philadelphia: University of Pennsylvania Press, 2013).

[137] NYLAS, *Domestic Employment*, 6.

stood in the gray, undefined area between real wage employment and domestic life.[138]

Using long-established tropes, Briesen described the home as composed of harmonious relationships and lamented that any girl would choose industrial employment rather than domestic work. He advised that for a young woman there was "no better calling... than the privilege of assisting in the affairs of the home of cultured men and women. In such a home she finds every means of development."[139] In Briesen's view, domestic work provided an opportunity to be educated in the ways of the upper classes. Unlike factory work, which allowed women some leisure time, domestic employment supposedly ensured that the servant was supervised constantly – one of the very reasons that many working-class women disliked it.[140] He approvingly noted that the young servant could save her money so that one day she too could marry and employ her own servants. Thus, for Briesen, upward mobility for working-class women occurred in the home, under its pure influences and with practical training for marriage. He so romanticized domestic work that he urged all young women, even those of the middle and upper classes, to spend time engaged in such work. Briesen's perspective was not an unusual one, since many believed such work to be wholesome employment.[141] More troubling is that Briesen's decades of experience with legal aid should have made him well aware of domestic servants' difficult working conditions, their constant complaints to the society, and the reality that many women spent their entire lives, not just their youth, as domestic workers.

Briesen's remarks also were in tension with the substance of the *Domestic Employment* manual, which attempted to establish legal norms for addressing the difficulties in the relationship between employer and

---

[138] See Vanessa H. May, *Unprotected Labor: Household Workers, Politics, and Middle-Class Reform in New York, 1870–1940* (Chapel Hill: University of North Carolina Press, 2011); Peggie R. Smith, "Regulating Paid Household Work: Class, Gender, Race, and Agendas of Reform," *American University Law Review* 48 (April 1999): 851–923.

[139] NYLAS, *Domestic Employment*, 6.

[140] See Elizabeth Ewen, *Immigrant Women in the Land of Dollars* (New York: Monthly Review Press, 1985); Kathy Lee Peiss, *Cheap Amusements: Working Women and Leisure in Turn-of-the-Century New York* (Philadelphia: Temple University Press, 1986); Faye E. Dudden, *Serving Women: Household Service in Nineteenth-Century America* (Middletown, CT: Wesleyan University Press, 1983); May, *Unprotected Labor*.

[141] On this traditionalist view of household labor, see May, *Unprotected Labor*; Smith, "Regulating Paid Household Work."

servant. One of the most contentious questions concerned the wages due a servant who quit without notice – a practice that was very irksome to mistresses, who would then refuse to pay the worker for the time that she had worked before quitting. Mistresses saw servants who departed without notice as displaying the height of irresponsibility, and often accused them of timing their departure to inflict chaos on the household. For servants, however, quitting was an active form of resistance against exploitive employment conditions.[142] In addressing this issue the manual made it clear that the employer did not generally owe the employee her wages for the full time worked. An employer owed wages only in cases where the contract was for an "indefinite time."[143] If the contract was for a definite time and the employee left without cause before that time expired, no wages were due. The manual noted, however, that the generous mistress might decide to pay such wages even though the law did not require it.[144]

The manual's advice on this important issue is troubling: rather than simply stating the law as it existed, or recognizing the law's ambiguity, the manual advocated a norm advantageous to employers and skewed against employees. In fact in 1904, four years before the publication of the *Domestic Employment* manual, a New York court had ruled that an employee who had a month-to-month contract but quit before the end of the contract term was entitled to payment for the days actually worked. In the next decade, two more New York court decisions supported that legal position.[145]

---

[142] In her study of African American women domestic workers in the South, Tera Hunter argues that quitting without notice constituted a form of resistance and was an exercise in freedom. Tera Hunter, *To 'Joy My Freedom: Southern Black Women's Lives and Labors after the Civil War* (Cambridge, MA: Harvard University Press, 1997); Vanessa May, in *Unprotected Labor* (65–68), makes the same point in connection with domestic servants in New York City.

[143] NYLAS, *Domestic Employment*, 9.

[144] See ibid., 5–6.

[145] In Wheaton v. Higgins, 90 N.Y.S. 1041, 1042 (N.Y. App. Div. 1904), the plaintiff had a month-to-month contract; having left his employment in the middle of the month, he argued that he was nevertheless entitled to the payment of wages for the full month. In a per curiam decision, the New York Supreme Court disagreed, ruling that the payment should be limited to the actual wages earned during the month (1042). In Godt v. Henigson, 135 N.Y.S. 666, 667 (N.Y. App. Div. 1912), the plaintiff sought to recover $175 from the defendant employer, who argued that withholding the wages was justified because the plaintiff had abandoned his employment. The court ruled that the plaintiff was entitled to what he had faithfully earned, even though he quit before the end of the term. (667). Similarly, in a per curiam decision in Koch v. Siff, 154 N.Y S. 223 (N.Y. App. Div. 1915), the New York Supreme Court ruled that a strikebreaker

Even the various lawyers who reviewed drafts of the manual could not agree on what constituted definite versus indefinite employment, whether wages were owed in the case of resignation, or when notice had to be given. Questions such as these were so contentious, and lawyers and others who had read drafts of the manual were themselves in such significant disagreement, that there was serious discussion within the society of cancelling publication of the manual.[146] To break the stalemate, the authors and the society's publication committee eventually chose to interpret the absence of law specifically regarding domestics to the disadvantage of servants.[147]

The manual also advised employers and servants to enter into written contracts and provided a model contract. The contract, however, worked primarily to the disadvantage of the servant. It contained a penalty clause for failure to give one week's notice of termination of employment. If the terminating party failed to give such notice, then that party owed a sum of "not less than one week's wages to cover expenses and loss of time."[148] Thus, not only would the servant who quit without due notice not receive pay for time worked, but she would also owe damages to her employer. Although this clause applied to both parties, the odds were that it would impose a significant hardship on servants, who often found themselves on the margins of solvency. Equally troubling, neither the manual nor the contract addressed the employee's specific work hours or duties, something that domestic employees had long sought. Instead, the model contract assumed what was the general practice, that the servant's hours and work were unlimited and set at the discretion of the mistress. Such contracts – and the norms that they reflected and created – implied a view that the servant was selling not her specific labor but, rather, herself.[149]

The society hoped that the manual would discipline servants to at least give notice before quitting, but it did not, and in 1910 the society took more drastic measures. Leonard McGee, its chief attorney and former head of the Seaman's Branch, explained that, owing to pressure exerted on the society by employers, the board of directors had adopted

---

who quit his job for fear of being attacked by strikers was entitled to receive the amount that he had earned during the days that he was on the job.

[146] Charles F. Wiebusch to Arthur von Briesen, October 19, 1908, Briesen Papers, box 5, folder 4.

[147] Ibid.

[148] NYLAS, *Domestic Employment*, 10.

[149] On issues of hours and duties, see May, *Unprotected Labor*; Smith, "Regulating Paid Household Work."

a resolution that servants who left without notice or cause would be "deemed unworthy and refused our assistance." He explained that the society enforced the rule "very strictly, notwithstanding the fact that as a matter of law where the hiring is for an indefinite period, the applicant would be entitled to compensation for the time actually worked."[150] In other words, even when there was no doubt that the servant was legally entitled to wages, the society would not accept the case.[151]

McGee claimed that the society's relatively new Harlem Branch, which saw a growing number of African American applicants, had rejected 900 such cases in 1910, representing 12 percent of the branch's total applications.[152] Briesen explained that the policy was, in part, adopted in response to "colored" domestic workers who had created a "nuisance" that was "getting very serious."[153] He accused such workers of quitting without a minute's notice, leaving their employers with food uncooked, tables unset, and guests untended.[154] McGee later claimed that the society's policy and the large number of cases that it had refused had "greatly improve[d] the servant problem in the city."[155] On its face this was a racially neutral policy, but it must have prevented African American women, who filled the ranks of domestics, from obtaining the society's assistance in collecting the wages legally due to them.[156]

The society treated sailors and domestic workers in entirely different ways. Sailors were rights-bearing individuals entitled to all remedies and protections that the law allowed. Moreover the Seaman's Branch did not accept the status quo but tried to reshape, remake, and reinterpret law in ways most favorable to sailors.[157] A more subtle difference was that the branch's lawyers gave the benefit of doubt to the sailor. When shipmasters

---

[150] NYLAS, *Thirty-Seventh Annual Report of the President, Treasurer, and Attorneys of the Legal Aid Society for the Year 1912* (New York: Richardson Press, 1913), 25; "Copy of Resolution Passed at the Meeting of the Board of Directors of the Legal Aid Society on September 22, 1910," Briesen Papers, box 5, fol. 16.

[151] NYLAS, *Forty-First Annual Report of the President, Treasurer and Attorney for the Year 1916* (New York: Manger, Hughes & Manger, 1917), 10.

[152] NYLAS, *Thirty-Seventh Annual Report*, 26; NYLAS, *Thirty-Fifth Annual Report of the President, Treasurer, and Attorneys of the Legal Aid Society for the Year 1910* (New York: Richardson Press, 1911), 8.

[153] Arthur von Breisen to A. L. Everette, May 19, 1913, Briesen Papers, box 4, folder 4.

[154] Ibid.

[155] NYLAS, *Fortieth Annual Report*, 15.

[156] See, e.g., Brenda Clegg Gray, *Black Female Domestics during the Depression in New York City, 1930–1940* (New York: Garland Publishing, 1993).

[157] See, e.g., NYLAS, "Report," *Legal Aid Review* 4 (1906): 2–4; and "Introduction," *Legal Aid Review* 4 (1906): 2, 1.

accused sailors of desertion (the seaman's equivalent of quitting without
cause or notice) and withheld wages or property, the branch willingly
represented the seamen. Lawyers advocated for the sailors by arguing
either that they had left with cause or that they had planned to return to
their ship.[158] By contrast, the society saw domestic servants as having few
legal rights, even when legal precedent and custom could be interpreted
to confer some minimum protection. In other words, the society did not
represent primarily the interests of servants but instead often sided with
employers, even while proclaiming its own neutrality.

Through much of the society's history, it studiously avoided discussing
African Americans and the larger role that race played in American society, but a brief story written by a society attorney in the Harlem Branch
reveals the metrics of race and gender the society used. In the attorney's vignette, he contrasted the Jewish male client, now more Americanized, with the immature, undisciplined African American male client.
Such comparisons were part of an ongoing discourse in American life
that fortified ideas of whiteness.[159] Set in terms drawn from the minstrel
shows that made audiences laugh, the story was written in dialect, which
transformed the client's legal claim into a jest for a white audience tired
of hearing about wages unpaid and women abandoned.[160]

   The story also reflects that clients at the society's Harlem Branch would
have included a large number of African Americans and Jews, as African
Americans migrating from the South and Jews seeking to escape the
crowded tenements of lower Manhattan had moved into that neighborhood. Under the heading "An Amusing Incident," the attorney described
his client as, "[A] perfect specimant [*sic*] of the proverbial jolly, good
natured chuckling colored man, the come-day-go-day type who has no
thought for the morrow as long as today is here."[161] The client had a
wage claim against a bowling alley that the society had settled. While the
man waited patiently to receive his money from the settlement, another
"young business man of Semitic extraction" harangued the attorney with
a continuing stream of questions relating to his business, refusing to
leave and thus delaying the lawyer. This situation prompted the African

---

[158] See, e.g., NYLAS, *Twenty-Ninth Annual Report*, 10, 34–35; NYLAS, *Forty-First Annual Report*, 19–21.

[159] See Goldstein, *The Price of Whiteness.*

[160] See "Specimen Cases: An Amusing Incident," *Legal Aid Review* 15 (January 1917): 7–9.

[161] Ibid.

American man to laugh loudly. The attorney rebuked him for disrupting the dignity of the office. He responded, "Deed Boss, I doan mean to start no vaudeville show, but I jis nachally cain't help exploding."[162] Eventually he was called to speak to the lawyer himself and collect his settlement. The payment was, however, in the form of a check, which he had no way of cashing. The lawyer agreed to have the society cash the check but informed the man that it would take time. The crestfallen client explained, "Oh Boss, yo' all says as how yo' cain't pay me until next Wednesday and ah wants to take mah gal out Sunday."[163] Moreover, he could not take off more time from work to return to the branch. When the attorney offered to mail him the money, he explained that he was behind on his rent and that the landlady would confiscate it. The punch line was that the man was focused more on taking out his girlfriend than on paying his landlord.

This story set up a dichotomy between two types of problematic legal aid clients. On the one hand, the Jewish client, now a small businessman, asked too many questions of the lawyer and appeared demanding and neurotic. He was completely self-interested, and ignored the long line of waiting clients. Unending questions rolled from his tongue, all in pursuit of profit. On the other hand, the African American client was irresponsible and without self-discipline – more concerned with spending his money on pleasure (perhaps even sexual pleasure) than with paying his bills. Both men infringed on the time, patience, and rights of others. From the attorney's perspective, the African American client's poverty, his lack of a bank account (which prevented him from accepting a check), and his need to be at work provided only comic relief. The man perhaps intuited his attorney's viewpoint, as he recognized and denied the role that he was expected to perform, as if in a "vaudeville show."[164]

From the 1890s to the first decade of the twentieth century, the New York Legal Aid Society categorized and segregated its clients based on gender, nationality, occupation, and the kind of claim for which they sought assistance. By picking and choosing who received legal aid and who did not, which claims were worthy and which were not, the society

---

[162] Ibid.

[163] Ibid.

[164] Ibid. On the role of blacks in performing both pleasure and pain, see Sadiya V. Hartman, *Scenes of Subjection: Terror, Slavery, and Self-Making in Nineteenth-Century America* (New York: Oxford University Press, 1997); Eric Lott, *Love and Theft: Blackface Minstrelsy and the American Working Class* (New York: Oxford University Press, 1995).

sought to discipline those seeking assistance as well as the defendants with whom they negotiated or brought suit. Selection was based on whether clients conformed to gender norms, functioned appropriately within the wage labor system, and had a legal claim that could be clearly monetized. But this categorization was not straightforward. Instead, the Legal Aid Society's effort to discipline, educate, and vindicate the rights of some of its clients produced tensions and contradictions. Sailors, whom it saw as possessing an immature but nonetheless powerful masculinity, became favored clients. In contrast, at the turn of the century eastern European Jewish men were seen as lacking the self-discipline needed in a capitalist economy. Ironically they were also viewed as selfish, acrimonious, and mistaken in their understanding of the rights to which they were entitled. Likewise the society viewed female servants as pampered and irresponsible employees who took advantage of their mistresses. Within these categories and stereotypes, and in part as a function of them, for a decade the society hired women lawyers, in part to handle the cases of women clients. Yet as we see in the next chapter, women lawyers would soon disappear as a result of a larger change in who was considered an appropriate client and who an appropriate provider of legal aid.

4

Reinventing Legal Aid

During the second decade of the twentieth century, male legal aid lawyers gained prominence, and as they did so they sought to move legal aid from local organizations rooted in particular cities to the national stage. These leaders hoped to create a national association of legal aid societies, expand legal aid societies across the country, standardize the provision of legal aid, and generally promote the stature of legal aid. In the process, they tried to reduce and even eclipse women's visibility and their work in the field as lay lawyers and professional lawyers. During this same period, social work was emerging as a distinct profession. Women lay lawyers became strongly associated with social workers, and as a result, at least some of the new men leading legal aid argued that social workers also should have little or no role in its provision.[1] Although the crystallization of these organizing efforts was the publication in 1919 of Reginald Heber Smith's *Justice and the Poor*, the groundwork was laid in 1911 with the first national conference on legal aid. The ensuing decade saw significant conflict as men sought to redefine the nature of legal aid and lay claim to its foundation. *Justice and the Poor*, in many ways the culmination of that process, was an imagined history.

As new legal aid societies were established in major cities across the North and Midwest, some male legal aid attorneys experienced an identity

---

[1] Daniel Walkowitz writes that the term *social work* began to be used at the turn of the century. Walkowitz also discusses the large number of women drawn to the field of social work. Daniel J. Walkowitz, *Working with Class: Social Workers and the Politics of Middle Class Identity* (Chapel Hill: University of North Carolina Press, 1999), 27, 88.

crisis. Arthur von Briesen had long imagined a national legal aid organization that would articulate legal aid's history, mission, and policies,
and the 1911 national legal aid conference constituted a small first step
toward that goal.[2] No women were invited to speak at the conference,
nor were women's legal aid organizations represented. This was not
an accident. An officer of Boston's Women's Educational and Industrial Union, Carolina Cook, wrote to Briesen asking him whether one
of the union's representatives might attend. Briesen replied that he was
unaware of the organization, and that Boston was already being represented by the still-young Legal Aid Society of Boston (BLAS). Continuing, he suggested to Cook that if the attorney for the Boston society was "satisfied that your Union seeks to secure justice to the poor
and helpless on the lines of the Legal Aid Societies, he might, if he
desires, appoint a delegate of your Union."[3] One can imagine the sense
of insult. The WEIU, a women's organization that had been providing legal assistance since 1878, was not being recognized as a legal
aid organization and was excluded from participating in the national
conference.

Briesen's response to Cook was less than candid. He was well aware of
the existence of women's legal aid organizations and he disapproved of
them. Regarding such an organization in Washington, D.C., he wrote: "It
was in the hands of ladies only, who did not understand its real object,
and who would not take interest in the sufferings of men, and who
confined their attention to cases brought by women, who complained of
their husbands."[4] Instead, Briesen hoped that legal aid would be elevated
and enshrined in the corridors of power – a place where weighty legal
issues might be addressed among men.

Briesan and other male lawyers had high hopes and expansive ambitions for the future of legal aid. Having been introduced as "the father of
the Legal Aid movement," Briesen spoke of opening a Washington, D.C.,
office:

---

[2] *First Conference of Legal Aid Societies of the United States* (Pittsburgh: Pittsburg Legal
Aid Society, 1911), 38.
[3] Arthur von Briesen to Carolina Cook, April 27, 1912, and Arthur von Briesen to Thomas
Clafin, September 27, 1912, Arthur von Briesen Papers, Public Policy Papers, Department
of Rare Books and Special Collections, Princeton University Library (hereinafter Briesen
Papers), box 5, folder 19.
[4] Arthur von Briesen to Hariette J. Hifton, June 11, 1913, Briesen Papers, box 4,
folder 3.

Just imagine that we should succeed in finding the right man.... The man I would imagine for that place would be one who would have high social position; he should be gladly seen in the White House; he should gladly be seen by the justices of the Supreme Court; he should be gladly be seen by senators and members of congress.[5]

He envisioned that legal aid work could be raised above the powerlessness and poverty of its clients and the everyday grind of domestic relations and wage cases.

Samuel Scoville, head attorney of the Legal Aid Society of Philadelphia, was the first speaker at the 1911 conference.[6] The Philadelphia Society had its roots in the Philadelphia Committee for the Protection of Women and Children, an organization run by women lay lawyers. These women, along with a number of male attorneys, had founded the Philadelphia Legal Aid Society in 1901, and its first staff attorney was a woman.[7] Scoville did not discuss these facts nor did he mention that the society's early clientele was predominantly female.

Yet the male would-be reformers of legal aid could not ignore entirely the day-to-day work of legal aid. As soon as speakers addressed the kinds of cases that legal aid actually handled, women's wage claims and domestic relations cases resurfaced. Likewise, the mundane routine of legal aid work occurred in the office and not in the courtroom. In discussing the real work of legal aid offices, conference speakers commented on how they seldom filed suits but instead quickly settled clients' claims.[8] If bringing cases to trial was, in part, what separated the manly practice of law from what women lay lawyers had been doing for almost half a century, better distinctions would have to be found elsewhere; the work of female lay lawyers and male lawyers looked similar. Louis Stoiber, chief attorney of the Legal Aid Society of New York, described his days as filled with "deadening, routine work, which would kill any sensible, ambitious man

---

5 *Proceedings of the First Conference of Legal Aid Societies of the United States* (Pittsburg: Legal Aid Society of Pittsburg, 1911), 4; Arthur von Briesen, "Necessity for National Committee of Legal Aid Societies," in ibid., 35–36.

6 Samuel Scoville, "The Practical Working of the Legal Aid Society," *Proceedings of the First Conference of Legal Aid Societies of the United States* (Pittsburg: Legal Aid Society of Pittsburg, 1911), 7.

7 *First Annual Report of the Legal Aid Society of Philadelphia* (Philadelphia, 1904). Francis Anne Keay, a graduate of the University of Pennsylvania Law School, was the society's first attorney.

8 See Scoville, "The Practical Working of the Legal Aid Society," 7.

in two months."[9] From his perspective, legal aid work was insufficiently manly and robust for an ambitious male lawyer.[10]

Masculinizing legal aid required deciding what to do with poor women who continually brought domestic relations cases to legal aid offices. Even when such organizations tried to discourage them, women persisted. Many male legal aid lawyers viewed these cases with dread – they did not involve real law, and women applicants in domestic relations cases took time and energy away from more "pressing" cases. At the legal aid conference, William Sabine of the Boston Legal Aid Society addressed the issue: "Endless time is used in obtaining bonds, securing the consent of the Judge, and otherwise attending to details. In separate support cases, many are contested when at times hours are wasted merely waiting for the case to be reached."[11] Paradoxically, Sabine complained about having to appear in court, something that legal aid lawyers welcomed when cases did not involve domestic relations claims. Rather than having legal aid societies accept such cases, Sabine insisted that social workers in charity organizations could handle them more effectively. "Great success has attended the efforts of social workers in Boston by making a personal visit upon the putative father... and almost without exception she obtains a confession of responsibility. It is then not difficult to make an arrangement for reasonably small weekly payments."[12] Indeed, though neither Sabine nor his colleagues were willing to acknowledge these facts, women lay lawyers had done such work within legal aid organizations for years.

No social worker spoke at the legal aid conference. This silence was palpable, especially because Maud Parcells Boyes of the Chicago Legal Aid Society (and former superintendant of Chicago's Protective Agency for Women and Children) was in attendance. Boyes had spent almost a decade handling women's domestic relations claims, as well as many other cases, and she was also the only woman delegate at the conference. The women's board of directors of the Chicago Legal Aid Society had specifically granted the funds for Boyes to attend, perhaps

---

[9] Letter from Louis Stoiber to Professor Racca, December 25, 1912, quoted in Jerold S. Auerbach, *Unequal Justice: Lawyers and Social Change in Modern America* (New York: Oxford University Press, 1976), 58.

[10] Kenneth W. Mack, *Representing the Race: The Creation of the Civil Rights Lawyer* (Cambridge, MA: Harvard University Press, 2012).

[11] William Sabine, "Character of Litigation to Be Undertaken," *Proceedings of the First Conference of Legal Aid Societies of the United States* (Pittsburgh: Legal Aid Society of Pittsburg, 1911), 45.

[12] Ibid., 47.

understanding that she would be the lone woman representative. Boyes must have realized that, with the sole exception of Briesen, she was the most experienced legal aid worker in the room.[13]

These national conferences were important, for legal aid history was being made – and remade. Legal aid's genesis story set the framework for who would be considered appropriate providers and appropriate clients of legal aid. Speakers repeatedly asserted that the Legal Aid Society of New York was the first legal aid organization in the country, and only a handful of speakers rejected this claim. In a 1916 speech to the National Alliance, Rudolph Matz, president of the Chicago Legal Aid Society, asserted that Chicago's Protective Agency for Women and Children had been the first such organization.[14] But such corrections fell on deaf ears. This quest for origins by male leaders was not an antiquarian search for roots – it was a normative search for precedent that would justify the reconfiguration of legal aid, allowing the expulsion of women as clients, providers, and even patrons. Legal aid leaders were so anxious to disassociate women from legal aid that the Legal Aid Society of Pittsburgh prohibited women from serving on its board of directors.[15]

The methods these new leaders used to promote legal aid to a larger audience reflected a similar agenda of masculinization. Before and during the turn of the century, the quintessential legal aid client was a woman, as illustrated in a 1903 article in the *Green Bag*, a popular journal for lawyers that published stories about the legal profession. The article

---

[13] Women's presence at national legal aid conferences remained low. Only three women attended the conference in 1916: Boyes again; Paula Laddey, an attorney for the New Jersey Legal Aid Society; and an investigator from the Legal Aid Bureau of Saint Louis. See *Proceedings of the Third Biennial Convention of the National Alliance of Legal Aid Societies* (Cincinnati: Legal Aid Society of Cincinnati, 1917). For years it also remained rare for any woman, no matter her experience, to hold office in the National Alliance or its successor organizations. By contrast, in 1922, when the first official national legal aid organization was incorporated as the National Association of Legal Aid Organizations (NALAO), John Hassrick of the Bureau of Legal Aid of Philadelphia was elected to its national executive committee after only nineteen months as a legal aid attorney. *Proceedings of the Fifth National Conference of Legal Aid Bureaus and Societies under the Auspices of the Department of Public Welfare, City of Philadelphia, Friday, March 24, and Saturday, March 25, 1922* (Philadelphia: G. H. Dean, 1922), 10.

[14] *Proceedings of the Third Biennial Convention of the National Alliance of Legal Aid Societies* (Cincinnati: Legal Aid Society of Cincinnati, 1917), 137. Boyes also corrected the assertion in a 1914 article that portrayed the PAWC as a full-blown legal aid society that had handled a wide variety of cases on behalf of women. Maud Parcells Boyes, "Legal Aid Societies: For the Protection of Home and Family," in *The Woman Citizen and the Home*, ed. Shailer Mathews (Chicago: Civics Society, 1914), 31–37.

[15] *Proceedings of the Third Biennial Convention of the National Alliance*, 149.

highlighted the female clients of the Legal Aid Society of New York and their wage and domestic relations claims.[16] By 1914, however, a second *Green Bag* article proclaimed that legal aid clients were entitled to a free lawyer "by reason of their manhood."[17] The male client's status as head of the family, caring for his wife and children, created his right to an attorney. The article observed, "However poor a man may be, there are always two points where he is vulnerable. Whatever touches his wages or his family goes home directly to his life and to his soul."[18] Legal aid allowed the wage-earning husband and father to maintain his manliness by helping to preserve his ability to support his family. The article also assured readers (incorrectly) that legal aid societies rarely accepted divorce or paternity cases.[19]

The ongoing debate over whether legal aid organizations should charge clients a small fee marked legal aid's distance from charity. Fees allowed lawyers to trumpet their own professionalism while supposedly enhancing the manhood of their clients. Scoville explained, "The Legal Aid Society of Philadelphia does not give its services free to the poor, believing that a poor man does not wish to be pauperized, but simply to be able to retain an attorney for the same proportion of his income as that paid by his wealthier neighbor."[20] By paying for legal services, the client could establish an appropriately professional and masculine relationship. In *Justice and the Poor*, Reginald Heber Smith claimed that such a fee puts the "relationship between client and [legal aid] society on a more businesslike basis, it tends to maintain self-respect, it prevents a tendency to pauperization, and it gives the client a greater sense of responsibility toward the society."[21]

The greatest opponents of fees were those women who had long provided legal aid to women. At one legal aid conference, Maud Parcells Boyes spoke against charging fees: "We surely believe that justice should

---

[16] Waddill Catchings, "The Work of the New York Legal Aid Society," *Green Bag* 15 (1903): 316.

[17] William E. Walz, "Legal Aid Societies: Their Nature, History, Scope, Methods, and Results," *Green Bag* 26 (1914): 98–99.

[18] Ibid., 100.

[19] Ibid., 101.

[20] Scoville, "Practical Working of a Legal Aid Society," 7.

[21] Reginald Heber Smith, *Justice and the Poor: A Study of the Present Denial of Justice to the Poor and of the Agencies Making More Equal Their Position before the Law with Particular Reference to Legal Aid Work in the United States* (New York: Carnegie Foundation, 1919), 167.

not be a purchasable commodity but a right."[22] She explained that the Chicago Legal Aid Society initiated a fee in 1905 and discontinued the practice in 1916. In that year, the Women's Committee, which had long objected to fees, recommended that it be abolished because the clients were too poor and it was unjust. Boyes pointed out that the fees made legal aid look too much like the work of a "private attorney who makes small charges and has a large practice."[23] Having worked with the Protective Agency and then the Chicago Society, Boyes did not see lawyers as meriting an exalted status, nor did she view the professional lawyer-client relationship as the ideal model for legal aid.[24] Rather, in her view, legal aid was philanthropic. Yet the forces of professionalization swirled all around her: on one side, legal aid lawyers sought to professionalize the service fully, and on the other, social workers were themselves undergoing a similar process of professionalization.

When Maude Parcells Boyes first became the superintendent of Chicago's Protective Agency for Women and Children, she might have called herself a paid charity worker. By the 1910s, her professional identity had morphed into that of a social worker. Where law was a male profession, enshrining ideals of masculinity, social work was a female profession.[25] From the prospective of male legal aid attorneys, social workers ranked low on the professional hierarchy, if they were on it at all.

Historians of welfare and social work are well aware that organized social work began in the 1870s with the creation of the charity-organization movement, which sought to systematize the delivery of charity to the poor and to prevent what was called "indiscriminate alms-giving."[26] Central to the movement was an understanding that poverty was in large part caused by individuals' own moral and character flaws.[27] Charities thus needed to minimize material aid and instead concentrate

---

[22] Ibid., 92.

[23] Ibid., 91.

[24] See Chapter 2.

[25] See Mark C. Carnes and Clyde Griffen, *Meanings of Manhood: Constructions of Masculinity in Victorian America* (Chicago: University of Chicago Press, 1990). Susan P. Kemp and Ruth Brandwein, "Feminism and Social Work in the United States: An Intertwined History," *Affilia* 25 (2010): 341.

[26] See, e.g., Josephine Shaw Lowell, *Public Relief and Private Charity* (New York: G. P. Putnam and Sons, 1884), 88–96.

[27] Elizabeth N. Agnew, *From Charity to Social Work: Mary E. Richmond and the Creation of the American Profession* (Urbana: University of Illinois Press, 2004); Lori D. Ginzberg, *Women and the Work of Benevolence: Morality, Politics, and Class in*

on uplifting the poor spiritually and morally through friendly visiting.[28] The friendly volunteer visitor was often a middle-class woman who called on poor families with the intention of introducing discipline (and perhaps hope) into their households. One of the basic tenets of the movement was that charity had to be organized efficiently and effectively to prevent families from receiving duplicate aid, especially as excessive material support fostered dependence.[29]

By the 1890s a younger cadre of women and men began founding and working in settlement houses to study, document, and help change the conditions of the poor.[30] Their version of what would come to be called social work increasingly viewed poverty as the result of economic and structural relationships, and social workers slowly engaged in a wide variety of progressive reforms. They criticized earlier charity workers for emphasizing individuals' moral qualities as the cause of poverty and for focusing too intensely on the importance of self-sufficiency.[31] By the turn of the century even charity workers were reevaluating their character-based understanding of poverty – but they still emphasized the need for the poor to adopt habits of thrift, sobriety, independence, and hard work. As many scholars have pointed out, such concepts of self-sufficiency were gendered, revolving around the familial model of an independent male

---

the *Nineteenth-Century United States* (New Haven, CT: Yale University Press, 1992); Walkowitz, *Working with Class.*

[28] See Josephine Shaw Lowell, *Public Relief and Private Charity* (1884; repr., New York: Arno Press, 1971).

[29] Ibid. See also Joan Waugh, *Unsentimental Reformer: The Life of Josephine Shaw Lowell* (Cambridge, MA: Harvard University Press, 1997); Agnew, *From Charity to Social Work.*

[30] The literature on settlement houses is vast. Some of the most important scholarship includes Doris Groshen Daniels, *Always a Sister: The Feminism of Lillian D. Wald* (New York: Feminist Press, 1989); Mina Carson, *Settlement Folk: Social Thought and the American Settlement Movement* (Chicago: University of Chicago Press, 1990); Allen F. Davis, *Spearheads for Reform: The Social Settlements and the Progressive Movement, 1890–1914* (1967; repr., New Brunswick, NJ: Rutgers University Press, 1994); Elizabeth Lasch-Quinn, *Black Neighbors: Race and the Limits of Reform in the American Settlement House Movement, 1896–1945* (Chapel Hill: University of North Carolina Press, 1993); Edward T. Devine, *When Social Work Was Young* (New York: Macmillan, 1939); Mary Kingsbury Simkhovitch, *Neighborhood: My Story of Greenwich House* (New York: Norton, 1938); Vida Dutton Scudder, *On Journey* (New York: E. P. Dutton, 1937); Lillian D. Wald, *The House on Henry Street* (New York: Henry Holt, 1915); Jean Bethke Elshtain, *Jane Addams and the Dream of American Democracy: A Life* (New York: Basic Books, 2002); Rivka Shpak Lissak, *Pluralism and Progressivism: Hull House and the New Immigrants, 1890–1919* (Chicago: University of Chicago Press, 1989); Jane Addams, *Twenty Years at Hull House* (New York: Macmillan, 1910).

[31] Agnew, *From Charity to Social Work,* 84–85.

breadwinner and his dependent wife and children.[32] According to this model, social work was to prop up, not impede, a husband's incentive to be a breadwinner.[33]

Social work thus took two often overlapping forms: one that focused on large-scale social reforms and another that stressed meeting the immediate needs of the poor. Those who focused on reform became deeply involved in the law. One scholar describes social work around the turn of the century as having one foot in twentieth-century concepts of professional culture, social science, and expertise, and the other foot in nineteenth-century ideas of personal influence, individual moral reform, and citizen participation.[34] At their best, social workers functioned as reformers while mediating between their clients' needs and urban resources such as employment, relief agencies, schools, housing, medical care, the courts, and municipal and state agencies.[35]

As part of social work's professionalization, reformers and charity organizations founded schools of social work, in which students were overwhelmingly female.[36] One of these schools was the Chicago School of Civics and Philanthropy; under the direction of Graham Taylor, in 1908 the school hired onto its faculty Edith Abbott and Sophonisba Breckinridge, both one-time residents of Jane Addams's Hull House. Breckinridge was from a prominent Kentucky family of generations of politicians and lawyers. She had studied law in her father's office and then passed the Kentucky bar examination, becoming the first woman lawyer in Kentucky. She spent a short time as a practicing lawyer before abandoning the work, deciding it was too difficult for a woman lawyer to attract clients.[37] Instead, she entered the University of Chicago as a

---

32 See, e.g., Agnew, *From Charity to Social Work*; Linda Gordon, *Pitied but Not Entitled: Single Mothers and the History of Welfare 1890–1935* (Cambridge, MA: Harvard University Press, 1998).

33 Agnew, *From Charity to Social Work*, 101–2.

34 Ibid., 7.

35 Michael Katz, *In the Shadow of the Poorhouse: A Social History of Welfare in America* (New York: Basic Books, 1986), 165.

36 The first school of social work was created in 1898 in New York, and in 1904 it began to function as the New York School of Philanthropy. By 1915 there were five schools of social work in the United States, and the organization of other schools quickly followed. Walkowitz, *Working with Class*, 27, 53–54.

37 See Anya Jabour, "Relationship and Leadership: Sophonisba Breckinridge and Women in Social Work," *Affilia* 27 (2012): 22. On the difficulty for women lawyers of attracting clients, see Jill Norgren, *Belva Lockwood: The Woman Who Would Become President* (New York: New York University Press, 2007); Barbara Babcock, *Woman Lawyer: The Trials of Clara Foltz* (Stanford, CA: Stanford University Press, 2011).

graduate student and, in 1903, earned a doctorate in political science. Edith Abbott, originally from Nebraska, had studied law and political science and received a doctorate in economics from the University of Chicago in 1905. Both women were avidly interested in law and brought that interest to social work.

The mission of the Chicago School of Civics and Philanthropy was to "promote through instruction, training, investigation and publication the efficiency of civic, philanthropic, and social work, and the improvement of living and working conditions."[38] The school focused on teaching students how to do fieldwork and introducing them to a vast array of urban problems and Chicago's social service agencies and institutions, including the Chicago Legal Aid Society. By 1913 Maud Parcells Boyes was teaching on the school's summer faculty along with Mary Barthleme of Chicago's juvenile court and Ida B. Wells, the famed civil rights activist.[39] Breckenridge and Abbott embraced the idea of producing credentialed social workers who understood poverty as a structural problem, and many of the school's graduates worked in a variety of social service institutions, including the Chicago juvenile court and the Chicago Legal Aid Society.[40] Breckinridge, a director on the society's board, once wrote a chastising letter to Boyes, admonishing that she did not want her name to appear on any society literature stating that the society limited its services to "worthy cases." "I do not understand that we are helping people who are worthy any more than a doctor asks whether his patient is worthy. We ask what they need and how we can help."[41] In drawing an analogy between the legal aid worker and a physician, she highlighted the fact that social workers were learned professionals with a duty to assist those in need, no matter their moral character.

For decades after the turn of the century, the term *social worker* referred to both those who were professionally trained and those who were not; those who still believed in the importance of a client's character and intimate one-on-one contact and those who found such an approach unscientific; those who endorsed the need to professionalize social work

[38] Chicago School of Civics and Philanthropy, "Announcements," *Bulletin* 9 (April 1913).

[39] Ibid., 3.

[40] Chicago School of Civics and Philanthropy, *Alumni Register 1903–1913* (Chicago, 1912).

[41] Sophonisba Breckinridge to Maud Boyes, July 14, 1914, Sophonisba Breckinridge Papers, microfilm reel 1, University of Chicago Library.

and those who fought it.[42] These internal debates, however, did not question the value of social work as a whole.

In contrast, some professionals outside the discipline did not see the value of social work, nor did they view it as a profession.[43] In 1915 Abraham Flexner, a self-appointed expert on professionalism who wrote an influential report on medical education, criticized social work as lacking a core set of skills. The social worker merely called upon real professionals and experts, acting only as an intermediary.[44] Flexner and others saw the ideal social worker as possessing the qualities of sympathy, devotion, altruism, and resourcefulness rather than knowledge, expertise, and skill.[45] These characteristics were gendered: sympathy and altruism were associated with women, skill and knowledge with men. Flexner further faulted social workers for being too confident and verbose, and for failing to respect adequately real professionals.[46] Female social workers were attempting to claim too much authority, trespassing on the terrain of the truly male professions of medicine and law.[47]

Social workers responded to Flexner's critiques and continued their own process of professionalization, often turning to law and lawyers for

---

[42] Historian Robyn Muncy writes that Breckinridge and Abbott denigrated the traditionally female methodology of social work that was based on personal contact between the individual in need and the social worker. Muncy, *Creating a Female Dominion*, 73–78. Other social work leaders, such as Mary E. Richmond, rejected certain norms of professionalization, emphasizing the continued need for volunteer "friendly visitors" who would engage in personal and emotional contact with a family in need. Richmond further challenged the assumption that laypersons were unable to understand the needs of the poor without specific classroom instruction. Agnew, *From Charity to Social Work*, 135–7.

[43] Walkowitz, *Working with Class*, 7.

[44] Abraham Flexner, "Is Social Work a Profession?" *Proceedings of the National Conference of Charities and Corrections at the Forty-Second Annual Session* (Chicago: Hildmann, 1915), reprinted in *Research on Social Work Practice* 11 (March 2001): 152–65. For a full critique of Flexner, see Agnew, *From Charity to Social Work*.

[45] John H. Ehrenreich, *The Altruistic Imagination: A History of Social Work and Social Policy in the United States* (Ithaca, NY: Cornell University Press, 1985), 57–58. See also Daniel Walkowitz, "The Making of a Feminine Professional Identity: Social Workers in the 1920s," *American Historical Review* 95 (October 1990): 1051–75.

[46] Flexner, "Is Social Work a Profession?" 152–65.

[47] See Elizabeth N. Agnew, "Shaping a Civic Profession: Mary Richmond, the Social Gospel, and Social Work," in *Gender and the Social Gospel*, ed. Wendy J. Deichman Edwards and Carolyn De Swarte Gifford (Urbana: University of Illinois Press, 2003), 127; Patricia McGrath Morris, "Reinterpreting Abraham Flexner's Speech, 'Is Social Work a Profession?' Its Meaning and Influence on the Field's Early Professional Development," *Social Service Review* 82 (March 2008): 29–60.

advice. Ironically, lawyers themselves were in a quandary over their own professionalization and the related issue of legal education. In the early twentieth century many law schools did not require an undergraduate degree, and most states allowed lawyers to sit for the bar examination after an apprenticeship rather than attendance at a law school.[48] Some states did not even require those minimal qualifications. Law, however, looked like a mature profession compared with social work, filled as it was with women and volunteer workers. As lawyers reflected on and spoke about social work and social workers, their own identity as lawyers became stronger.

Felix Frankfurter, then a Harvard Law School professor, spoke on professionalism at a national social work conference. In his talk he sought to use the legal profession as a model for social workers, confidently explaining that a legal education, which was the foundation of the legal profession, entailed the orderly study of law, which was itself a science – that is, a systematized body of knowledge. Such professional study had began in earnest in the United States in 1817, with the opening of Harvard Law School, and reached full maturation in 1896, when Harvard adopted the requirement of an undergraduate degree for admission to its law school.[49] According to Frankfurter, for social work to become a real profession, it needed schools attached to research universities. Such schools of social work would create an organized course of study and would centralize the collection and development of social facts and knowledge. Frankfurter also saw the connection between law and social work as one in which social workers would become the administrators of the emerging administrative state. Together, lawyers and social workers would be the new social engineers of society.[50]

Other elite, progressive legal thinkers, such as Roscoe Pound, who in 1917 became dean of Harvard Law School, sought to create a sociological

---

[48] See Bruce Kimball, *The Inception of Modern Professional Education: C. C. Langdell, 1826–1906* (Chapel Hill: University of North Carolina Press, 2009); Robert Bocking Stevens, *Law School: Legal Education in America from the 1850s to the 1980s* (Chapel Hill: University of North Carolina Press, 1983), 37–38. See also *Rules for Admission to the Bar in the Several States and Territories of the United States* (Saint Paul: West Publishing Co., 1901).

[49] Felix Frankfurter, "Social Work and Professional Training," *Proceedings of the National Conference on Charities and Corrections, 1915* (Chicago: Hildmann Printing Co.), 591. For a discussion of early legal education at Harvard and the idea that law was a science, see William LaPiana, *Logic and Experience: The Origin of Modern Legal Education* (New York: Oxford University Press, 1994).

[50] Frankfurter, "Social Work and Professional Training," 595.

jurisprudence that would be concerned with the living conditions of the poor. Pound, who had spent time at Jane Addams' Hull House and knew Breckinridge well, saw social workers as already having such knowledge, as well as the ability to collect social facts that lawyers could then use to shape the law. Other progressive lawyers, such as Louis D. Brandeis, began collaborating with social workers to produce legal briefs and social policy based (as they saw it) on social facts rather than abstract legal knowledge. Through a combination of these advances and social processes, social work and law entered into a dialogue.[51]

Although these legal luminaries saw social work as a rising profession, legal aid lawyers, fearful for their own status and professional identity, entertained no such idea. Moreover, even legal elites never believed that social work would be the equal of law. Instead, social workers would be lawyers' handmaidens – engaged in the collection of facts, the day-to-day care of clients, and the midlevel administrators of the bureaucratic state.

By the late 1910s Reginald Heber Smith emerged as the most prominent leader of legal aid – and an adamant opponent of social work and social workers' involvement in law and the provision of legal assistance. Head attorney of the Legal Aid Society of Boston from 1914 to 1916 and author of the influential *Justice and the Poor*, he created a history of legal aid in which women lay lawyers played no role in legal aid and in which the modern social worker had no place.

Smith attended Harvard Law School and spent two summers clerking for the Boston society; after graduating, he became its head attorney. Although a relatively young organization – it was founded in 1900 – the Boston society had significant connections with the Boston Bar

---

[51] On Roscoe Pound, see N. E. H. Hull, *Roscoe Pound and Karl Llewellyn: Searching for an American Jurisprudence* (Chicago: University of Chicago Press, 1997), 72. For a canonical discussion of legal progressivism, see Morton J. Horwitz, *The Transformation of American Law, 1870–1960: The Crisis of Legal Orthodoxy* (New York: Oxford University Press, 1992), 189. On Louis Brandeis's and Felix Frankfurter's work with Florence Kelley and the National Consumers League, see Susan D. Carle, "Gender in the Construction of the Lawyer's Persona," review of *Florence Kelley and the Nation's Work: The Rise of Women's Political Culture, 1830–1900*, by Kathryn Kish Sklar, *Harvard Women's Law Journal* 22 (1999): 258; Clement E. Vose, "The National Consumers' League and the Brandeis Brief," *Midwest Journal of Political Science* 1 (1957): 283; Nancy Woloch, *Muller v. Oregon: A Brief History with Documents* (Boston: Bedford Books, 1996); Felice Batlan, "Notes from the Margin: Florence Kelley and the Making of Sociological Jurisprudence," in *Transformations in American Legal History*, vol. 2: *Law, Ideology, and Methods: Essays in Honor of Morton J. Horwitz*, ed. Daniel W. Hamilton and Alfred L. Brophy (Cambridge, MA: Harvard University Press, 2011).

Association. Yet for ten years, the organization had neither a permanent office nor a permanent staff; instead it paid a series of law firms to handle its legal work. Poor women flocked to the Boston society, as they did to many legal aid organizations, hoping to pursue claims against husbands and employers.[52] Lacking an office, staff, and affiliation with another organization, BLAS recognized the need to work with established social welfare organizations. "If the various and innumerable charitable organizations in Boston could be induced to send all their cases to us, we should have exactly the class of applicants we most desire and could best serve," the Legal Aid Society declared in its sixth annual report.[53] The society established close relations with Boston Associated Charities and the Massachusetts Society for the Prevention of Cruelty to Children.[54] It regularly identified and referred to itself as a charitable organization working in full cooperation with other philanthropic institutions.[55] It even hired a social worker, Alice Palmer, to conduct investigations and handle domestic relations cases.[56]

Tensions emerged within the organization, however, between charity and legal practice. Like other lawyer-run legal aid societies, the Boston society was trapped between economic efficiency and justice in individual cases. Society lawyers insisted that it must make economic sense to pursue a case, and they were willing to drop a case if the cost of prosecuting it exceeded potential damages. Likewise, the society charged 10 percent on any claim collected over ten dollars, as "it did not wish to pauperize those whom it benefits."[57] Exempted from this policy was money collected from husbands for the support of women and children, as they were not likely

---

[52] In its first year, 138 BLAS clients were women, as compared with 60 men; about half of the women's cases involved domestic relations claims and the other half, wage claims. There were also twenty divorce cases, which, when compared with figures for other legal aid societies, was quite high. By 1905 BLAS's domestic relations cases made up its single largest category of cases and represents almost twice the number of wage claim cases. BLAS, *Eighth Annual Report of the Boston Legal Aid Society, 1907–1908* (Boston: George H. Ellis, 1908), 22.

[53] BLAS, *Sixth Annual Report of the Boston Legal Aid Society, 1905–1906* (Boston: George H. Ellis, 1906), 5.

[54] BLAS, *First Annual Report of the Boston Legal Aid Society, 1900–1901* (Boston: Alfred Mudge and Son, 1901), 10.

[55] BLAS, *Eighth Annual Report*, 5.

[56] Women's Educational and Industrial Union, *Forty-Third Annual Report of the Women's Educational and Industrial Union, 1920–1921* (Boston, 1921), 6.

[57] Arthur Dehon Hill, "The Boston Legal Aid Society," *Legal Aid Review* 3 (October 1905): 2.

"to be injured by receiving charity."[58] Such women, the thinking went, were already dependent.

One of Reginald Heber Smith's first acts as the society's new head attorney in 1914 was to terminate its full-time social worker and replace her with a male lawyer. Giving effect to his profound interest in efficiency, also Smith reduced by almost half the amount that the society spent on each case, and he created a series of elaborate charts to account for the office's output and dollars spent per client.[59]

Smith, however, was not content to be just a legal aid attorney. By his second year at the society, he had written a short history of legal aid describing its role and purpose, which he published as part of the society's annual report. It was blunt and critical: "We have developed a system of justice which in practical operation results in an absolute denial of justice to millions of people."[60] Striking an even more radical note, Smith declared, "In numberless cases the law itself has been twisted by unscrupulous persons into a weapon of oppression and means of prey."[61] These flaws in the legal system, he continued, led to the popular perception that "there is one law for the rich and another for the poor."[62] Smith was impassioned, and he articulated a powerful class-based argument about the legal system's denial of substantive and procedural justice to the poor.

Since the turn of the century, second-generation legal aid societies had often made the argument that if poor immigrants could not settle disputes through legal channels, their anger and frustration would lead them to embrace radicalism. Smith made a stronger argument, claiming that law and legal process actually oppressed the poor. He called for legal aid societies to agitate for wide-ranging legal reforms and to act as centers for experimentation, through which a study of their thousands of individual cases would lead to a greater understanding of how law worked in action. Such knowledge could be used to enact new laws designed to address systemic problems. Smith's report became the outline for *Justice and the Poor*. It also drew the attention of BLAS board member

---

[58] Ibid.

[59] BLAS, *Fourteenth Annual Report of the Boston Legal Aid Society, 1913–1914* (Boston: Fort Hill Press, 1915). For excellent background information regarding Smith and BLAS, see Michael Grossberg, "Altruism and Professionalism: Boston and the Rise of Organized Legal Aid, 1900–1925, *Boston Bar Journal* 22 (May 1978): 21 and (June 1978): 11.

[60] BLAS, *Fifteenth Annual Report of the Boston Legal Aid Society, 1914–1915* (Boston: Fort Hill Press, 1916), 8.

[61] BLAS, *Sixteenth Annual Report of the Boston Legal Aid Society, 1915–1916* (Boston: Fort Hill Press, 1917), 7.

[62] Ibid.

Robert Hale, who hired Smith to work at his Boston law firm, Hale and Dorr.[63] He urged Smith to write a book on legal aid and introduced him to people at the Carnegie Foundation, which agreed to fund Smith's work as part of its series on legal education.[64]

Justice and the Poor changed how American lawyers and politicians viewed legal aid. For almost a century now, it has been the standard text on legal aid's history and its state at the time of the book's publication.[65] In fact, however, *Justice and the Poor* set forth what Smith and the new leaders of legal aid hoped legal aid organizations would become in the future – not what it was then or had been. Before its publication, legal aid providers communicated primarily with one another but not with the legal profession as a whole or with the general public. *Justice and the Poor* expanded awareness of the importance of legal aid and redefined the provision of legal aid to the poor as a national issue connected to the efficacy of democracy and the stability of the nation.[66] Yet Smith had written out the story of women as legal aid providers.

Justice and the Poor was intended to be critical in urging reform without appearing subversive or offending potential supporters of legal aid. Smith eliminated many of the blunt criticisms of law and legal process that were part of his original report on legal aid. From the beginning of their collaboration, Smith and the Carnegie Foundation were concerned that *Justice and the Poor* would appear too radical. They further worried that Smith's youth and inexperience would provoke criticism. One prepublication reviewer, an elite New York lawyer named J. F. Bowie, urged the Carnegie Foundation not to publish the manuscript: "Doubtless revision to the existing system is desirable but the publication of a book calculated to support the charge that the law as applied discriminates against the poor is unjustified."[67] In response, Smith revised his manuscript so it no

---

[63] See ibid., 16–18.

[64] Reginald Heber Smith to Dr. Clyde Furst, May 1, 1919, Reginald Heber Smith Papers, Harvard Law School Library, MS. 1377 (hereinafter Smith Papers); Reginald Heber Smith to Henry Pritchett, January 29, 1918, Justice and the Poor Correspondence, 1913–1921, Smith Papers.

[65] See, e.g., Earl Johnson Jr., "Three Phases of Justice for the Poor: From Charity to Discretion to Right," *Clearinghouse Review* 42 (2009): 487.

[66] See Michael Grossberg, "The Politics of Professionalism: The Creation of Legal Aid and the Strains of Political Liberalism in America, 1900–1930," in *Lawyers and the Rise of Western Political Liberalism: Europe and North America from the Eighteenth to Twentieth Centuries*, ed. Terence C. Halliday and Lucien Karpik (Oxford: Clarendon Press of Oxford University Press, 1997).

[67] Memorandum from J. F. Bowie regarding *Justice and the Poor*, April 11, 1918, Justice and the Poor Correspondence, 1913–1921, Smith Papers.

longer implied that the poor needed to be protected against exploitation by the rich or that law substantively favored the wealthy.[68] To ward off further criticism, the foundation convinced the noted lawyer Elihu Root to write the foreword. With Root's imprimatur, they believed, the book would be more acceptable to leaders of the bar.[69]

As published in 1919, *Justice and the Poor* reflected some of the central arguments of a deradicalized and dying progressivism. Prewar progressivism had encompassed a wide range of reformers, including those who engaged in serious critiques of class, but World War I, the Russian Revolution, and the censure and intimidation of reformers had devastated progressive communities and coalitions. Instead of mounting significant critiques of market liberalism and class inequality, post–World War I progressivism focused on efficacy, expertise, professionalization, a fear of immigrant and working-class disorder, an abhorrence of class-based arguments, and a desire for elites to control whatever reforms might be undertaken. To be sure, such themes always had been part of progressivism, but after the war they were increasingly dominant.[70]

Smith, his editors, and the Carnegie Foundation understood this new environment well. *Justice and the Poor* set up the issue of access to courts as crucial to the Americanization of millions of immigrants. It also asserted that the principal problems regarding justice for the urban poor were procedural and not substantive. These procedural problems included significant delays in litigation stemming from the inefficient organization of the court system, the high cost of court fees, and the expense of counsel. In other words, it was the court system that needed to become more efficient: substantive law itself required little reform.

---

[68] Reginald Heber Smith to Dr. Clyde Hurst, March 17, 1919, Smith Papers.

[69] A. Z. Reed to Henry S. Pritchett, July 29, 1918, Smith Papers.

[70] The literature on progressivism is vast. See, e.g., John Fabian Witt, *Patriots and Cosmopolitans: Hidden Histories of American Law* (Cambridge, MA: Harvard University Press, 2007); Daniel T. Rodgers, *Atlantic Crossings: Social Politics in a Progressive Age* (Cambridge, MA: Belknap Press of Harvard University Press, 2000); Michael E. McGerr, *A Fierce Discontent: The Rise and Fall of the Progressive Movement in America, 1870–1920* (New York: Oxford University Press, 2005); Maureen A. Flanagan, *Progressives and Progressivisms, 1890s–1920s* (New York: Oxford University Press, 2006); John White Chambers II, *The Tyranny of Change: America in the Progressive Era, 1890–1920* (New Brunswick, NJ: Rutgers University Press, 2000); Nell Irvin Painter, *Standing at Armageddon: A Grassroots History of the Progressive Era* (New York: Norton, 2008); Elizabeth J. Clapp, *Mothers of All Children: Women Reformers and the Rise of Juvenile Courts in Progressive-Era America* (University Park, PA: Penn State University Press, 1998).

Justice and the Poor's mission was to continue the process of professionalizing, rationalizing, and masculinizing legal aid, and Smith borrowed heavily from the agenda set forth by the new leaders of legal aid. *Justice and the Poor* strongly argued that justice and efficiency required that legal aid work be conducted by attorneys who specialized in legal aid. Smith repeatedly emphasized that any other structure for legal aid wasted resources, duplicated effort, and created multiple inefficiencies. He vigorously maintained that bar associations must control legal aid societies, which needed to be cleaved from welfare organizations, charities, and social work.

Smith's research for *Justice and the Poor* reflected his agenda. Particularly important were what he chose to ask and whom he chose to interview. As part of his research Smith visited fourteen cities, where he met with local leaders of the bar, judges, and legal aid attorneys. He interviewed few social workers, lay lawyers, or women involved in legal aid, and even when he did meet with them, he did not incorporate their ideas and comments into his manuscript.[71] Often he simply ignored the existence of women's legal aid organizations. *Justice and the Poor* did not even mention the Boston Women's Education and Industrial Union, an organization that in 1919 was still active and providing legal aid to women. In fact, the Boston Legal Aid Society and the union were even discussing merging their legal services, which the union refused to do until the Legal Aid Society hired a female attorney.[72]

Smith's written research questionnaire, which he sent to dozens of legal aid organizations, focused on whether an organization was connected to a charity or operated as a stand-alone institution. It queried, "Is the executive in active charge of your work an attorney? If so, how many years has he been a member of the bar? If not, who is in active charge? Please state the reasons for not having an attorney in charge."[73] These questions reflect Smith's vision that the ideal legal aid society was controlled by a male attorney and that any deviation required an explanation. Some recipients were aware of Smith's agenda-driven research. In response to

---

[71] Reginald Heber Smith, "Memorandum on Study of Legal Aid Work to the Carnegie Foundation," February 24, 1917, 1–4, Study of Legal Aid Work, vol. 1, Harvard Law School Library, MS 1254 (hereinafter Smith Study).

[72] WEIU, *Forty-Third Annual Report of the Women's Educational and Industrial Union* (Boston, 1920–21), 16, Women's Educational and Industrial Union, Schlesinger Library, Radcliffe Institute, Harvard University (hereinafter WEIU Papers).

[73] Reginald Heber Smith, Preliminary Survey of the Legal Aid Society of Chicago, July 29, 1916, 4, Smith Study.

the question of who was in charge of the Chicago Legal Aid Society, Maud Parcells Boyes wrote of herself, "A woman and a social worker."[74]

As Smith visited various legal aid organizations, he became further convinced of the necessity of separating legal aid from philanthropic organizations and of the importance of having a lawyer in charge. He was unimpressed by the Rochester Women's Educational and Industrial Union, for example, finding that its records were in "wretched condition." He wrote, "The [Rochester Union] offered little of instructive value except [that] it demonstrated some of the dangers of permitting legal aid to be controlled by [a charity]."[75] Smith then described how he explained to one of its male directors the importance of "making the bar feel its responsibility towards this work and of securing from the bar suitable persons to control and guide the Society."[76]

Smith could easily dismiss the small Rochester union. The Legal Aid Society of Chicago, however, created significant problems for him. It was the second largest legal aid society in the nation, the society still had a women's board of directors, and social workers conducted much of the actual work. Smith explained that his visit to the society produced "difficulty."[77] According to him, "[The] Chicago method of handling the work is totally different from ours in Boston and their view point on many questions is diametrically opposed to ours. . . . Mrs. Boyes, the executive in charge, had an idea that I would use my position to further my personal views at the expense of hers."[78] Boyes's concern was justified. Rather than explain the Chicago society's different approach to legal aid, Smith downplayed its importance, history, guiding convictions, and methods of operation. Amazingly, he wrote Boyes herself out of the history of legal aid.

While in Chicago, Smith also visited the Bureau of Personal Service, an organization that provided a wide range of social services, including legal aid, to Chicago's Jewish community. Smith interviewed the director, Minnie Low, and took extensive notes. Although Smith did not seem to realize it, Low was a renowned social worker, often dubbed the "Jewish Jane Addams."[79] She firmly believed that the provision of legal aid should

---

74 Ibid.
75 Smith, "Memorandum on Study of Legal Aid Work to the Carnegie Foundation," February 24, 1917, 1–2, Smith Study.
76 Ibid., 2–3.
77 Ibid., 3.
78 Ibid., 3–4.
79 On Minnie Low, see Hasia R. Diner and Beryl Lieff Benderly, *Her Works Praise Her: A History of Jewish Women in America from Colonial Times to the Present* (New York:

be controlled by social workers and radically opposed the involvement of lawyers. Low understood modern-day law as a series of technicalities that prevented "moral adjudication" and "real justice."[80] Low opined that the social worker is "deeply interested in that side of a case, which conserves the moral issue, for the moral side is positive – it is vital, while the legal side is more or less negative and traditional."[81]

Smith was bewildered by this small Jewish woman who had no formal education. His notes of this meeting read:

No lawyers used.... All of staff are women. Social workers. Not trained in law. They do, however, perform all the functions of an attorney. They go into court and advise clients, etc. This is the extreme type of social service legal aid office. The law is trusted to what the social workers pick up through experience. I examined them and they appear very intelligent. They follow current decisions, etc.[82]

Smith also highlighted how the organization fully integrated law and social work and, when necessary, provided material relief to clients: "They follow the case and keep after it doing anything that is necessary.... They try to cover everything."[83] Smith clearly recognized that the bureau's female social workers were engaged in legal work and that they were competent to do so. He even seemed satisfied with how they handled their cases. This material, however, never found its way into *Justice and the Poor.*

In his early manuscript drafts Smith had included at least some discussion of Minnie Low and her agency, Maud Parcells Boyes, and Boston's Women's Educational and Industrial Union. Later, however, he removed such references. In commenting on the manuscript, Alfred Z. Reed, a law professor and one of Smith's Carnegie Foundation editors, wrote to Smith, "If I am right in thinking that women have had nothing to do with this [legal aid] movement, you might consider the desirability of deleting them. That sentence, as it stands, reduces the whole movement, as it

---

Basic Books, 2002), 235–6; Shelly Tanenbaum, "Minnie Low," in *Jewish Women in America: A Historical Encyclopedia*, ed. Paula Hyman and Deborah Dash Moor (New York: Routledge, 1998); Mary Jo Deegan, "Minnie Low," in *Women Build Chicago, 1790–1990*, ed. Rima Lunen Schultz and Adele Hast (Bloomington: Indiana Press, 2001), 521–2.

[80] Minnie F. Low, "Legal Aid," *Proceedings of the Sixth Biennial Session of the National Conference of Jewish Charities in the United States Held in the City of St. Louis May 17-19th* (Baltimore: Kohn and Pollock, 1910), 183.

[81] Ibid.

[82] Reginald Heber Smith, "Preliminary Survey of Bureau of Personal Service," January 30–31, 1917, 3, vol. 1, Smith Study.

[83] Ibid., 7.

seems to me, to the level of charity work in general."[84] Reed's editorial advice highlights both Smith's awareness of women as legal aid providers and Smith and Reed's shared fear of associating legal aid with charity and women. So delete, Smith did.[85]

Justice and the Poor effectively severed the provision of legal aid from the world of women, lay lawyers, and social workers. Instead, Smith situated legal aid firmly in the masculine realm of lawyers and law: "The societies are engaged in the practice of law and not in social service work as that phrase is generally used. More closely than anything else, the work resembles an attorney engaged in general practice."[86] Seeking to identify the essence of "real" legal aid societies, Smith explained, "The most important thing is the fact that its initial impulse came entirely from the bar."[87] Again, Smith's subtext was to reject any idea that legal aid arose from women's work and philanthropy. He asserted, "The scope of the work is confined to the field of legal action."[88] And reaching for an elusive distinction between legal aid work and social work, Smith contended, "Legal aid work is a distinct thing from general charity work, it requires the legally trained mind acting in the light of a knowledge of legal affairs."[89] This explanation clashed directly with reality: social workers untrained in law were delivering legal aid – and were doing it effectively.

Justice and the Poor assumed that charity perpetuated dependence. After reading Smith's draft manuscript, Arthur von Briesen urged him to emphasize even more strongly that legal aid was entirely distinct from charity.[90] Even without Briesen's advice, Smith wanted to put as much distance as possible between legal aid and charity, and the latter's connection to social work and dependence. The irony here is that it was early social

---

[84] Alfred Z. Reed to Reginald Heber Smith, June 11, 1919, Smith Papers.

[85] In 1916 Smith asserted in an article in the *Massachusetts Law Review* that the Legal Aid Society of New York was the first legal aid society in the country. John Wigmore, an eminent legal scholar who was dean of Northwestern Law School and a longtime board member of the Legal Aid Society of Chicago, wrote an angry letter to the editor of the *Review* in response to Smith's article: "This is an error of history. Already in 1888 *two societies* had been incorporated in Chicago – one, the Bureau of Justice; the other, the Protective Agency for Women and Children. Both of these were purely legal aid societies, as now understood." John H. Wigmore, "Letter to the Editor – Note on the History of Legal Aid Work," *Massachusetts Law Quarterly* 1 (1916): 288.

[86] Smith, *Justice and the Poor*, 152.

[87] Ibid., 141.

[88] Ibid., 152.

[89] Ibid., 178.

[90] Arthur von Briesen to Reginald Heber Smith, March 12, 1918, Smith Papers.

workers who had stigmatized material relief as creating dependence. To ensure the separation of charity from legal aid, Smith positioned access to legal aid as a right belonging to the independent male citizen. If the feminized world of charity and social workers created dependence, the newly imagined male world of legal aid created independence. Thus Smith saw the clients of charities and those of legal aid agencies as two entirely separate populations, rather than as the same population receiving two kinds of help.

With legal aid now properly situated, Smith placed the responsibility for founding, financing, and managing legal aid societies squarely on the established bar. He criticized the organized bar for failing to live up to its responsibility in the past:

> Where there ought to be the closest possible alliance, there is not a semblance of ordered and sustained cooperation. It is profitless to attempt to fix or apportion the blame of the past; but it is of high importance both to the cause of legal aid work and to the reputation of the profession, that the wholly unsatisfactory nature of the present situation be stated and that steps, calculated to improve it, be suggested.[91]

Smith emphasized that since legal aid societies were dispensing law and not charity, morality should play no role in whether an organization would accept or decline a case. He even interpreted the stance of many societies, that cases had to be "worthy," as meaning that the potential client needed a plausible legal claim, not that the claim had to be substantively just or that the claimant be of good character. He explained that if the worst man in the world was owed ten dollars by the best man in the world, a legal aid society would accept the worst man's case against the best man. Smith did, however, note two exceptions. One situation was that of domestic workers who failed to give employers notice of their resignation but still claimed wages owed. Like the Legal Aid Society of New York, Smith viewed such cases – which primarily involved wage claims brought by African American and immigrant women – as distinct from regular wage claims, but he did not explain why they should be considered unworthy. The second type of exceptional case involved mothers' child custody claims. Without elaborating, Smith claimed that such cases always involved questions of character, morality, and worth. What Smith failed to acknowledge was that both of these kinds of cases primarily concerned women.[92] If morality was to play a minimal

---

[91] Smith, *Justice and the Poor*, 226.
[92] Ibid., 160–2.

role in connection with men's cases, it still had an impact on women's cases.

Smith further cautioned that any aid organization's director who was not an attorney could not be competent to handle legal matters. "The general secretary of a charity is disqualified from passing expert opinion on such matters, [because] he lacks the legal training to apply them, and he approaches them from an entirely different background."[93] In other words, legal knowledge could be possessed and wielded only by a lawyer. Smith also claimed that a legal aid office attached to a social service agency reached fewer people, as the poor did not want to ask for legal services from a charity.[94] He even asserted that the physical proximity of a legal aid office to a charitable organization reduced the numbers of those who sought legal aid. The mere presence of a charitable organization would contaminate legal aid societies, which had to be strenuously "independent." Just as an attorney would be harmed by dependence on others, so, too, would the man in need of legal aid, who would be unwilling to seek such aid if it made him feel dependent – that is, less than a true man. The relationship between the legal aid attorney and his client needed to be between equally independent and autonomous men. The legal aid society, its lawyers, and its clients were like a series of magnifying mirrors, reflecting and enhancing each other's masculinity.[95]

In some quarters, readers rejected *Justice and the Poor* as potentially fueling class warfare.[96] Several New York judges and lawyers also criticized *Justice and the Poor* for implying that the administration of justice was not impartial.[97] Charles Evans Hughes wrote, "Any charge that, on account of the lack of impartiality, American courts do not give equal justice

---

[93] Ibid., 178.

[94] Ibid.

[95] On the importance of independence and masculinity, see Barbara Young Welke, *Recasting American Liberty: Gender, Race, Law, and the Railroad Revolution, 1865–1920* (Cambridge: Cambridge University Press, 2001); Gail Bederman, *Manliness and Civilization: A Cultural History of Gender and Race in the United States, 1880–1917* (Chicago: University of Chicago Press, 1995).

[96] See, e.g., "Justice and the Poor," *New York Times*, December 26, 1919; William D. Guthrie to Henry S. Pritchard, December 6, 1919, and A. Z. Reed, "Memorandum Regarding *Justice and the Poor*," December 24, 1919, 3, Smith Papers; Michael Grossberg provides an account of reactions to *Justice and the Poor* in "Counsel for the Poor? Legal Aid Societies and the Creation of Modern Urban Legal Structures, 1900–1930," Legal History Papers, 1994–5, University of British Columbia.

[97] "Summary of New York State Bar Association Pamphlet Discussing 'Justice and the Poor,'" April 2, 1920, and "Hughes Says Poor Get Full Justice," February 27, 1920, Smith Papers.

to the poor would be absolutely groundless."[98] Alfred Z. Reed mocked such critics' attitudes in a memorandum to his colleagues at the Carnegie Foundation: "[Conservative lawyers] usually convince themselves that the poor have no grievances – certainly no grievances comparable to those the rich have against the poor. The Carnegie Foundation has betrayed its class by publishing this bulletin."[99]

In contrast, the legal progressive Roscoe Pound embraced *Justice and the Poor*. In his review for the *Harvard Law Review*, Pound praised Smith for examining how law affected people on the ground. According to Pound, Smith's argument was ultimately about how court procedures and legal processes buckled under the pressure of modern urban life.[100] Other reviewers were sympathetic to Smith's argument that, on the whole, there was little wrong with substantive law, and that the problem was instead primarily one of bringing needed reforms to lower courts. Further, they lauded Smith's description of the history of and the need for legal aid societies, and his distinctions between charitable organizations and legal aid societies.[101] Almost all agreed that Smith struck an important chord in arguing for greater responsibility on the part of lawyers and bar associations to support the provision of free legal aid.[102]

Justice and the Poor succeeded on multiple levels. The Carnegie Foundation distributed the work widely, and Smith soon became the leading expert on legal aid, poised to lead it into the future. Male leaders of legal aid happily endorsed *Justice and the Poor*, treating it as a bible that gave

[98] "Hughes Says Poor Get Full Justice," February 27, 1920, Smith Papers. Hughes, an elite New York City attorney, was elected governor of New York in 1905. In 1910 he was appointed to the Supreme Court but he resigned in 1916 to run for president on the Republican ticket. In 1921, he became U.S. secretary of state. Herbert Hoover later reappointed him to the Supreme Court as chief justice.
[99] "Justice and the Poor," *New York Times*, December 26, 1919; A. Z. Reed, "Memorandum Regarding *Justice and the Poor*," December 24, 1919, 3, Smith Papers.
[100] Roscoe Pound, review of *Justice and the Poor*, by Reginald Heber Smith, *Harvard Law Review* 33 (February 1920): 621–6.
[101] See, e.g., H. M. Alderson Smith, review of *Justice and the Poor*, by Reginald Heber Smith, *Journal of Comparative Legislation and International Law* 2 (1920): 298–301.
[102] Reviewing the book for the *Columbia Law Review*, Harlan F. Stone wrote: "Mr. Smith has compiled an extremely interesting and valuable history of Legal Aid Societies in the United States.... They have not received adequate support from the legal profession, principally because they have not made an organized and systemic appeal to members of the bar. This report, printed and widely circulated by the Carnegie Foundation, will spread knowledge of the Legal Aid Movement." Harlan F. Stone, review of *Justice and the Poor*, by Reginald Heber Smith, *Columbia Law Review* 20 (January 1920): 113, 116–17. See also Thomas Reed Powell, review of *Justice and the Poor*, by Reginald Heber Smith, *Political Science Quarterly* 35 (March 1920): 152–4.

legal aid a reformulated history and a blueprint for the future.[103] Reed wrote to Smith, "How does it feel to have become a national character over night?"[104] He continued, "If you aspire ... to lead the scattered hosts of your advancing army, ... a very important part of your work is ... to keep your following from quarreling among themselves."[105]

To capitalize on *Justice and the Poor*'s momentum, Smith, other legal aid leaders, and a number of prominent jurists agreed that a new national legal aid organization was needed. The old National Alliance of Legal Aid Societies, which functioned without a treasury, was too weak, decentralized, and "impotent," they said.[106] In 1923, with money from the Carnegie Foundation, Smith and other prominent lawyers created the National Association of Legal Aid Organizations (NALAO), designed as a centralized organization that would promote the establishment of legal aid societies. NALAO's constitution proclaimed that it would set minimum standards for local legal aid societies and if such standards were not met, the offending organizations would be expelled from the national organization and reported to the local bar for disciplinary action.[107] NALAO's hopes, however, were a far cry from the reality of legal aid.

John Bradway, chief attorney at the Legal Aid Society of Philadelphia, was handpicked by Smith to serve as NALAO's executive secretary, a position Bradway held for eighteen years.[108] If Smith was the high priest of legal aid, Bradway was the missionary on the ground, spreading the gospel of legal aid as articulated by Smith. Under Smith's direction, Bradway began with a grand tour of legal aid. He started in the Harvard Law School Library, reading reports of the Legal Aid Society of Boston, carefully studying *Justice and the Poor*, and reviewing all of Smith's correspondence and files regarding legal aid, as well as the background material Smith had used in writing *Justice and the Poor*. Examining this material confirmed for Bradway the bar's important role in legal aid.

[103] Grossberg, "The Politics of Professionalism," 308.
[104] Alfred Z. Reed to Reginald Heber Smith, October 31, 1919, Smith Papers.
[105] Ibid.
[106] Smith, *Justice and the Poor*, 197.
[107] Reginald Heber Smith to John Wigmore, November 6, 1923, John Henry Wigmore Papers, Northwestern University Archives, Northwestern University (hereinafter Wigmore Papers), box 93, folder 4.
[108] Born in Swarthmore, Pennsylvania, in 1890, Bradway attended Haverford College and the University of Pennsylvania Law School. He had spent approximately six years as an attorney with the Philadelphia Legal Aid Society when he was hired for the NALAO position, at a salary of $5,000 a year.

Next, he visited Boston's Legal Aid Society and then continued to Chicago and New York. Bradway understood his job as learning how these societies functioned, assessing their policies, and creating standardized procedures and rules for legal aid societies' organization and operations. He also sought to delineate further why lawyers were responsible for legal aid, how legal aid was not charity, and why social workers should not be involved in legal aid. Bradway understood his goals well; he kept detailed notes in which he tried to elaborate on and provide theoretical justification for the distinctions among law, social work, and philanthropy. He excitedly wrote to himself, "Why not get the theory of Social Service, the theory of the Bar and Bench worked out? This should show the dividing line between the two."[109]

As Bradway went about his work, he was shocked by the gulf between legal aid as presented by Smith and what was actually happening. Social workers and women were everywhere: "It is not right to have 'Legal Aid Society' over the door and a social worker inside.... Only a lawyer can tell whether the facts present a legal problem or not.... Also a social service worker makes the client feel that it is charity."[110] Even employing a female attorney to investigate cases degraded legal aid: "To my mind what you need instead of a social service secretary (which is a popular idea to a woman attorney) is a man of 40 or 50 years of age who can go out and get the facts just the same as a large trial office has investigators."[111] Only a man could bestow the necessary prestige, and in Bradway's view, legal aid needed to attract the "best men."[112] In significant contrast, the Legal Aid Society of Chicago had always used female social workers to interview prospective clients. As one Chicago memorandum explained regarding the type of person who should fill that position, "These should be persons, probably women, of sympathetic manner, accurate and clear,... with full appreciation of the social importance of the work we do."[113]

Bradway also tried to reconcile the actual history of women lay lawyers who provided legal aid with Smith's newly created history of legal aid. In an unpublished outline on the history of legal aid, Bradway wrote that organized legal aid began in 1863 with the establishment of New York's

---

[109] John S. Bradway, "Legal Aid Material Indicating My Work from June 1, 1922, to about August 1, 1922," 2, John S. Bradway Papers, David M. Rubenstein Rare Book and Manuscript Library, Duke University (hereinafter Bradway Papers), box 5, vol. 3.

[110] Ibid., 5.

[111] Ibid., 7.

[112] Ibid., 2.

[113] CLAS, untitled memoranda (n.d.), Wigmore Papers, box 84, folder 2.

Working Women's Protective Union. He then tried to explain why such a fact was irrelevant:

If a gold mine were discovered by a group of Mexicans, it would still be a gold mine and not a Mexican mine.... The same holds good in Legal Aid. It happened that people charitably inclined discovered the need for legal aid and made up the goldmine as a society.... It is no less part of justice because it was discovered by social and philanthropic workers. The credit is due them for the discovery and the work done.[114]

Perhaps, like a Mexican gold mine, legal aid was ripe for foreigners to expropriate, and – like the imagined primitives who first opened the gold mine – social workers did not have the knowledge to understand their discovery fully or exploit it efficiently. That women lay lawyers had always been involved in legal aid was, for Bradway, an unfortunate historical accident without significant meaning.

As Bradway's tour continued, he struggled to articulate a grand theory of legal aid as a constitutional right. Legal aid was necessary pursuant to the Equal Protection Clause of the U.S. Constitution's Fourteenth Amendment because without legal aid, the poor would not have equal access to the courts. The administration of law was a government function, and lawyers were, he claimed, public officers of the courts. Thus they had to deliver legal aid as part of their public function. By contrast, social workers were "outlaws" – the law gave them no legal function or recognition. He even questioned the use of the word *society* in the term *legal aid society* because it smacked of the "social" rather than individual rights. Bradway continued, stating that social services as a whole were "un-American," led to socialism, and derogated "the theory that we must stand on our own feet."[115] Law was "fundamentally American."[116] Bradway concluded, "Legal aid deals with normal Men. It should be identified with normal government."[117] Social work needed to be limited to those clients who were "abnormal."[118]

According to Bradway's theory, when lawyers delivered legal aid it enhanced clients' sense of independence, whereas social workers dealt

---

[114] Bradway, "Legal Aid Material Indicating My Work," 10, Bradway Papers, box 5, vol. 3.
[115] Ibid., 3.
[116] Ibid.
[117] John Bradway, "Relation of Legal Aid and Social Service," July 27, 1922, 7, Bradway Papers, box 5, vol. 5.
[118] Ibid., 4–5.

with those who were either born dependent or who had failed at independence. He observed, "In our law the normal man is supposed to take care of himself."[119] Exempted from the category of "normal man" were women, infants, and "the insane."[120] For the normal man, law in part consisted of constitutional rights and the common law, which was based on rules, reason, and precedent. Legal aid was the technology that could deliver the rule of law to the common man. Social work, in comparison, was private, discretionary, and pure charity – or, as Bradway noted, "pity translated into action."[121] Protected legal rights, which should be in the hands of male lawyers, were distinct from unprotected social and economic issues, areas in which the social worker might intervene. Bradway wrote, "The mind of the lawyer naturally revolts at the idea of a giving and withholding at the discretion of a group of social service workers on the basis of the individual conscience."[122] Social work, according to Bradway's logic, was lawless – an uncontained, amorphous, feminized, ever-growing field that sought to subsume law and usurp its functions.

For Smith and Bradway, the key to the expansion and success of legal aid was support from bar associations. From his perch at Hale and Dorr, and with the backing of the Carnegie Foundation, Smith began to organize elite lawyers. His work paid off when a special committee of the American Bar Association (ABA) presented a report on legal aid to a meeting of the ABA in 1921. The report claimed, "To the extent that legal aid work has become a national movement the American Bar Association alone has adequate jurisdiction to sponsor, aid, and *direct* it."[123] Now sympathetic to Smith's agenda, Secretary of State Charles Evan Hughes, the original chairman of the special ABA committee, added, "While the legal aid organizations are instruments of the entire community, they perform a service which lawyers should regard as peculiarly their own."[124] In return for the ABA's support, legal aid organizations would accept the association's oversight. ABA sponsorship theoretically would infuse needed funds as well as lend prestige to legal aid societies, and it would

---

[119] Ibid., 3.

[120] John S. Bradway, "Notes on the Relation of Legal Aid and Social Service," July 27, 1922, 3, Bradway Papers, box 5, vol. 5.

[121] Bradway, "Legal Aid Material Indicating My Work," July 24, 1922, 6, Bradway Papers box 5, vol. 3.

[122] Ibid.

[123] ABA, "Report of the Special Committee on Legal Aid Work," *Report of the Forty-Fourth Annual Meeting of the American Bar Association* (Baltimore: Lord Baltimore Press, 1921), 495 (emphasis in original).

[124] Ibid., 497. Hughes resigned as chairman of the committee before the 1921 convention because of his appointment as secretary of state by President Warren G. Harding.

firmly position legal aid within its professional, conservative, and male realm.[125]

How the ABA was to provide oversight and leadership was never fully delineated, especially because legal aid was delivered on a local level, but the National Association of Legal Aid Organizations was in part intended to fulfill this mission. NALAO saw its role as assisting local bar associations in creating legal aid organizations, and it recommended that no legal aid society should be formed without the cooperation of the local bar. It declared that "earnest and sincere men will be found for these respective bar associations' legal aid committees and the combination of our technical equipment plus their influence and position affords the best possible method for obtaining rapid results."[126]

In general, NALAO and the ABA promoted the plan that, in small cities and towns, bar association committees on legal aid would directly provide representation to those unable to afford an attorney. In larger cities, bar associations would establish legal aid societies. In both cases, the bar associations, with advice from NALAO, would decide controversial matters of policy, such as what kind of cases would be accepted, and would ensure that legal aid societies did not compete with the bar.[127] Legal aid thus would become part of the monopoly that bar associations sought to exert over the practice of law. As the New York State Bar Association explained, "The local legal aid bureau... and its activities should be as carefully and as jealously supervised as are those of the association's Grievance Committee."[128] In this new scheme, no place existed for the older model of lay lawyering or even community-based legal aid that did not involve bar associations.

Smith and Bradway campaigned far and wide, seeking to make the bar aware of its responsibility for legal aid. They lectured to bar association meetings, shared copies of their speeches with lawyers, and published those speeches in journals and magazines, where lawyers might read them. If an attorney or bar association wrote to NALAO expressing interest in legal aid, Bradway would respond by sending a copy of *Justice and the*

---

[125] On the conservative nature of the ABA at this time, see Auerbach, *Unequal Justice*, 102–29.

[126] "First Report of the National Committee on Legal Aid Work to the Carnegie Corporation," 1922, 32, Wigmore Papers, box 93, folder 4.

[127] "Report of the Legal Aid Committee of the American Bar Association" (1922), in John S. Bradway, *The Work of Legal Aid Committees of the Bar Association* (Chicago: American Bar Association, 1938), 15.

[128] New York State Bar Association, "Report of the Committee on Legal Aid Societies, Oct. 2–4," 1924, 6, Bradway Papers, box 3, vol. 25.

Poor along with the advice that the most respected lawyers involved in the local bar association should be recruited to serve on a legal aid committee. Such a committee, under the auspices of the bar association, was then expected to establish and finance a legal aid organization.[129] This formula, of course, was easier to prescribe than to effectuate.

NALAO's new national model of legal aid suffered from significant flaws, as legal aid was intensely local. The ABA, state bar associations, and NALAO might attempt to assert power, but they could not reach down to the grassroots level where people sought and received assistance. Prestigious members of the bar across the country touted legal aid at national and state bar association conventions, yet their active involvement often did not go beyond making approving speeches and lending their names to honorary boards.[130]

Elite lawyers (Charles Evans Hughes is a prominent example) could support legal aid because it posed no economic threat to them. In contrast, nonelite lawyers feared that legal aid would deplete their clientele. Harrison Tweed, former president of the Legal Aid Society of New York, recalled, "Lawyers were suspicious; they thought [legal aid] was taking the bread out of their mouths."[131] Even successful lawyers who served on the boards of legal aid societies pressured their societies to adopt stringent income eligibility requirements for clients. One lawyer involved in legal aid and the local Chamber of Commerce, hardly a radical organization, wrote, "Legal Aid extension is a very slow process. It would seem that the Bar Association would be the logical organization to take the initiative and support such an organization. However, Bar Associations are constitutionally organized for conservative purposes, to-wit, to preserve conditions and prevent radical innovations."[132] Despite dozens of laudatory speeches by legal luminaries, bar associations' ground-level support for legal aid societies did not materialize quickly or consistently. Bradway became frustrated with the bar and NALAO's strategy: "The Bar has had its chance, it [has] left the poor litigant. No one has come

[129] "First Report of the National Committee on Legal Aid Work," December 22, 1922, Wigmore Papers, box 93, folder 4.

[130] See, e.g., "The Reminiscences of Allen Wardwell Oral History" (1952), 73, Columbia University Center for Oral History, Columbia University; Bradway, *The Work of Legal Aid Committees*. Wardwell was an elite New York City lawyer and one-time president of the Legal Aid Society of New York.

[131] "The Reminiscences of Harrison Tweed Oral History" (1970), 99, Columbia University Center for Oral History, Columbia University.

[132] J. L. M. Boyd to Louise Bignall, February 25, 1927, Bradway Papers, box 1, vol. 36.

along to take the place except the charitable organizations and it is not peculiar that they want to hold on, having once found it." He continued, "The Bar is not sold."[133] Legal aid was not moving in the direction that NALAO, Smith, and Bradway had envisioned.

Instead, social workers retained significant influence and growing power in some cities. In 1919, the same year that *Justice and the Poor* was published, the Legal Aid Society of Chicago merged with United Charities of Chicago, that city's largest social service agency. The society justified the merger on a number of grounds, declaring, "There would be a special advantage in that the policies and methods of relief could all be organized under a single management and thus better service to the community be rendered."[134] Just when Smith began preaching that legal aid and social service agencies must be separate, the Chicago Legal Aid Society became part of a social service agency. It understood legal aid to be part of a continuum of services that United Charities provided, and that social workers had a significant role to play in providing legal aid.

The Chicago merger was a marriage between the old and the new, lawyers and social workers. The United Charities' board of directors appointed Joel Hunter as its new superintendent, to whom the renamed Legal Aid Bureau would now report. The son of a minister of the Dutch Reformed Church, Hunter had intended to follow in his father's footsteps but abandoned the clergy after a year in seminary. He moved to Chicago and worked as a probation officer in the Chicago courts, where he became familiar with Chicago's leading social workers, social service agencies, judges, philanthropists, and lawyers. Perhaps equally important, Hunter was the brother-in-law of John Wigmore, dean of the Northwestern University School of Law and a long-time director of the Legal Aid Society of Chicago. He was exactly the kind of social worker against whom Smith railed, a nonlawyer who directed a legal aid organization. The Chicago Legal Aid Bureau now stood as a visible rebuke to Smith's vision of how an appropriate legal aid society should run, and it set the stage for a decade-long conflict between lawyers and social workers.

---

[133] Bradway, "Legal Aid Material Indicating My Work," 16, 17, Bradway Papers, box 5, vol. 3.

[134] John H. Wigmore, "Memorandum as to Amalgamation of Legal Aid Society and the United Charities of Chicago," June 28, 1919, Wigmore Papers, box 82, folder 11. For a discussion of the new emphasis on the efficiency of charities after World War I, see Agnew, *From Charity to Social Work*.

PART III

DIALOGUES: LAWYERS AND SOCIAL WORKERS, 1921–1945

5

Constellations of Justice

Lawyers did not achieve their goal of removing social workers from legal aid organizations. Instead, social workers demonstrated that attorneys' professionalization of legal aid was neither preordained nor linear. Many social workers developed their own understanding of how legal aid should be conceived, challenging Reginald Heber Smith's theories of the rule of law and what constituted justice. Social workers and their allies embraced a more substantive concept of justice, free from legal technicalities. Throughout the 1920s, lawyers and social workers battled over professional authority, competencies, the meaning of justice, and the various ways of providing legal aid. The National Association of Legal Aid Organizations, led by John Bradway, became the key site for these confrontations and negotiations.

These opposing views of legal aid raised two central questions: what services should legal aid provide and which clients should legal aid serve? Scholars have long noted legal aid societies' conservative nature, but social workers and some lawyers presented an alternative and potentially more expansive vision. Lawyers also never had the monopoly over law that they sought. Social workers (and the new schools of social work that they created) taught law to their primarily female students, and social workers staffed many legal aid organizations. These women blurred the boundary between law and social work, and they insisted on raising larger questions about the nature of justice.

In 1922 at the first convention of the new National Association of Legal Aid Organizations, NALAO president Leonard McGee, who was also chief attorney for the Legal Aid Society of New York, called social work and social workers "the most dangerous" issue ever faced by legal aid organizations. Their presence in legal aid organizations could "destroy public confidence," he said, and "deter the poor" from seeking help.[1] McGee presented the conflict in stark terms. One side believed that a legal aid society was a law office for poor people and should function like any other law office. The other side believed that legal aid was part of social services and had a duty to the community and the client that extended beyond providing legal services. McGee was not engaging in hyperbole: leaders of the lawyer-based model of legal aid believed that social workers were besieging legal aid and destroying lawyers' attempts to professionalize it. In other words, social workers had refused to disappear into the woodwork, and their resistance endangered the new law-based model of legal aid.

To address the issue, NALAO appointed a committee to examine the question of legal aid's relationship to social service agencies, and John Bradway, the executive secretary of NALAO, selected Alice Waldo to head the committee. Waldo was a social worker employed by the Volunteer Defenders Office, which was part of NYLAS; she was the only woman to head a NALAO committee and one of two women who attended the 1922 convention. Bradway first met her during his visit to NYLAS, and the two struck up a close friendship, with Waldo looking to him as her mentor. Bradway's selection of Waldo indicates the gap separating him from social workers generally. Waldo was young, she was not a professionally trained social worker, and she was little known in the social work community. But she was one of the few social workers he knew and with whom he felt comfortable.

Waldo was charged with writing a report on legal aid and social work, and she clearly understood that she was writing for an audience of male lawyers who endorsed Reginald Heber Smith's negative assessment of social workers.[2] The report recognized the heated nature of the debate. It urged readers to look past "prejudices" and "stereotypes" and find a middle ground from which to reconcile the opposing camps.[3] Yet Waldo's report was full of contradictions. She suggested that legal aid might be considered one element of social service work. Unlike Smith's *Justice and*

---

[1] Leonard McGee, "Preface," *Proceedings of the Fifth National Conference of Legal Aid Bureaus and Societies* (March 1922), viii.

[2] Alice Waldo, "Report of the Committee on Relationships between Social Service Work and Legal Aid Work," *Record of Proceedings at the Meetings of the Central Committee of the National Alliance of Legal Aid Societies* (December 15, 1922), 35. (The National Alliance of Legal Aid Societies was about to become the NALAO.)

[3] Ibid., 36.

the Poor, Waldo's report recognized the wide use of social workers in legal aid organizations. She called "untenable" the claim that legal aid societies were like any other law office.[4] Instead, the report insisted, legal aid lawyers, unlike private lawyers, had a duty to ensure that a client received all available and necessary social services.

Later in the report Waldo backed away from these claims. Accepting certain questionable statistics in *Justice and the Poor*, she reported that few legal aid clients needed social services; yet her report's assessment of such clients was highly gendered. Although the male worker with a personal injury claim needed only legal aid in order to collect the damages rightly owed him, Waldo saw domestic relations cases as being properly in the field of social work rather than law:

A dispute between any married couple may involve elements very different from a simple legal claim.... In marriage there is a large social interest and the law recognizes it. Therefore, even if the parties need purely legal relief, the legal relief itself involves questions of social interest which may properly be within the field of the social worker.[5]

Having recognized the role that social workers might play in such cases, however, the report criticized social workers who claimed that they alone should determine a client's legal needs and requirements. Rather, Waldo imagined a new cadre of professionals – trained legal-social workers. The female lay lawyer of the past would now become the professional legal-social worker of the future. Waldo's idea came to dominate the later thinking of legal aid leaders, who took a moderate position regarding social workers' role in legal aid compared with Smith's more conservative position.

Waldo's report also warned that the most radical social workers posed a danger to the American legal system. In what would become a well-worn trope, she complained that social workers sought too much substantive justice in individual cases, and yet at other times placed societal good ahead of individual rights. Such thinking, she insisted, was "subversive and dangerous" to democracy.[6] The report concluded that legal aid's alignment with bar associations was more advantageous than its association with social workers and social service agencies. She explicitly masculinized legal aid and its history, claiming that bar associations were

---

[4] Ibid., 43.
[5] Ibid., 41.
[6] Ibid., 45.

the rightful "foster father" of legal aid, but added that in the future social workers might become their "foster mother."[7]

Robert Kelso, president of the National Conference on Social Work, responded to Waldo's report. He argued that social workers constantly saw clients who also needed legal help, and he stressed that social workers should conduct the initial interviews with clients in legal aid organizations so that all of the clients' needs could be assessed. He also viewed law and lawyers with considerable hostility. At the heart of law, he argued, stood contracts and property, which elevated the individual above ideas of societal and community welfare. Likewise, lawyers protected contract and property rights through inflexible rules that often failed to produce substantive justice. By contrast, social workers brought the idea of the "social" into law, especially in creating juvenile courts, workers' compensation boards, zoning boards, and other institutions that treated the individual as part of a larger community. These institutions challenged both the formality of law and the protection of individual rights that prevented government regulation of labor, contracts, and property. Legal education, Kelso continued, should include the study of social conditions regarding how people, especially the poor, actually lived and how law created such conditions.[8] In sum, social workers offered a radically different argument about the nature of law and its normative goals than did lawyers.[9]

---

[7] Ibid., 45–46. Waldo herself was situated in the gray area between the professions of law and social work. Although she did not have formal legal training, she was the head of investigations for the Volunteer Defenders Office, a position steeped in criminal law and one that gave her significant discretion in handling cases. In this way, she was a lay lawyer working in a legal aid society. Personally she yearned to attend law school, and she enrolled in a correspondence law school that turned out to be a sham. She eventually resigned her position at the defenders office, believing that it did not give her the opportunity to use the "brains" that "Nature" gave her. She complained that the lawyers she worked with refused to heed her advice or consider her ideas seriously. As she wrote, "The facts don't seem to be acceptable if they come from one who is not counsel. That kind of thing is deadly to me." Letter from Alice Waldo to John S. Bradway, July 13, 1926, John S. Bradway Papers, David M. Rubenstein Rare Book and Manuscript Library, Duke University Library (hereinafter Bradway Papers), box 10, vol. 7.

[8] Robert Kelso, response to "Report of the Committee on Relationship between Social Service Work and Legal Aid Work," *Record of Proceedings at the Meetings of the Central Committee of the National Alliance of Legal Aid Societies* (December 15, 1922), 46.

[9] Karen Tani, in exploring differences between lawyers' and social workers' conception of rights stemming from New Deal programs, argues that social workers understood rights as entailing government responsibility for substantive and material human needs. In contrast, lawyers had a more procedural understanding of rights. Karen M. Tani, "Securing a Right to Welfare: Public Assistance Administration and the Rule of Law,

The 1922 conference and its aftermath compelled Bradway to revisit his justifications for distinguishing law from social work. Bradway agreed with Kelso that law and the Constitution primarily protected contract, property, and the individual's right to be free of government intrusion. What for Kelso was a target of criticism, however, was for Bradway an ideal to be defended. In distinguishing legal aid from social work, Bradway defined legal aid more and more narrowly and in purely procedural terms: "Legal Aid is exclusively interested in providing a machinery by which legal rights may be enforced. Social service is interested in developing and enforcing moral and social rights."[10] Law did not exist to produce justice in the individual case: "Laws which are molded in their application to every set of facts in this way approximate the justice administered by the potentates of the Eastern nations of Asia. It is the essence of our form of government that we should rely in the main on well thought out[,] clearly devised rules of action."[11] To do otherwise would create a "hodge-podge of absurdities" that would destroy the rationality of law.[12] Bradway accused social workers of being too concerned with "natural justice" and therefore of dismissing the need to respect the integrity of law.[13] Both Smith and Bradway understood law as a rational science that, viewed with the trained eye, created an internally logical system. Social workers, untrained in the logic of the law, could not see the whole as lawyers could.[14]

Legal scholars have long identified a period in which "classical legal thought" dominated scholarship as well as judicial opinions. Classical

1935–1960," PhD diss., University of Pennsylvania, January 1, 2011, chap. 3. See Felice Batlan, "Notes from the Margin: Florence Kelley and the Battle against Laissez-Faire Constitutionalism," Social Science Research Network working paper, December 1, 2010, http://ssrn.com/abstract=1721725.

[10] John S. Bradway, "Memorandum with Reference to the Difference between Legal Aid and Social Service," 13, Bradway Papers, box 5, vol. 5.

[11] John S. Bradway, "Draft of Handbook of Legal Aid Work," chap. 11, 14, Bradway Papers, box 10, vol. 8.

[12] Ibid., 15.

[13] John S. Bradway, "Memorandum for the Joint Meeting of the Committees of the American Association for Organizing Family Social Work and the National Association of Legal Aid Organizations, Chicago, February 13, 1925," November 19, 1924, Bradway Papers, box 5, vol. 5.

[14] On law as a science, see William LaPiana, *Logic and Experience: The Origin of Modern Legal Education* (New York: Oxford University Press, 1994); Daniel W. Hamilton and Alfred L. Brophy, eds., *Transformations in American Legal History*, vol. 2: *Law, Ideology, and Methods: Essays in Honor of Morton J. Horwitz* (Cambridge, MA: Harvard University Press, 2011).

legal thought privileged abstract thinking that treated law as a logical system that could not be measured by substantive justice in any one case.[15] Clearly, this view of law permeated the ideas of leaders of legal aid, men who did not sit within the ivy-covered halls of academia or on appellate courts. Moreover, these men *were* concerned with the poor and the reform of the court system. Yet in their view, giving the poor access to this formal system of law was the epitome of equality between the poor and the rich. They looked at the law through a prism shaped by law school, seeing rules as often trumping justice. At the same time, these were men who truly believed in the rationality and power of law to create justice as a whole. In contrast, social workers at the grass-roots level grappled with the real inequalities that abstract theories of law generated.

Bradway often uncritically defended law, lawyers, and the rule of law. He proclaimed, "The law is the ultimate repository of most of the worthwhile ideas of our social thinking."[16] In another speech that represented the thoughts of many legal aid attorneys, he exclaimed, "There is no fault to find with the laws of our country. They are remarkably fair and are designed to operate with absolute equality on all classes of persons in our community."[17] Bradway's narrow definition of the role of legal aid as purely providing procedural justice and his sustained unwillingness to critique the law led him to believe that NALAO had no role in some of the day's most pressing issues. Regarding the civil rights of African Americans, Bradway wrote, "It does not seem to me that social rights for colored people have anything at all to do with legal aid."[18] Along with other legal aid leaders, Bradway defined legal rights so narrowly that they did not even encompass issues such as Jim Crow and desegregation. In fact, Bradway was involved in drafting North Carolina's revised 1933 sterilization law, which now provided significant legal process, including notice, the appointment of a guardian, and the ability to appeal the

[15] See, e.g., William M. Wiecek, *The Lost World of Classical Legal Thought: Law and Ideology in America, 1866–1937* (New York: Oxford University Press, 1998).

[16] John S. Bradway, "The Use by Social Workers of Legal Resources in Constructing Social Programs," *Proceedings of the National Conference of Social Work at the Fifty-Fourth Annual Session Held in Des Moines, Iowa, May 11–18, 1927* (Chicago: University of Chicago Press, 1927), 630.

[17] John S. Bradway, "Legal Aid Service and Social Work: The Legal Point of View," *Proceedings of the National Conference of Social Work at the Fiftieth Anniversary Session Held in Washington, D.C., May 16–23, 1923* (Chicago: University of Chicago Press, 1923), 188.

[18] John S. Bradway to Emmet Field, March 28, 1929, Bradway Papers, box 1, vol. 36.

decision.[19] Yet under that law, thousands of black Americans, most of them poor, were involuntarily sterilized.[20]

On a more mundane level, some lawyers dismissed social workers as annoying meddlers.[21] Bradway repeated a common complaint, that social workers "will tell you where you were born, when you must work, whom you must marry, why you must divorce, what you must eat."[22] Such stereotypes depicted the social worker as an overbearing mother. Lawyers also chastised social workers for being too sympathetic to their clients, too idealistic, for giving too much legal advice, and for not knowing the law.[23] "They presented the law to others," declared Bradway, "when they are strangers to it themselves."[24] One legal aid attorney wrote about his interactions with a social worker: "Miss Smith seemed suspicious that Ethel would not get her share of the money. I tried to point out to Miss Smith what guardians' bonds were for. Likely she does not yet understand it. It is a usual experience to be obstructed, balled up, inconvenienced in attempts to deal with women's clubs, women [sic] societies and women's bureaus."[25] Here the attorney directed his frustration at ignorant and meddling women who failed to submit to the (male) lawyer's greater knowledge and authority.

Lawyers' constant chiding of social workers for too often sympathizing with their clients was in reality another attack on social workers' professionalism. One hallmark of professionalism is objectivity, a trait often associated with masculinity. Criticisms of partiality and sympathy called

---

[19] North Carolina Sterilization Statute, Chapter 224, Public Laws of 1933 as Amended by Chapter 463 Public Laws of 1935. See also Victoria Nourse, *In Reckless Hands: Skinner v. Oklahoma and the Near-Triumph of American Eugenics* (New York: Norton, 2008).

[20] John Bradway, "The Legality of Human Sterilization in North Carolina," *North Carolina Medical Journal* 11 (May 1950): 25. Well through the 1950s, Bradway was a proponent of sterilization and failed to see its connection to white supremacy or basic individual rights.

[21] See Daniel J. Walkowitz, "The Making of a Feminine Professional Identity: Social Workers in the 1920s," *American History Review* 95 (October 1990): 1051–75.

[22] John S. Bradway, "Memorandum of the Joint Meeting of the Committees of the American Association for Organizing Family Social Work and the National Association for Legal Aid Organizations, Chicago, February 13, 1925.

[23] Otto G. Wismer, "A Lawyer Looks at Social Workers," *Survey* (February 15, 1925): 585.

[24] John S. Bradway, "Memorandum of the Joint Meeting of the Committees of the American Association for Organizing Family Social Work and the National Association for Legal Aid Organizations, Chicago, February 13, 1925.

[25] "The Law and the Lawyer in Social Work" (1923), 13, Bradway Papers, box 5, vol. 4.

into question the social workers' professionalism while also highlighting the feminine nature of social work. In the minds of male lawyers who criticized social workers, the link between social work and women in part precluded the necessary objectivity that would raise the social worker to a professional status akin to that of the lawyer.[26]

As much as some lawyers believed that social workers should have no role in legal aid, many social workers now claimed that *lawyers* should get out of the way. Minnie Low, director of the Bureau of Personal Service in Chicago, employed only social workers. Low adamantly refused to hire lawyers, believing that their legal training made them incapable of taking a social viewpoint. One report explained, "If trained and licensed attorneys were to do the court work of the organization[,] they would prefer to be known as attorneys and argue their cases on the basis of the legal elements involved rather than on a humane and equit[able] basis.... This would threaten the loss of all that has been accomplished."[27] Low could not countenance that a legal aid bureau merely provided access to courts and remained unconcerned with substantive justice. Moreover, almost all of her social workers were women, and she was not going to give male lawyers power over her organization.

Although NALAO, through Bradway and others, continually lambasted social workers, it did not have any control or even professional sway over them. This lack of power frustrated Bradway, who complained that social workers ignored the distinction between law and social work, and that they refused to engage in dialogue with NALAO regarding their role in legal aid – one that ideally (in his eyes) would be limited to referring clients. To try to bridge the divide, Bradway spent significant time attending conferences on social work. There, he lectured social workers on how they should support legal aid societies but not be directly involved in their work. Ironically, Bradway's increasing exposure to social workers and their ideas enlightened him. He privately noted, "The charities' point of view is more progressive than that of the bar. The [social] worker has read progressive books and can apply the ideas presented in them better

---

[26] On gender, objectivity, and the professions, see Helene Silverberg, ed., *Gender and American Social Science: The Formative Years* (Princeton, NJ: Princeton University Press, 1998); Regina Morant-Sanchez, *Conduct Unbecoming a Woman: Medicine on Trial in Turn-of-the-Century Brooklyn* (New York: Oxford University Press, 1999).

[27] Maurice J. Karpf, *A Social Audit of a Social Service Agency: The Jewish Aid Society and the Jewish Social Service Bureau of Chicago, 1919–1925* (Chicago: Jewish Aid Society and Jewish Social Service Bureau of Chicago, 1925), 85. For a discussion of Smith's reaction to his visit to the bureau, see Chapter 4.

than the average lawyer."[28] In a parallel development, he began to see that bar associations might welcome him and Smith to come and give speeches, but they were slow to create legal aid societies.

Bradway also received a constant stream of letters from women interested in establishing legal aid organizations. Margaret Laing, general secretary of the Associated Charities of Columbia, South Carolina, wrote in 1923 that a Mrs. Reamer was intending to create a legal aid organization under the auspices of the charity group and that she wanted advice from Bradway.[29] In 1927 Louise Bignall of the Associated Charities of Knoxville, Tennessee, wrote to inform Bradway that the local social workers club was interested in establishing a legal aid organization.[30] A more detailed letter from an Ohio social worker specified the subjects Bradway should address in an upcoming visit:

I thought if you could talk about the social significance of problems of law and give us some idea of how the social case worker can do better case work when she knows how to go about getting legal justice for her clients... [t]hen if you will talk just a little while on how to go about organizing the resources in any community to bring about the proper functioning of the Legal Aid Society as a social service agency.[31]

Even after Bradway's talks, in which he stressed to social workers the difference between legal aid and social services, they still wanted to create legal aid societies.

Also, NALAO, always desperate for dues and funds, was willing to accept paying members even from social service organizations. Of greater importance, NALAO received a number of grants from the social work–dominated Russell Sage Foundation, under leaders such as Mary E. Richmond and her protégée Joanna Colcord. Bradway was in constant discussion with Colcord and relied on her to support NALAO's many grant requests.[32] Likewise, Chicago's Legal Aid Bureau, which was filled with

---

[28] John S. Bradway, "Legal Aid Material Indicating My Work from June 1, 1922, to about August 1, 1922," Bradway Papers, box 5, vol. 3, 16.

[29] Margaret Laing to John S. Bradway, October 24, 1923, Bradway Papers, box 1, vol. 36.

[30] Mr. McLean of the American Association for Organizing Family Social Work to John S. Bradway, February 25, 1927, Bradway Papers, box 1, vol. 36.

[31] Unknown sender to John S. Bradway, September 6, 1926, Bradway Papers, box 2, vol. 19.

[32] Olivia Sage, the millionaire widow of a railroad baron, created the Russell Sage Foundation in 1907 to promote research, education, and legislative efforts related to eliminating poverty, disease, and crime. See Elizabeth N. Agnew, *From Charity to Social Work: Mary E. Richmond and the Creation of an American Profession* (Urbana: University of Illinois Press, 2004), 134.

social workers, was still the second largest legal aid organization in the country. Thus material reality, for NALAO, prevented it from rejecting social workers outright. All NALAO could do was try to limit social workers' influence.

NALAO's Committee on Relations with Social Service Agencies soon became its most progressive group, and it consistently supported social workers' involvement. Exactly what that involvement should be, however, remained a topic of debate. Marguerite Raeder Gariepy, the chief attorney at Chicago's Legal Aid Bureau, succeeded Alice Waldo as head of the committee when Waldo left the Volunteer Defenders Office to pursue other work. Gariepy was better suited than Waldo to the task, with her years of experience as a legal aid attorney at an organization deeply immersed in social work. The committee immediately undertook a survey of legal aid societies and social service agencies to determine their day-to-day interactions and the attitudes of lawyers and social workers toward each other. Not surprisingly, the survey found that social workers did not fully appreciate the value of legal aid lawyers, and that legal aid attorneys did not see the value of social workers.[33]

The survey further revealed that social workers in cities without legal aid societies did not see the need to create a separate legal aid society, as they did their own legal work and relied on attorney board members when they required additional legal advice. Even where legal aid societies existed, social workers complained about the quality and attitudes of legal aid attorneys. One social worker wrote, "There has been little confidence in the advice or ability of the Legal Aid Department; the lawyer in charge is said to be erratic and undependable."[34] Another complained, "We find the Legal Aid Society perfunctory and uncooperative, often adopting a contemptuous attitude toward social problems and opinions of social workers."[35] Still others charged that legal aid lawyers were impatient and untrained.[36] Social workers' remarks make it clear that at times they trusted their own legal knowledge more than that of lawyers.

Gariepy endorsed the use of social workers in all legal aid organizations. At the least, she said, legal aid attorneys had a duty to refer clients to social service agencies when needed. She further recommended that

---

[33] Marguerite Raeder Gariepy, "Report of the Committee on Relations with Social Agencies," *Reports of Committees of the National Association of Legal Aid Organizations, 1923–1924* (Boston: NALAO, 1924).

[34] Ibid., 103.

[35] Ibid.

[36] Ibid., 103, 104.

legal aid societies have social workers on staff: "The fact that so few cases are referred to Social Agencies by Legal Aid Agencies doubtless shows that legal aid workers do not recognize social problems or if they do, do not feel any responsibility for seeing that they are solved."[37] The report recommended that social workers receive more formal training in law, a radical idea at a time when bar associations were consolidating their monopoly over the practice of law and putting into place specific requirements for law school education. The committee's report challenged this growing monopoly, claiming that, with some training, social workers could provide legal advice. This posed a direct challenge to the male nature of the legal profession by asserting that female social workers had the ability and capacity to engage with law openly and independently.

Gariepy emerged an ardent supporter of a combined social and legal approach to legal aid. Under this model, social workers and lawyers worked closely together, with social workers giving legal advice, investigating cases, determining the client's needs, and engaging in mediating and settling cases. She explained that under the Chicago model, the legal aid attorney was regularly available for social workers to call on when they needed answers to complex legal questions. Lawyers also educated social workers on points of law and coordinated with them on actions to be taken by an attorney.[38] Gariepy expounded, "Clients receive not only legal assistance, but also assistance in solving their social problems which are often at the root of the legal difficulty." She made it clear that social workers were practicing law and that they were doing it well.[39] At the Chicago Legal Aid Bureau, no clear hierarchy existed between lawyers and social workers. Rather, the social workers reported to Gariepy (a lawyer), and she reported to the executive director (a social worker).

A social service agency that provided legal aid also had advantages over an independent legal aid society. Such agencies could provide clients with immediate financial relief. They could also pay court costs, which stand-alone legal aid societies often lacked the resources or the will to do. Further, as state welfare programs became available, lawyers working closely with social workers could help clients meet those programs' eligibility requirements. For example, in Illinois the mother's pension statute declared applicants ineligible if they owned a certain amount of property.

---

[37] Ibid., 104.
[38] Marguerite Raeder Gariepy, "Legal Aid as Part of a Community Program," *Annals of the American Academy of Political and Social Science* 205 (September 1939): 75.
[39] Marguerite Raeder Gariepy, "The Legal Aid Bureau of the United Charities of Chicago," *Annals of the Academy of Political and Social Science* 124 (March 1926): 39.

Legal aid lawyers, working with social workers, helped women who had small interests in property to dispose or transfer them so that they could qualify as claimants. Gariepy insisted that only through close cooperation between lawyers and social workers could legal aid "fulfill what would seem to be its highest purpose, that of securing equal justice and equal opportunity for the poor."[40]

There were real differences between how lawyers, such as Smith, imagined legal aid and how some social workers and their lawyer allies envisioned it. The law-based model of legal aid saw a lawyer's involvement with clients as strictly bounded. The lawyer addressed only a specific legal issue, and, after settlement or a decision by a court, that case was closed. Social workers, however, took a more holistic approach, seeking out information on additional problems that a client faced, and a settlement or judgment in a legal matter did not necessarily end the social worker's relationship with the client. Gariepy pointed out that a social worker might even try to "persuade" families "to expend the money [from a judgment] wisely."[41] In other words, social workers could be intrusive, both as to the range of issues and the duration of the involvement.

Social workers, at times, were also biased toward wives, an attitude that lawyers found offensive. Social workers might seize funds from judgments obtained by husbands, for example, rather than allowing "irresponsible husbands" control. The social worker would then use those funds to pay the family's expenses. Such involvement, especially when the husband was himself a client of the legal aid society, violated an attorney's duty of loyalty to the client. Moreover, the lawyer would see this kind of action as increasing the family's dependency on outside support rather than returning the husband, the head of the household, to independence. Gariepy admitted that there were no clear-cut rules regarding such cases, and said the Legal Aid Bureau's lawyers and social workers tried to do what was in the "best interest of the client in the long run" – with the understanding that their client was the family unit.[42] This approach gave the legal aid provider wide discretion and allowed her to substitute her own judgment for that of the head of the family.

Additionally, lawyers complained that social workers would sometimes arrange for husbands to be arrested while wives spirited away their children, despite joint custody orders. Others criticized social workers

[40] Ibid., 33.
[41] Ibid., 29.
[42] Ibid., 34.

who wanted to have men barred from their homes and their wages garnished for failure to pay support, when, from the lawyer's standpoint, insufficient legal grounds existed.[43] In part, these complaints reflected the fact that many social workers understood that husbands and fathers were morally and legally bound to support their wives and children, whether or not they were capable of doing so. From 1909 to 1915 the Legal Aid Society of Chicago handled some 9,000 cases against men who failed to support their wives and children.[44] Although some social workers were comfortable bringing civil and criminal cases against errant husbands, and then further policing their conduct, some legal aid lawyers began to have qualms about the strict enforcement of such laws, especially criminal sanctions, believing that they constituted overreaching by the state and endangered men's individual rights.[45]

The story of social workers' role in legal aid complicates our understanding of social work. Scholars have demonstrated the substantial control that social workers asserted over poor women's lives and how they misunderstood and even condemned working-class, immigrant, and African American women's lives and domestic practices.[46] The social work model, however, provided women with resources and services that the lawyer-based model of legal aid did not. Social workers at times were much more willing to believe their female clients' stories than were male legal aid lawyers. Poor women often were willing to submit to a social worker's supervision in return for her policing their husbands' behavior.[47]

---

[43] "Report of the Sub-Committee of the Committee of the American Association for Organizing Family Social Work on Relations with Legal Aid Societies," *National Association of Legal Aid Organizations Reports of Committees for Discussion at the Convention in Detroit, Michigan, October 4 and 5, 1928* (Boston: NALAO, 1927–8), 90–91, available at Gallagher Law Library, University of Washington. See Michael Willrich, "Home Slackers: Men, the State, and Welfare in Modern America," *Journal of American History* 87 (September 2000): 460–89.

[44] Willrich, "Home Slackers," 469, 471.

[45] Ibid.

[46] See, e.g., Leslie Margolin, *Under the Cover of Kindness: The Invention of Social Work* (Charlottesville: University of Virginia Press, 1997); Michael Willrich, *City of Courts: Socializing Justice in Progressive-Era Chicago* (New York: Oxford University Press, 2003).

[47] On this point see, e.g., Willrich, "Home Slackers"; Gordon, *Pitied but Not Entitled*. In connection with her study of the Massachusetts Society for the Protection of Children, Linda Gordon writes, "One of the most striking findings is how often the objects of social control themselves asked for intervention." Linda Gordon, *Heroes of Their Own Lives: The Politics and History of Family Violence* (New York: Penguin Books, 1988), 6. A similar dynamic is present in connection with legal aid.

Other differences between lawyer-based models and social worker–based models of legal aid existed as well, specifically in their ideas of whom they were helping. For the social worker, the focus of attention was the family and, where the husband was missing, the mother-child dyad. In the lawyer-based model of legal aid, the focus of attention was the individual rights-bearing man. Historian Michael Willrich writes, "In the progressive rhetoric of socialized law, the identity of the family as the 'social unit' of the state – the engine of racial reproduction, the wellspring of life's necessities, the nursery of child welfare – created a social interest in the family that trumped the interests of its individual members."[48] This triumph of the family over the individual, especially when it involved men's rights, is precisely what the lawyer based-model of legal aid objected to and feared.

Joel Hunter of the United Charities of Chicago stressed the difference between lawyers and social workers as they might manifest in a client interview: "The Legal Aid interviewers will direct the interview so that all irrelevant material is eliminated and so that everything relating to the particular legal problem is covered. The Family Service worker will do everything possible to put the client at ease so that he will talk freely and in his own way about his feelings and attitudes relating to the problems on his mind."[49] On its most basic level, social casework required an intense focus on an individual's relationships with her environment and with other people. The social worker was to gather all available information in order to determine what the individual client required. Social work was highly grounded in the specific case – one rule did not, could not, and should not fit all.

Where Bradway, Smith, and other lawyers understood the rule of law as crucial to democracy, social workers spoke of democracy in a different key. They viewed abstract and inflexible rules as incompatible with modern democracy. Mary E. Richmond, a founder of social work, observed: "As a matter of fact there is more than a trace of autocracy left in our traditional public policy of the 'same thing for everybody.'"[50] For Richmond and others, sameness in the law erased the substantive differences among people, inevitably leading to injustice. By treating rich and poor, and men and women, the same, the law was perpetuating inequalities.

---

[48] Willrich, *City of Courts*, 129.

[49] Joel D. Hunter, "Social Agencies and Legal Aid Theory," *Annals of the American Academy of Political Science* 205 (September 1939): 129–33, 131.

[50] Mary E. Richmond, *What Is Social Case Work? An Introductory Description* (New York: Russell Sage Foundation, 1922), 150.

Richmond cited the continuing need for protective legislation regulating women's industrial employment: to treat working-class women the same as working-class men was to deny the reality of women's material lives and the wage market. Only when substantive equality existed could procedural equality have meaning. For Richmond, democracy therefore required "administrative policy" that "does different things for and with different people."[51] Minnie Low's phrase, that legal aid provided by social workers was "personal service," recognized that the uniform application of the same law to all could not create real justice. Instead, Low insisted, the social worker's vision brought "the human equation" to an otherwise inhumane "technical legal vision."[52]

Their fundamentally different understandings of equality, justice, and the rule of law affected how social workers and lawyers dealt with the everyday practice of legal aid. One goal of those who supported even moderate cooperation between lawyers and social workers was shared client information. Social workers created central registries in which cases handled by social service agencies were recorded, to prevent duplication of effort, provide information, and ensure that families did not receive overlapping aid.[53] Proponents of the social work model of legal aid believed that legal aid societies should register their cases with such exchanges. Social workers could thus give lawyers information that would help their clients' cases, they claimed, including assistance in locating witnesses, family members, and financial and medical records. Likewise, social workers could obtain information about clients' pending cases and potential liabilities and judgments.

Some lawyers strenuously objected to this exchange of information, believing that sharing any information with social service agencies was a breach of attorney-client confidentiality. They refused to register their legal aid cases or provide information to social workers.[54] In response, a number of social workers asserted that much of the client information possessed by lawyers regarding their cases was not protected and was

[51] Ibid.
[52] Minnie F. Low, "Legal Aid," *Proceedings of the Sixth Biennial Session of the National Conference of Jewish Charities in the United States Held in the City of St. Louis May 17–19th* (Baltimore: Kohn and Pollock, 1910), 185–6.
[53] NALAO, "Report on the Use of the Social Service Exchange by the Legal Aid Society," February 1927, Bradway Papers, box 10, vol. 7 (1925–32).
[54] Ibid. See also, *Report, Joint Committee for the Study of Legal Aid of the Association of the Bar of the City of New York and the Welfare Council of New York City* (New York, 1928), 91–93.

already available in public records.[55] Thus lawyers' arguments against registering cases, they said, masked their real unwillingness to cooperate with social workers, who had their own duties of confidentiality to clients.[56] For social workers, such confidentiality was part of what made their profession akin to law and medicine. Lawyers' refusal to acknowledge this cast aspersions on social work as a profession as well as on the professionalism of individual social workers. The debate about whether lawyers should share information with social workers festered for decades.

Social workers and their allies were at times dumbfounded by legal aid attorneys' hostility. In direct response, some social workers engaged in a public critique of the lawyer-based model of legal aid.[57] Kate Holladay Claghorn set forth one of the most cogent and hard-hitting criticisms of legal aid in *The Immigrant's Day in Court* (1923), which, like Smith's *Justice and the Poor*, was a publication sponsored by the Carnegie Foundation. One of Claghorn's fundamental criticisms was legal aid's focus on legal technicalities rather than on the client as a whole: "The legal mind trained in analyzing technical distinctions in laws . . . tends to regard legal protection as the task of fitting a given law to a set of circumstances shown in a given case, without reference to the personality of the client, or to any service rendered him other than that of securing the technical right involved."[58] Such a constricted approach resulted in legal aid lawyers' failure to communicate with, or to understand, their clients' problems and lives.

Claghorn also criticized the absence of female attorneys in legal aid offices and how some male legal aid attorneys treated their female clients. She remarked that the Legal Aid Society of New York had few women lawyers. When she questioned the organization's chief attorney about this, he replied, "The clients prefer to tell their troubles to a man, the Europeans especially feeling greater respect and confidence in a man in regard to legal matters."[59] Although Claghorn did not press the matter,

---

[55] Kate Holladay Claghorn, "Lower Court Justice and the Immigrant," *Proceedings of the National Conference of Social Work at the Fifteenth Anniversary Session Held in Washington, D.C., May 16–23, 1923* (Chicago: University of Chicago Press, 1923), 182.

[56] Ibid. Mary Richmond wrote, "In the whole range of professional contacts there is no more confidential relation than that which exists between the social worker and the person or family receiving treatment." Richmond, *What Is Social Case Work?* 29.

[57] See Claghorn, *The Immigrant's Day in Court*, 469–71, 481–3, 486, 489–90.

[58] Ibid., 470.

[59] Ibid., 480–1.

this had not proved to be the case in the earlier part of the century, when Rosalie Loew, Bertha Rembaugh, Mary Quackenbos, and other female attorneys worked for the society.[60]

The interactions that Claghorn observed between male attorneys and their female clients at the New York society were especially disturbing. She commented on a number of instances in which male attorneys failed to believe or were uninterested in women's claims. She observed a waitress telling an attorney that her employer had docked her wages and terminated her because she refused to work nine hours a day and on Sunday; the attorney advised the waitress to accept the money offered by the employer for back wages and not to press any claim. Wrote Claghorn, "The attorney was apparently not interested in the laws regarding hours of women's labor."[61] Speaking of women domestic workers who sought legal aid, she wrote chidingly that the Legal Aid Society's chief attorney believed that "the fault is often with the employees in these cases, as they are undisciplined and irresponsible." She further pointed out that the law often was on the servant's side in such cases.[62] Claghorn believed that these legal aid attorneys were failing to counsel their female clients adequately and concluded that more women attorneys, as well as social workers, were necessary.[63]

The acceptance of social workers and women attorneys went hand in hand. In legal aid societies that adopted the social-work model of legal aid, women attorneys were abundant. By 1924 eight of the eleven attorneys at the Chicago Legal Aid Bureau were women. The Legal Aid Society of Philadelphia, which adopted a strong lawyer model of legal aid, trumpeted its rule of hiring only male lawyers.[64]

In a *New Republic* review of *The Immigrant's Day in Court*, John MacArthur Maguire, a Harvard Law School professor and an ardent supporter of Boston's and New York's legal aid societies, harshly criticized Claghorn's arguments regarding social workers providing legal aid. "Social workers wish to absorb the legal aid organizations, or at least permeate them with the theories and practice of social services.... It is fair to state the reasons for the legal aid worker's wish to remain separate

---

[60] See Chapter 3.
[61] Claghorn, *The Immigrant's Day in Court*, 482.
[62] Ibid.
[63] Ibid.
[64] Roman Hassrick to John Wigmore, February 9, 1921, John Henry Wigmore Papers, Northwestern University Archives, Northwestern University (hereinafter Wigmore Papers), box 82, folder 10.

and distinct. He is a lawyer and proud of it."[65] Bradway had a more difficult time dismissing Claghorn's conclusions, as he saw them as pointing to fundamental distinctions between the two professions. He wrote, "Social workers are inclined to regard the legal profession as a distinctly backward social group."[66]

By the end of the 1920s, Bradway was convinced that lawyers and social workers should cooperate in creating, maintaining, and providing legal aid. In part, Bradway's changed viewpoint represented his increasingly substantive understanding of what the legal aid client needed, his continuing exposure to social workers, and a growing distance between him and Reginald Heber Smith. He was also playing a game of catch-up: social service agencies were still creating legal aid bureaus, without concern for the opinions of the leaders of legal aid or the bar. Social service agencies were also part of a network of organizations, such as United Way, United Charities, and local community chests, that provided funding.[67] Stand-alone legal aid societies had to conduct their own fund-raising activities, relying heavily on bar associations for support.

While writing a how-to manual on legal aid for NALAO, Bradway began describing legal aid as an interstitial field between law and social work, accepting the idea that there was more than one model for legal aid. He astutely noted that the social work model was "most common in the middle west, where the line between legal aid and social work is not drawn so rigidly as in the East."[68] What he did not mention was that this geographical diversity was the result of the long history of women creating and working in legal aid as lay lawyers, as well as Chicago's rich history of women's reform institutions. Comparing the legal aid model with the social work model, Bradway pointed out the benefits and disadvantages of each. Although Bradway still preferred the lawyer-based model, he recognized the difficulty of raising funds for a stand-alone legal aid organization. He also acknowledged the importance of the social point of view in legal aid work.[69]

---

[65] John MacArthur Maguire, review of *The Immigrant's Day in Court*, by Kate Holladay Claghorn, *New Republic*, April 18, 1923, 218.

[66] Bradway, "Draft of Handbook of Legal Aid Work," Bradway Papers, box 10, vol. 8.

[67] Stanley Wenocur and Michael Reisch, *From Charity to Enterprise: The Development of American Social Work in a Market Economy* (Urbana: University of Illinois Press, 1989), 107–14. See Chapter 6 for a discussion of community chests.

[68] Bradway, "Draft of Handbook of Legal Aid Work," Bradway Papers, box 10, vol. 8.

[69] Ibid.

Social workers and progressive lawyers, such as Marguerite Raeder Gariepy, regularly sought common ground with legal aid attorneys while arguing for the crucial role of social workers. J. Prentice Murphy stated at the 1927 National Proceeding of Social Workers, "It is no new thing to say that the lawyer and the social worker are engaged in fields of labor which are closely related and which cross and recross and overlap in countless situations."[70] Social workers sought a reciprocal relationship in which they learned the basics of law and lawyers learned the foundations of social work. They refused, however, to recognize any hierarchy between the professions and reserved the right to be critical of law. As Murphy put it, "There should be a readiness to question the law, and no reason why we should not question the opinions and decisions of lawyers and judges, just as they question us."[71]

A pivotal 1928 report on legal aid in New York City acknowledged the long-standing importance of social workers. In an unusual act of cooperation, the Joint Committee for the Study of Legal Aid, composed of members of the Association of the Bar of the City of New York and the Welfare Council of New York City, with the financial support of the Russell Sage Foundation, issued the report. The report described legal aid services in New York City, assessed whether social welfare organizations had unfulfilled legal needs, and looked at how such agencies viewed the quality of legal services provided to the poor. The report was a breakthrough on multiple levels. It defined legal aid broadly to include advice, arbitration, conciliation, and representation – whether it occurred in a legal aid office or a social service agency and whether a lawyer or a social worker provided it. It also reconciled the ideas of progressive lawyers and those of social workers: "The accomplishment of the aims of individual justice and of social justice gives the legal aid agency a distinct place in the social welfare field[,] since the fundamental basis of the work is the attempt to solve human problems."[72] This statement both placed legal aid within the field of welfare and recognized that it was not solely about an abstract or procedural understanding of justice but also involved human relations and social justice – an understanding long sought by some social

---

[70] J. Prentice Murphy, "The Use by Social Workers of Legal Resources in the Practice of Case Work," *Proceedings of the National Conference of Social Work at the Fifty-Fourth Annual Session Held in Des Moines, Iowa, May 11–18, 1927* (Chicago: University of Chicago Press, 1927), 622.

[71] Ibid., 623.

[72] *Report, Joint Committee*, 4.

workers. The report further positioned stand-alone legal aid societies and those that were part of social agencies as equally important and legitimate. Incorporating many of the suggestions in Claghorn's *Immigrant's Day in Court*, going beyond a reliance on *Justice and the Poor*, and broadening the literature on which it drew, the joint committee's report reached different conclusions – and created a different history of legal aid.

Within its first five pages, the 1928 report identified New York's Working Women's Protective Union as an organization that provided legal aid to women.[73] It also discussed the famed Women's Trade Union League, an organization of working-class, middle-class, and elite women that fought for a host of reforms and provided (nonlawyer) legal representation for women with workers' compensation claims.[74] The report then raised and addressed, for the first time, the question of whether social workers were practicing law without a license. Perhaps the authors felt that they could not ignore the issue, as it clearly identified many places where social workers were functioning as attorneys. Without fully exploring the question, the report concluded that where social workers represented clients before administrative agencies or specialized courts, and not in general courts, they were not practicing law.[75] This reflected the long-standing belief that practicing law meant appearing in court. The report recognized that social workers provided legal advice and that this practice was appropriate, especially in such "specialized" areas as immigration, workers' compensation, and domestic issues.[76]

The report directly criticized the Legal Aid Society of New York's refusal to take personal injury cases and its stringent income ceilings for accepting clients. "Where an organization, such as the Legal Aid Society, is ostensibly broad in scope but by rule, tradition, practice, or necessity narrows that scope so that the poor man with a worthy cause finds justice denied . . . there is occasion for serious reflection."[77] More specifically, it recommended that no strict eligibility rules exist, and concluded that

[73] Ibid., 5, 7, 87. For a full discussion of the Working Women's Protective Union, see Chapter 1.

[74] *Report, Joint Committee*, 31. For some time Maude Schwartz, who later became president of the Women's Trade Union League and an important labor activist, provided legal advice and representation to women appearing before compensation boards. On the WTUL, see Nancy Schrom Dye, *As Equals and Sisters: Feminism, the Labor Movement, and the WTUL* (Columbia: University of Missouri Press, 1980).

[75] See *Report, Joint Committee*, 32.

[76] Ibid., 76.

[77] Ibid., 104.

individual circumstances should dictate whether a client could afford a *competent* attorney, not just any attorney. Likewise, the report urged legal aid societies and bar associations to produce lists of reliable and affordable lawyers for people who had been refused legal aid and urged that such lawyers be diverse in terms of nationality and their ability to speak other languages, so that they might adequately serve New York's immigrant population.[78]

The report called for greater cooperation between legal aid societies and social service agencies. Legal aid organizations, it declared, often failed to recognize social welfare problems, and social welfare agencies were at times reluctant to send cases to legal aid. Regarding social workers' attitudes, the report explained, "There was a very general feeling that organized legal aid service left so much to be desired both as to scope and quality of service that it was inadvisable to attempt to use it."[79] The report also explicitly commented on women working as legal aid attorneys: "In these days of increasing numbers of women lawyers the choice of them as opposed to men is a worthwhile consideration.... Women last longer, are more conscientious in office detail and attention to clients, and [are] good interviewers."[80] Clearly making the connection between women social workers and women lawyers, it found that lawyers comfortable with the socio-legal viewpoint were more helpful to clients.[81] In its final recommendations it urged legal aid societies to hire more women, following the Chicago model of legal aid. To create such a model legal aid society, the report concluded, law schools and schools of social work must add such courses in the other discipline to their offerings.[82]

Despite its understanding of the breadth of legal aid, the role of women, and the need to break down professional hierarchies – and like much of the literature produced by major legal aid organizations – the report of the joint committee was silent on race. It made no mention of the role of African Americans in providing legal services, the acceptance of African American clients, or legal aid organizations' refusal to address the discrimination faced by African Americans in almost every arena of life.[83]

[78] Ibid., 112.
[79] Ibid., 82.
[80] Ibid., 112.
[81] Ibid.
[82] Ibid., 85.
[83] John S. Bradway to Emmet Field, March 28, 1929, Bradway Papers, box 1, vol. 36; John S. Bradway to Rabbi Milton Ellis, April 12, 1926, Bradway Papers, box 1, vol. 36.

Through its omission of race, the 1928 report overlooked the presence of African American organizations that were providing legal aid to African Americans. Commenting on the need for African American attorneys to provide such aid, famed civil rights lawyer Charles Hamilton Houston found a "general apathy" on the part of the African American bar. He explained: "The younger men tend to respond to suggestions of legal aid work, but they shrink from having any considerable portion of it directed to their offices."[84] This would seem to make sense, as African American lawyers had to struggle mightily for their own legitimacy and livelihood.[85]

Yet Houston's generalization was incorrect. African American lawyers in fact handled a wide range of cases involving civil rights, and they did so pro bono. Additionally, Chicago's African American lawyers had ensured representation for those African Americans charged with crimes as a result of the city's infamous 1919 race riot.[86] More organized efforts were also made after the African American Cook County Bar Association established its own legal aid bureau in the late 1920s.[87] African American women attorneys in Chicago, such as Edith Sampson, formed the Portia Club for the purpose of providing free legal assistance to African American women and children.[88] Women social workers who were African American also responded to the need for legal aid. In 1928 Bertha Perry created the Princitian organization in Waukegan, which provided a variety of services – including legal aid – to African American migrants from the South.[89] Even earlier, the civil rights activist Ida B. Wells established the Negro Fellowship League in Chicago in 1910 as part settlement house and part community center. The league provided pro bono lawyers to African American men accused of serious crimes and even protected them from lynch mobs. The Negro Fellowship League may have also provided civil legal assistance, because Wells herself was legally sophisticated, was

---

See Susan Carle, *Defining the Struggle: National Organizing for Racial Justice* (Oxford: Oxford University Press, 2013), 277.

[84] Charles Houston, "Tentative Findings of Survey of Negro Lawyers," January 23, 1928, Laura Spelman Rockefeller Memorial Papers, Rockefeller Archive, box 101, folio 1019 (courtesy of Kenneth Mack).

[85] Kenneth Mack, *Representing the Race: The Creation of the Civil Rights Lawyer* (Cambridge, MA: Harvard University Press, 2013).

[86] Houston, "Tentative Findings of Survey of Negro Lawyers."

[87] "Bar Assn. Gets Books: Has Legal Aid Bureau," *Chicago Defender*, July 14, 1928, 10.

[88] "Women Offer Expressions of Gratitude," *Chicago Defender*, December 1, 1928.

[89] Anne Meis Knupfer, *Reform and Resistance: Gender Delinquency and America's First Juvenile Court* (Routledge: New York, 2001), 63; James Dorsey, *Up South: Blacks in Chicago's Suburbs, 1719–1983* (Bristol, IN: Wyndham Hall Press, 1986), 64.

a parole officer in the Chicago courts, had ties to Chicago's progressive community of social workers and lawyers, and was married to a leading member of the African American bar.[90]

In all of these cases, however, documentation is scarce, and it is difficult to know how long these organizations lasted, how active they were in providing civil legal assistance, and what types of cases they handled.[91] Such assistance may not have focused on the same quotidian issues that primarily white legal aid organizations provided. Instead, African American organizations likely focused on a range of civil rights issues and criminal cases. A deeply biased criminal justice system and the white supremacy that African Americans encountered in their everyday lives made such cases particularly pressing – often a matter of life and death.[92]

In the same way that the 1928 report does not speak about African Americans, NALAO proceedings are equally silent on the subject. In the multiple debates that occurred in NALAO meetings over the role of lawyers and social workers in providing legal aid, African American lawyers and social workers did not participate. As NALAO began to open its doors to white women, it did not put out a welcome mat for male or female African Americans.

Even with its failure to include African American organizations in its assessment of legal aid, the joint committee's report was groundbreaking. It recognized that social workers were already learning law at the University of Chicago's School of Social Service Administration.[93] In particular, Sophonisba Breckinridge grasped the central importance of law to social structures, while also condemning much of the common law as an oppressive and outdated system that could be corrected only through systemic legislation.

---

[90] Mia Bay, *To Tell the Truth Freely: The Life of Ida B. Wells* (New York: Hill and Wang, 2009), 285–9; Ida B. Wells, *Crusade for Justice: The Autobiography of Ida B. Wells* (Chicago: University of Chicago Press, 1970).

[91] For works that briefly refer to the provision of some form of legal aid service by grassroots African American organizations, see St. Claire Drake and Horace R. Clayton, *Black Metropolis: A Study of Negro Life in a Northern City* (New York: Harcourt, 1945), 428; Theda Skocpol, Ariane Liazos, and Marshall Ganz, *What a Mighty Power We Can Be: African American Fraternal Groups and the Struggle for Racial Equality* (Princeton, NJ: Princeton University Press, 2006); Susan Carle, *Defining the Struggle: National Organizing for Racial Justice* (Oxford: Oxford University Press, 2013), 277.

[92] See Carle, *Defining the Struggle.*

[93] Breckinridge was on the board of the Chicago Legal Aid Society, a member of NALAO, and a member of the NALAO subcommittee that examined law courses taught in schools of social work.

Breckinridge's view of the relationship between law and social work appears most clearly in her textbooks for social workers. *Family Welfare Work in a Metropolitan Community: Selected Case Records* (1924) presents case files from a variety of social work agencies.[94] The law permeates the book, and the appendix is filled with state and local statutes and regulations concerning families. Breckinridge may have chosen the cases in the book for their legal complexity, for they included issues of residency, juvenile delinquency, mother's pensions, insurance, property, tenant and landlord relationships, loans, and estates. In her introduction to *The Family and the State*, another edited volume of documents, she wrote, "In general, as in a law course, the chief sources of information are judicial decisions and statutory enactments. They are, however, supplemented by some statistical data, by commentaries, and by the results of certain social investigations which throw light upon the source of the not infrequent conflict between the legal and social work point of view."[95] Unlike a law school casebook, Breckinridge's text primarily focused on legislation and legislative history rather than on court cases and judicial decisions. The material often highlighted how law failed to address people's needs and perpetuated injustices. In contrast to Smith and Bradway, Breckinridge pointedly criticized law, lawyers, and judges, claiming that social workers ultimately sought to reform law in the interest of substantive justice.[96]

Breckenridge had little patience for abstract legal doctrine. In her view, the social worker needed to be familiar with law in order to engage in the "manipulation of those agencies and institutions for the accomplishment of her immediate purpose, namely, that of bringing relief to persons in special need of service and aid."[97] Her social work students were urged to analyze legal cases and statutes as well as to draft legislation. At one point Breckenridge hired a female law professor to teach law to her students, and she advocated a sort of invasion of the law school by students of social work, encouraging them to make themselves at home in the law library and to learn how to use its resources.[98] One of her regular courses

94 Sophonisba P. Breckinridge, *Family Welfare Work in a Metropolitan Community: Selected Case Records* (Chicago: University of Chicago Press, 1924).

95 Sophonisba Breckinridge, *The Family and the State, Select Documents* (Chicago: University of Chicago Press, 1934) 6.

96 See, e.g., Sophonisba P. Breckinridge, "The Social Worker in the Courts of Cook County," *Social Service Review* 12 (June 1938): 230–1.

97 Breckinridge, *The Family and the State*, 9.

98 Sophonisba Breckinridge to Eleanor Bontecou, June 1, 1929, Sophonisba P. Breckinridge Papers, microfiche reel 5, University of Chicago Library. NALAO, "Report of the

was titled Social Work and the Courts, and she consistently brought law and its administration into her other courses. She even sent her top students to Professor Ernst Freund's classes at the University of Chicago Law School.[99] Through Breckinridge's work with the Legal Aid Society of Chicago, its successor the Legal Aid Bureau, and NALAO, she provided a crucial bridge between lawyers and social workers.[100]

As social work professors began to teach legal topics, they needed new course material. Surprisingly, it was Bradway who would write this text, with the support of Breckinridge. Bradway's *Law and Social Work: An Introduction to the Study of the Legal-Social Field for Social Workers* (1929) was underwritten by the School of Social Science Administration at the University of Chicago and the Chicago Legal Aid Bureau, and it appeared in a book series edited by Breckinridge.[101] *Law and Social Work* provides a fascinating study in contradictions and conflicts regarding the role of social workers in legal aid and what it meant to provide them with training in the law. Breckinridge and Bradway recognized that producing such a legal textbook for social workers was controversial. About teaching law within the social work school, Breckinridge wrote that there could be "possible misunderstanding on the part of... [my] legal brethren."[102]

Bradway's discomfort with the project emerges from the text. He declared that the book's purpose was "to prevent social workers from giving legal advice."[103] Social work was a newcomer that at times failed to respect the older field of law, he said, and some social workers did not

---

Committee on Relations with Social Agencies, March 16, 1928," *Reports of Committees, 1927–1928* (Boston: NALAO, 1928), 63.

[99] Sophonisba P. Breckinridge, "Ernst Freund," November 1932, Sophonisba P. Breckinridge Papers, microfiche reel 7, University of Chicago Library. Eulogizing Freund upon his death, Breckinridge wrote, "He always welcomed the Social Service contingent in his classes and showed a keen interest in the special questions they raised or special problems they proposed."

[100] Under the auspices of the American Association for Organizing Family Social Workers, Marguerite Raeder Gariepy, Joel Hunter, Sophonisba Breckinridge, and John Henry Wigmore devised a series of social work courses on law. A 1929 survey of professors in schools of social work found that a large majority supported teaching classes devoted to legal topics and that many professors already included an array of legal issues in their own courses. NALAO, "Report of Sub-Committee on 'The Extent to Which Courses in Law Are Taught in Schools of Social Work,'" *Reports of Committees, 1928–1929* (Boston: NALAO, 1929), 96–103.

[101] John S. Bradway, *Law and Social Work: An Introduction to the Study of the Legal-Social Field for Social Workers* (Chicago: University of Chicago Press, 1929).

[102] Sophonisba Breckinridge to Miss Bontecou, June 1, 1929, Sophonisba P. Breckinridge Papers, microfiche reel 5, University of Chicago Library.

[103] Bradway, *Law and Social Work*, xiii.

respect legal rules.[104] Simultaneously, he sought to define a "legal social field" in which lawyers and social workers had similar interests.[105] Seeking the blessing of lawyers, Bradway prevailed on Reginald Heber Smith to write the foreword, in which Smith extended an olive branch to social workers: "For a dangerously long period [law and social work] . . . have been held apart by ignorance, misunderstanding, and distrust. . . . All of this is unnecessary. It is a sheer waste and tragic folly."[106] Yet, as soon became clear, Smith also sought to establish strict disciplinary boundaries between law and social work. The heart of Smith's message was that law and social work were two distinct professions that, at discrete times, might cooperate.

With all these caveats and criticisms, the book is nonetheless a primer on law, covering procedure, contracts, torts, workers' compensation, criminal law, property, estates, and domestic relations. It is nuanced and complex, and its substance contradicts its warnings that social workers must stay away from the law. It provided a concrete manual of the basics of law and the types of claims that social workers might encounter in their daily work, especially involving clients of legal aid.

Law and Social Work was welcomed by many social workers, and those lawyers who sought cooperation with social workers praised it as creating an important new genre.[107] In fact, it was so well received that Bradway made plans for a second book that would present a series of legal aid case scenarios. These cases would teach social workers how to recognize and address a variety of legal problems, and how to draft reform legislation, lobby legislatures, and bring test cases.[108] As Bradway contemplated this additional work, some social workers commented that he should allow social workers to identify what topics were important. They further suggested the creation of texts on social work for law students and lawyers. Once again, social workers challenged lawyers' monopolization of law, insisting that their own experience and knowledge were equally valuable – and that they had something to teach lawyers.[109]

---

[104] See ibid., 8, 20–21.
[105] Ibid., 5–7.
[106] Reginald Heber Smith, "Foreword," in Bradway, *Law and Social Work*, vii.
[107] Emery Brownwell, "Summary of the Work of the Committee on Relations with Social Agencies of the National Association of Legal Aid Organizations, 1922–1934," United Charities of Chicago, box 40, Chicago History Museum.
[108] John S. Bradway, "Suggested Outline of a Case Book for Use by Students of Social Work in Courses in Law," n.d., Bradway Papers, box 6, vol. 29.
[109] NALAO, "Report of Committee on Relations with Social Agencies," *Reports of Committees, 1928–1929*, 89.

It is clear that social workers *were* being taught law with the idea that they would be providing clients with legal advice. By 1939, twenty-seven out of thirty-eight schools of social work taught courses on law. Marguerite Raeder Gariepy commented, "While there is some objection to such courses raised by lawyers who feel that social workers will feel qualified to practice law without a license, in general this is overbalanced by a realization of the injury which the client may suffer if his legal or social problems are not adequately diagnosed and treated."[110]

Although Bradway concentrated his first efforts on enabling social workers to learn law, he and other progressive lawyers and social workers believed that lawyers also needed to learn social work techniques. As early as 1927, NALAO's Committee on Relations with Social Agencies discussed the need for lawyers to be trained in social work. The lawyers and social workers on the committee viewed law not as a stand-alone discipline but as connected to the social sciences. One committee report noted, "Law... is not a closed system; it is more than a system of mere logic. It is a record of human aspirations and the organization of human interests.... Hence law and social work are inevitably bound together."[111] The report called on law schools to give every student training in social work. The committee's resolution suggesting that courses in social work be offered in law schools was transmitted to the American Association of Law Schools.

Hoping to write a book on social work for lawyers, Bradway told Breckinridge that he tried to teach his law courses in ways that enabled law students to become acquainted with social work.[112] Yet when speaking to lawyers (not social workers), Bradway's tone changed, reflecting his lack of optimism about the enterprise. He explained that, in those few instances when social work was introduced to law students, they proved uninterested and rebelled.[113] Bradway further described the effort as "too radical" and one that would be "voted down at once" by law school faculties.[114] As he wrote to a Columbia Law School professor,

[110] Marguerite Raeder Gariepy, "How the Family Case Worker and the Legal Aid Society Cooperate," *Social Work Technique* 1 (May–June 1936): 77.
[111] NALAO, "Report of Committee on Cooperation with Social Agencies," *Reports of Committees, 1926–1927 for Discussion in St. Louis, Missouri Oct. 6th and 7th* (Boston: NALAO, 1927), 64.
[112] John S. Bradway to Sophonisba Breckinridge, June 22, 1929, 2, Bradway Papers, box 2, vol. 23.
[113] John S. Bradway to Elliott Cheatham, March 9, 1931, 3, Bradway Papers, box 9, vol. 30.
[114] John S. Bradway to Alice Waldo, June 21, 1927, Bradway Papers, box 10, vol. 7.

"Speaking very frankly to you and in strict confidence, I have an impression that social workers... [have] some notion in their minds that they can make lawyers into social workers."[115] Clearly, some lawyers maintained a continuing understanding of the gendered hierarchy and disciplinary divisions separating law and social work.

Although law schools refused to budge in their opposition to teaching social work to law students, during the 1920s lawyers and social workers nonetheless made significant headway in learning how to cooperate with each other. Bradway recognized that lawyers were not going to create quickly and fund legal aid associations. Rather, the impetus for closer relations between the fields was coming, in many cases, from social workers. Remarkably, Bradway had learned to work with professional women and had come to appreciate social workers. He also saw that it was crucial for social workers to have legal training. Other lawyers, too, often with the help of social workers, began to understand that multiple kinds of organizations (some that employed lawyers and some that did not) provided legal aid outside of lawyer-run societies. At times such legal representation involved new state entities such as workers' compensation boards, family courts, and immigration agencies, that were not intended to have the legal formality of other courts and tribunals. Similarly, some legal aid lawyers clearly understood that their clients had needs that might best be met by a combined legal–social work approach. As a result, NALAO and those societies that had adopted a joint approach were well suited to deal with the onslaught of clients and issues brought by the Great Depression.

[115] John S. Bradway to Elliott Cheatham, March 9, 1931, 3, Bradway Papers, box 9, vol. 30.

6

Compromises

The Depression and federal New Deal programs produced a significant change in how leaders understood, shaped, and categorized legal aid.[1] Legal aid societies that isolated themselves from social service agencies found that they were increasingly out of step with the spirit of the age. New Deal programs and benefits also severed, at least for a time, the links between charity, dependence, and women. Yet some bar associations, increasingly anxious about the ability of their members to earn a living, expressed concern that free legal assistance siphoned off paying clients. To counter this fear, legal aid organizations increasingly identified themselves as social service agencies, a characterization they had long resisted.

During the Depression, the importance of the male breadwinner grew and frequently women were ousted from jobs that could go to men. Yet this did not happen in legal aid organizations, where instead female social workers and lawyers won growing acceptance as legal aid providers. Legal aid organizations also showed a new concern for women as clients, especially manifested in their increasing willingness to accept divorce cases, perhaps because so many men were unable to support their families.[2]

---

[1] On the central role played by social workers in the New Deal, see Karen M. Tani, "Securing a Right to Welfare: Public Assistance Administration and the Rule of Law, 1935–1960," PhD diss., University of Pennsylvania, 2011.

[2] On the argument that social service agencies placed a new emphasis on male breadwinners during the Depression, see Linda Gordon, *Heroes of Their Own Lives: The Politics and History of Family Violence, 1880–1960* (New York: Penguin, 1988); see also Nancy Cott, *Public Vows: A History of Marriage and the Nation* (Cambridge, MA: Harvard University Press, 2000). In contrast, Elaine Abelson argues that the poverty of white women became

These trends continued during World War II; the onset of the war and the widespread desire to ensure that those in the armed services, as well as their dependents, had access to legal aid brought Americans close to recognizing legal aid as a universal right.[3] Across the country, legal aid organizations suspended or relaxed eligibility requirements. Although it was through servicemen that dependents qualified for legal aid, it was soldiers' wives and mothers who now filled legal aid offices. Like female clients in the past, they sought help with divorces and domestic relations cases. The female legal aid lawyer also received new attention, becoming perhaps the professional equivalent of the iconic Rosie the Riveter.

The hard-fought battles of the 1920s between lawyers and social workers brought social workers new respect from legal aid lawyers. One sign of their acceptance was the appointment of Bruce Cobb as chief attorney of the Legal Aid Society of New York in 1930. Cobb, a former magistrate, was one of the principal authors of the 1928 report by the Joint Committee for the Study of Legal Aid, discussed in the last chapter.[4] Cobb had taught classes in law to social workers during the 1920s, and he was committed to collaboration between the two professions. Another indication of the growing alliance between social workers and legal aid lawyers was Joel Hunter (superintendent of United Charities of Chicago) taking the post of executive secretary of NALAO in 1940. Just fifteen years earlier it would have been unthinkable for NALAO to install a non-lawyer in that position. Yet with a growing need for funding on the part of NALAO in particular and local legal aid societies more generally, Hunter was able to expand the relationship between legal aid organizations and philanthropic sources of funding.[5]

As the Depression deepened and spread, legal aid organizations quickly became cash-strapped, owing to both a decline in donations and an increase in cases. In 1931, the Legal Aid Society of New York handled 7,000 additional cases, an increase of more than 22 percent from the

especially visible during the Depression; Elaine S. Abelson, "'Women Who Have No Men to Work for Them': Gender and Homelessness in the Great Depression, 1930–1934," *Feminist Studies* 29, no. 1 (Spring 2003): 103–27. For a complex discussion of race and gender in general during the Depression, see Linda Gordon, *Dorothea Lange: A Life beyond Limits* (New York: Norton, 2010).

[3] See Michael B. Katz, *In the Shadow of the Poorhouse: A Social History of Welfare in America* (New York: Basic Books, 1996), 149–50, 210–13.

[4] *Report, Joint Committee for the Study of Legal Aid of the Association of the Bar of the City of New York and the Welfare Council of New York City* (New York, 1928); for a full discussion see Chapter 5.

[5] "Harold F. Swift Is Elected to Charities Board," *Chicago Daily Tribune*, January 22, 1919, 11. The article also discusses Hunter's appointment.

previous year.[6] Facing a large deficit, NYLAS's board closed branch offices and consolidated its work in the main office, effectively ending its provision of neighborhood-based legal services.[7] Other legal aid organizations disappeared entirely; New York's Jewish Educational Alliance shut its legal aid bureau in order to apply its dwindling funds elsewhere.[8] For a brief period the Legal Aid Society of Philadelphia, which was funded by the city government, ceased functioning as well.[9]

All across the country legal aid organizations were looking for new funding, and many turned to local community chests, general charitable funds whose boards were dominated by leading businessmen. Community chests, which increased in number substantially following World War I, employed professional fund-raisers to solicit widely for contributions and then dispersed funds to various welfare organizations and philanthropies in local communities. Historians have generally criticized the conservative nature of community chest boards, but legal aid agencies were keen to receive funding from them.[10]

Those legal aid organizations seeking new sources of funding remade their identities to attract new supporters, now asserting that they resembled other social welfare agencies. The private law office model did not produce sympathy – or generate contributions – in the midst of an economic crisis and growing poverty. The president of the Legal Aid Society of New York began portraying his organization as a welfare agency: "Legal aid has definitely taken its place among the more essential welfare activities. This is recognized . . . by the participation of legal aid organizations in local community chests."[11] Thus a tautology now existed: legal aid needed to look like a typical welfare agency in order to receive funding

---

[6] NYLAS, *Fifty-Sixth Annual Report of the Legal Aid Society for the Year 1931* (New York: Manger, Hughes and Manger, 1932), 23.

[7] See, e.g., NYLAS, *Fifty-Eighth Annual Report of the Legal Aid Society for the Year 1933* (New York: Manger and Son, 1934), 7; NYLAS, *Sixtieth Annual Report of the Legal Aid Society for the Year 1935* (New York: Manger and Son, 1936), 43.

[8] "Minutes of the Executive Committee of the Educational Alliance, May 11, 1939," 2, Papers of the Educational Alliance, reel 6, YIVO Institute for Jewish Research, New York.

[9] NALAO, *Reports of Committees, 1933–1934, for Discussion at the Convention in New York City October 4th and 5th 1934* (Boston: NALAO, 1934), 25.

[10] NALAO, *Committee Reports and Proceedings 1941–1942*, A-3, A-7, 8 in *National Association of Legal Aid Organizations, 1939–1941* (Rochester, NY: NALAO, 1942), A-3, A-7, Cornell University Library. On community chests, see Katz, *In the Shadow of the Poorhouse*, 156–7, 214; Roy Lubove, *The Professional Altruist: The Emergence of Social Work as a Career, 1880–1930* (Cambridge, MA: Harvard University Press, 1965), 183–4.

[11] Ibid.

from community chests, and receiving funding from community chests demonstrated that legal aid was a welfare agency. The crafting of legal aid's identity had essentially come full circle from its beginnings, rooted in women's philanthropy, in the mid-nineteenth century.

Some legal aid organizations also started to receive funds from government sources, whether municipal, county, state, or federal. By 1940, at least twelve legal aid organizations received county funding. Government funding provoked concern among some lawyers, who saw any involvement by the state as a sign of potential interference with the legal profession as a whole. These lawyers further feared that legal aid would become dependent on government funding – a perilous situation should the government later withdraw funding because of budget cuts or, even worse, for political reasons. Legal aid had to be funded entirely by private donors, these lawyers insisted, to maintain the autonomy of the legal profession and the integrity of legal aid.[12]

For most lawyers, ideological qualms were overwhelmed by clients' needs.[13] Increasingly, clients could not afford court costs, giving rise to the issue of whether legal aid organizations should contribute such fees. Some lawyers stressed the importance of clients paying their own costs to demonstrate both their independence and their serious intent to pursue a case. The Legal Aid Society of Boston generally did not advance court costs, reasoning that for a truly meritorious case, the client could always borrow money. In contrast, legal aid providers that were part of social service agencies were more willing to absorb costs. A social worker from Chicago's Bureau of Social Service commented, "Our office regards these as any other necessary expenses in order to do a piece of case-work."[14]

Communication between legal aid lawyers and social workers also improved during the Depression. Chicago's Legal Aid Bureau and the Legal Aid Society of New York now answered telephone calls from social workers with legal questions, rather than insisting that the social workers' client travel to see the lawyer.[15] Lawyers had learned to trust social workers

---

[12] See NALAO, *Memorandum of Proceedings of the 1940 Annual Conference of the National Association of Legal Aid Organizations Held at Jacksonville, Florida, October 31st and November 1st, 1940*, 31–32.

[13] See, e.g., NALAO, "Bulletin No. 15: The Legal Aid Society of Rochester," May 17, 1933, John S. Bradway Papers, David M. Rubenstein Rare Book and Manuscript Library, Duke University Library (hereinafter Bradway Papers), box 6, vol. 29.

[14] Sarah Schaar to John S. Bradway, April 2, 1930, Bradway Papers, box 10, vol. 3. The Bureau of Personal Service had changed its name to the Bureau of Social Service.

[15] NYLAS, *Ten Years of the Legal Aid Society 1927 to 1937*, 6, John Henry Wigmore Papers, Northwestern University Archives, Northwestern University (hereinafter Wigmore Papers), box 83, folder 5.

as intermediaries, relying on their ability to recognize and articulate legal issues. The New York society hired a full-time social worker and emphasized that its lawyers needed to be "more social minded and more understanding of social workers, their methods and aims."[16] It also sought to educate social workers about law, issuing a steady stream of publications aimed at informing them.[17] NALAO recommended that every legal aid organization have a social worker on staff and that lawyers should work closely with social service agencies in connection with individual clients and in shaping larger reform agendas.[18]

Legal aid lawyers' acceptance of social workers also heralded a new attitude toward women lawyers. Allen Wardwell, president of the Legal Aid Society of New York, came close to apologizing for the society's all-male staff of lawyers, explaining that employing women as lawyers was "a custom which for a number of years, for no very good reason, was not followed."[19] Returning to a practice that had peaked at the turn of the century and then had been dormant for more than a generation, the New York society hired two women as attorneys in the early 1930s. A society publication explained that these attorneys were "unusually sympathetic and conscientious in the trying routine of listening to the troubles of all sorts and conditions of people."[20] Although the idea that female attorneys were better equipped to listen to clients was a pervasive stereotype, the ideal characteristics of the legal aid attorney also underwent a subtle transformation, softening and even feminizing the formerly hard-edged male role model. A later president of the New York society explained that, in general, a legal aid attorney "require[d] patience and tact above all else," specifically invoking traits long associated with women. The society's women attorneys regularly represented the society at events and meetings held by New York's social welfare organizations.[21] Women lawyers were to provide the bridge between legal aid and social workers.

In at least some places, legal aid providers and professional organizations openly acknowledged – even celebrated – the new presence of women attorneys in legal aid. In 1935 the *Women Lawyers' Journal*

---

[16] Ibid., 9.
[17] Ibid., 10.
[18] NALAO, *Reports of Committees, 1933–1934, for Discussion at the Convention in New York City, October 4 and 5, 1934*, 69, Bradway Papers, box 6, vol. 31.
[19] NYLAS, *Fifty-Sixth Annual Report*, 11.
[20] NYLAS, *Ten Years of the Legal Aid Society 1927 to 1937*, 8, Wigmore Papers, box 83, folder 5.
[21] NYLAS, *Fifty-Seventh Annual Report of the Legal Aid Society* (New York: Manger, Hughes & Manger, 1933), 11.

reported that female attorneys now headed seven large legal aid organizations. The newest legal aid society had just been established in Washington, D.C., under the auspices of the Washington Council of Social Agencies and the local community chest, with Beatrice Clephine as its head attorney. The *Women Lawyers' Journal* article was one of the first national public acknowledgments of women working as attorneys in legal aid since the turn of the century.[22] At least three women also served on NALAO's executive board during the 1930s.

To say that women had gained full acceptance and integration into legal aid would be an exaggeration. When the Legal Aid Society of New York held a dinner in 1936 in honor of the completion of Wardwell's term as president, the women on its board of directors were not invited, nor were its women attorneys. A speaker remarked that one of the woman directors was a "very pronounced feminist" and that she would be "deeply pained" not to have been invited.[23] Not even the director's personal wealth protected her from such exclusion, which was justified on the grounds that the dinner was not an "official" event. Two clients also spoke at the dinner – both male and one a seaman, even though seamen now represented a very small proportion of the society's clients.[24] Wardwell even used his speech that evening to stress the difference between lawyers and social workers, explaining that the legal aid attorney must act like an attorney and that the social worker must know her place.[25] He thus reassured his audience of men that the society had not been taken over by either social workers or women attorneys.

As white women lawyers and social workers gained a new acceptance, the provision of legal aid to African Americans became more visible and widespread in the 1930s. Leaders of legal aid recognized that the South had been slow to create legal aid organizations. John Bradway complained that southern bar associations were uninterested in establishing legal aid organizations, as they did not want to provide services to African Americans, who, they believed, would inundate any such organization.[26]

---

[22] Elaine Cogswell, "The Development of the Legal Aid Idea," *Women Lawyers' Journal* 21 (1934–1935): 16–17.

[23] *Dinner Given in Honor of Allen Wardwell, Esq., December 2, 1936*, 1, Wigmore Papers, box 83, folder 5.

[24] Ibid., 7–9.

[25] Ibid.

[26] John S. Bradway to Emmet R. Field, March 26, 1929, Bradway Papers, box 1, vol. 36; John S. Bradway to Francis H. McLean, May 11, 1925, and June 5, 1925; Francis

Accepting the claims of African Americans even in simple wage disputes could destabilize racial hierarchies and challenge African Americans' ongoing oppression.[27] The support that Bradway received from leaders in the South primarily emanated from women in social welfare organizations.[28] Yet with the Depression's onset, even the South began to witness the spread of legal aid agencies.

In 1913 a handful of attorneys joined with a number of charity organizations run by women to create New Orleans's first legal aid society. The New Orleans Legal Aid Society was entirely unfunded, relying on lawyers and social workers who volunteered their time. The society also was willing to accept African American clients.[29] Perhaps because of this, and because of its use of women volunteers, the society faced such hostility from the New Orleans and Louisiana Bar Association that even the American Bar Association scolded those organizations for their lack of support.[30] Without funds, personnel, or office space, the society ceased to function in the early 1920s.[31]

During the Depression, and under the leadership of New Orleans philanthropist Ida Weis Friend, social workers and women volunteers created the Prison Aid League, which originally provided material relief and "friendly visits" to the families of prisoners. With the support of social workers from Tulane University's School of Social Work, the league soon began providing legal aid and reestablished the New Orleans Legal Aid Society, now funded primarily by patrons of the Prison Aid League and

H. McClean to John S. Bradway, June 4, 1925, Family Service Association of America Records, box 12, folder 12, Social History Welfare Archive, University of Minnesota Library, Minneapolis (hereinafter Family Service Association Records).

[27] On race, labor relations, and civil rights, see Robin D. G. Kelley, *Hammer and Hoe: Alabama Communists during the Great Depression* (Chapel Hill: University of North Carolina Press, 1990); Risa L. Goluboff, *The Lost Promise of Civil Rights* (Cambridge, MA: Harvard University Press, 2010).

[28] John S. Bradway to Francis H. McLean, May 11, 1925, and June 5, 1925; Francis H. McClean to John S. Bradway, June 4, 1925, Family Service Association Records, box 12, folder 12. On gender, race, and social service organizations in the South, see Glenda Elizabeth Gilmore, *Gender and Jim Crow: Women and the Politics of White Supremacy in North Carolina, 1896–1920* (Chapel Hill: University of North Carolina Press, 1996). Although Atlanta had had a legal aid society since the 1920s, legal aid in the South did not exist on any large scale until the 1960s. See Kris Shepard, *Rationing Justice: Poverty Lawyers and Poor People in the Deep South* (Baton Rouge: Louisiana State University Press, 2007).

[29] See Esther Haskin, "A History of Legal Aid in New Orleans," master's thesis, Tulane University, 1941, 11, Tulane University Library.

[30] Ibid., 22.

[31] Ibid., 27.

the local community chest.[32] On the first day that its legal aid office opened, it accepted five clients – three white women, one white man, and one African American man.[33] By the mid-1930s the New Orleans Bar Association proclaimed that it needed to supervise the organization. The bar created an advisory board for the society composed entirely of male lawyers. Not even the prominent white women who had been involved in founding the organization and made large financial contributions were allowed to serve on it. The advisory board claimed that the society's work resembled the practice of law and needed to be supervised by attorneys.[34] The advisory board's conduct notwithstanding, even in New Orleans, where social workers and lawyers had to struggle so to create a legal aid organization, the Depression acted as a catalyst for the spread of legal aid. Moreover, the actual work of the society was in the hands of one male lawyer and two female social workers, and within the decade a woman would become its head attorney. Yet like legal aid organizations across the country, the providers of legal aid were white; accepting African Americans as clients was one thing, but allowing them to be providers was another.

In response to the dearth of legal aid societies willing to aid large numbers of poor African Americans, the continued migration of African Americans from the South, and the ongoing Depression, a number of new African American organizations sought to provide formal organized legal assistance. Like their pre-Depression counterparts, these organizations left behind little detailed documentation of their actual work. The Truth Church Institute in Birmingham, Alabama, announced in 1931 that it would establish legal aid centers in southern communities that had a population of more than 5,000 African Americans. Its centers would

---

[32] Ibid., 31. Ida Friend was a Jewish philanthropist and reformer in New Orleans whose immigrant father had become wealthy as a cotton broker. Holding positions in the General Federation of Women's Clubs and several Jewish women's organizations, she undoubtedly would have come into contact with legal aid organizations and the role of social workers in providing legal aid. In the 1890s she spent a brief time in Chicago after marrying a Milwaukee lawyer; given her social class, it is possible, even probable, that she came into contact with the women who founded Chicago's Protective Agency for Women and Children; she would certainly have known the Jewish social worker Minnie Low. In the 1930s Friend served on the Commission on Interracial Cooperation and the New Orleans Urban League. See Karen Trahan Leathem, "Ida Weis Friend: 1868–1963," in *Jewish Women: A Comprehensive Historical Encyclopedia*, http://jwa.org/encyclopedia/article/friend-ida-weis.

[33] Haskin, "A History of Legal Aid in New Orleans," 37.

[34] Ibid., 47.

address both quotidian legal claims and cases involving racial discrimination. Whether the church was actually able to open and run these centers is difficult to discern, but its proposal further highlights the larger possibility that a wide variety of African American community institutions were providing some form of legal assistance to African Americans.[35]

During the 1930s African American newspapers – both northern and southern – began to publish notices of the availability of free legal assistance to African Americans from both individual attorneys and organizations. A 1931 *Atlantic World* article, "Chicago Attorney Sets Example for Professionals," discussed Chicago's Macon Huggins, an African American attorney who announced that he would provide free legal services to unemployed African Americans and urged other lawyers to do likewise.[36] In fact, other African American lawyers did try to alleviate the suffering of poor African Americans who had to endure the double hardship of the Depression and discrimination. The Harlem Lawyers Association in the mid-1930s provided free legal assistance in civil and criminal cases. As the *New York Amsterdam News* opined, even though other legal aid organizations existed in New York City, such as the Legal Aid Society, their services were narrow and attorney-client relations could be strained. "Where such agencies attempt to render legal assistance to the Negro, the relationship between the agency and those assisted lacks the personal element that normally exists in the conventional relationship of the individual attorney and his client."[37] This statement gives a rare glimpse of what African American clients might have experienced in seeking legal aid. The decision by the Legal Aid Society of New York to close its branch offices, including its uptown Harlem Branch, undoubtedly contributed to the difficulty for American Americans of even reaching the society's office, which was located in the lower part of New York City. Continuing the decades-long struggle to provide African Americans with legal aid, the National Bar Association, an organization of African American attorneys, announced in 1941 that it had created free legal aid bureaus in multiple cities in the North and the South.[38] Such organizations attempted

---

[35] "Truth Church to Give Legal Aid: To Open Aid Centers in Large Cities," *Chicago Defender*, May 16, 1931, 4.

[36] "Chicago Attorney Sets Example for Professionals," *Atlanta Daily World*, December 20, 1931, 7.

[37] "Needed Legal Aid," *New York Amsterdam News*, June 30, 1934, 8.

[38] Erin L. Thompson, "National Bar Association," in *Encyclopedia of African American History: From the Age of Segregation to the Twenty-First Century*, vol. 1, ed. Paul Finkelman (New York: Oxford University Press, 2009), 442.

to deliver legal services to African Americans, but they relied primarily on volunteer attorneys – a model that could not be sustained. This was especially a problem where African American lawyers and social workers were few in number and community organizations were often in financial straits.[39]

As new organizations began providing legal aid and others closed their doors, the Depression also brought about changes in who sought legal aid and what kind of assistance they needed. Wage claims, which had been the largest category of cases, now decreased because of widespread unemployment. Claims involving landlords and tenants, home mortgages, and defaults on small loans increased dramatically, as did domestic relations cases.[40] Marguerite Raeder Gariepy, head attorney at the Chicago Legal Aid Bureau, explained, "Real estate cases that have come to us since the beginning of the depression have involved rather a different type of client than we were formerly acquainted with.... Many had put all their savings into their homes and would have managed without help, had it not been for the depression."[41] These clients were not the perpetually poverty-stricken clients of the past, but instead were members of the working class grappling with the effects of the Depression. Paradoxically, at the same time that legal aid organizations were backing away from the claim that their clients were self-sufficient men who had temporarily fallen on hard times, such clients actually materialized in legal aid offices.[42] These new clients were the very type that Reginald Heber Smith had earlier imagined as the ideal person for whom legal aid should be provided.

[39] See Kenneth Mack, *Representing the Race: The Creation of the Civil Rights Lawyer* (Cambridge, MA: Harvard University Press, 2013).

[40] See NYLAS, *Fifty-Seventh Annual Report*, 24. Coalition building with social service agencies, along with the new political environment, prompted legal aid providers to lobby for significant new legislation, including small-loan legislation, laws to prevent or limit wage garnishment on chattel mortgages, new in forma pauperis rules, and eventually more uniform divorce laws.

[41] Marguerite Raeder Gariepy, "The Relationship between Legal Aid Work and Social Work" (draft of speech, February 1, 1937), 10, United Charities of Chicago, box 40, Chicago History Museum (hereinafter UCC Papers).

[42] See, e.g., "Annual Report of the Legal Aid Bureau, January 1939–1940," 7, Wigmore Papers, box 93, folder 5. In a close analysis of Depression-era letters from people seeking help from Eleanor Roosevelt, scholar Michele Landis Dauber has found that people in need presented themselves as blameless, respectable, and responsible, and only temporarily in need of aid owing to the Depression. Michele Landis Dauber, *The Sympathetic State: Disaster Relief and the Origins of the American Welfare State* (Chicago: University of Chicago Press, 2013), chap. 7.

How legal aid providers handled cases and what cases they were willing to accept also changed. In the past, some legal aid lawyers refused to
accept cases without substantive legal merit, but now many took cases for
strategic purposes – especially cases involving home foreclosures. Legal
aid lawyers and social workers often could not prevent home foreclosures, as the client clearly was in default and the interest rate on the loan
was neither usurious nor unconscionable. These lawyers instead used
court procedures to try to secure additional time for their clients. One
lawyer explained that although often there were no legal grounds for a
stay of court proceedings or an extension of court days, lawyers asked
for them anyway and judges often obliged.[43] Some states instituted mortgage moratoriums, which delayed banks from foreclosing on borrowers
with delinquent mortgages.[44] These programs were not self-executing;
often they were complicated, involving a variety of court proceedings.
The Legal Aid Society of Minneapolis explained that its moratorium
work "required the drafting of voluminous legal documents and frequent
court appearances." It complained that such work "severely taxed" its
resources.[45]

In Chicago, the Legal Aid Bureau was directly involved in government
relief programs administered at the local level by social workers. Working with public and private relief agencies, legal aid attorneys provided
advice to administrators, social workers, and relief applicants. In one
coordinated effort, lawyers worked to prevent clients from being evicted
from homes while social workers found clients housing or public financial
relief that could be used to pay their back or future rent.[46]

Legal aid lawyers often worked with social workers and clients in connection with the 1933 federal Home Owners' Loan Corporation (HOLC),
which provided refinancing to those who had defaulted or were about
to default on their home mortgages.[47] Growing ties between HOLC and

43 NALAO, "Bulletin No. 27: Replies to Questionnaire Regarding Home Owner's Loan
    Corporation," March 7, 1934, 3, Bradway Papers, box 6, vol. 29.
44 See Price Fisherback, Jonathan Rose, and Kenneth Snowden, *Well Worth Saving: How
    the New Deal Safeguarded Home Ownership* (Chicago: University of Chicago Press,
    2013), 32–33.
45 Legal Aid Society of Minneapolis, *Annual Report 1939*, 2, United Way of Minneapolis
    Records, Social Welfare History Archive, box 204, folder Legal Aid Society, 1931–1939,
    University of Minnesota Library, Minneapolis (hereinafter United Way of Minn. Papers).
46 Marguerite Raeder Gariepy, "Legal Aid as Part of a Community Program," *Annals of
    the American Academy of Political and Social Science* 205 (September 1939): 72–78.
47 See Fisherback, Rose, and Snowden, *Well Worth Saving*; Rosalind Tough, "The Life
    Cycle of the Home Owners' Loan Corporation," *Land Economics* 27 (November 1951):

legal aid organizations led to one of the first instances in which legal aid organizations became involved in a federal benefits program, and those links set the tone for subsequent work in similar programs. Applying for and being accepted for an HOLC loan was not a straightforward process. Even simple HOLC cases required clients to understand the basics of a mortgage, what back taxes they owed, and how the program functioned – that is, the current mortgage holder had to agree to refinance a loan, often for a sum smaller than the outstanding amount on the current mortgage, and to accept payment in the form of HOLC bonds. Adding an additional layer of complexity, cities and counties had to be convinced to remove tax liens, and often home repairs were required.[48] What made the program so difficult was that HOLC appraised properties at the then-current – that is, depressed – value, an assessment that deprived many homeowners of the equity that they thought they had in their homes and, at times, made them ineligible for the program.[49] Legal aid providers became home-owners' intermediaries, negotiating with banks and with HOLC to convince them to agree to new loan amounts.[50]

Given their new and evolving roles, legal aid providers disagreed among themselves about assisting a client who wished to apply for HOLC assistance. Some lawyers saw their duty as determining whether repayment of a new loan was realistic, and they refused to file applications on behalf of those they believed HOLC would reject, or who would quickly default on a new loan.[51] Other providers, especially those involved with social welfare agencies, believed that every homeowner was entitled to apply for a loan and that the decision to grant it was up to HOLC. Those providers saw the matter in strategic terms, insisting that an application, even one that would be rejected, could buy the client time. Dallas legal aid attorney Mildred Douglas told fellow legal aid attorneys that they should not worry about whether HOLC should grant a particular loan. Refusing to file an application for a client, she said, was an "outstanding disgrace" that would put the client "out on the streets, homeless, penniless, jobless, sick in heart, body, mind and pocket-book."[52]

324–31; Price V. Fishback, Alfonso Flores-Lagunes, William C. Horrace, Shawn Kantor, and Jaret Treber Source, "The Influence of the Home Owners' Loan Corporation on Housing Markets during the 1930s," *Review of Financial Studies* 24 (2011): 1782–1813.

[48] Fisherback, Rose, and Snowden, *Well Worth Saving*, 4–8.

[49] Ibid., 57–59, 63–74.

[50] NALAO, "Bulletin No. 27: Replies to Questionnaire regarding Home Owner's Loan Corporation," March 7, 1934.

[51] Ibid.

[52] Ibid., 10.

Douglas's insistence notwithstanding, generally legal aid's relationship with HOLC was bifurcated, with legal aid acting sometimes as its ally and sometimes as its opponent. In some places, HOLC sent clients to legal aid agencies for assistance when their cases raised legal complications, such as questions about the competency of the parties or identifying a given property's legal owner, or to stave off foreclosure until HOLC was ready to act. Applicants might also call on legal aid to help them challenge HOLC's rejection of an application.[53] Thus, a given legal aid organization might work with HOLC for one client while also challenging HOLC on behalf of another client. Overwhelmingly, legal aid lawyers admired the HOLC program because they believed that preventing foreclosures and securing new mortgages was not charity but a market-based solution that benefited both homeowners and banks. On a more abstract level, HOLC supported the male homeowner's status as breadwinner, even if he was unemployed, and preserved the domestic space to which women were supposedly attached.

As the federal government launched other New Deal relief programs, legal aid societies increasingly represented clients in cases when it was unclear whether clients were entitled to benefits. Legal aid providers again acted as intermediaries, helping to flesh out the contours of eligibility. Some lawyers were willing to challenge government agencies that denied benefits to applicants. Others refused to contest such determinations because they saw benefits as being within the discretion of the agency, and appealing decisions wasted limited resources. Moreover, they did not want to alienate agency officials with whom they might later work. Eventually NALAO took the position that legal aid societies should take such appeals when they had merit.[54]

Even without directly challenging an agency's decision, legal aid organizations faced multiple issues in connection with government benefits. One case from the Chicago Legal Aid Bureau demonstrates the legal complexities of New Deal programs and how distinct programs interacted with one another. The bureau represented a sixty-four-year-old man whom the Works Progress Administration employed after he had been discharged from his railroad job, which he had held for twenty-seven

---

[53] Ibid., 3.

[54] NALAO, *Memorandum of Proceedings of the 1940 Annual Conference of the National Association of Legal Aid Organizations Held at Jacksonville, Florida, October 31st and November 1st, 1940*, 62. It is not clear whether legal aid lawyers represented clients under the "fair hearing provisions" of the Social Security Act or whether such representations were more informal. On fair hearings, understanding benefits as rights, and local administrators' opposition, see Tani, "Securing a Right to Welfare."

years. Because of the discharge and his current work with the WPA, it was unclear whether he qualified for a pension under the Railroad Retirement Act of 1935. Extended discussions between the Railroad Retirement Board and the legal aid attorney produced a resolution: after the worker reached sixty-five, he would quit his WPA job and be entitled to receive his railroad pension.[55] The Social Security Act presented similar new questions, such as guardianship issues for those who were incompetent and provisions for the payment of such guardians. Bureau lawyers and social workers sought to address these and related questions.[56] Functioning almost as a bureaucratic arm of the state, the bureau also helped clients with claims for unemployment compensation, including pursuing employers who attempted to evade coverage.[57]

Basic applications for New Deal benefit programs raised a host of administrative and legal problems that legislators and administrators had not anticipated. Historian Karen Tani writes that staffing the low-level bureaucratic jobs of New Deal benefit programs was difficult, often requiring the hiring of those without social work or legal training, such as nurses and teachers. The size of their caseloads and the extent of their knowledge (especially when the federal government first established such programs) did not always allow them to do the necessary hand-holding required in assisting applicants – nor were there ready-made answers to difficult questions.[58] In the absence of local administrators who had the capacity to devote time to each novel and individual problem, at least some applicants turned to legal aid. Legal aid providers and administrators at times puzzled together over how such problems might be solved.

Applicants often needed assistance even when unusual questions or complications were not at issue. One legal aid lawyer explained that some clients were "illiterate and helpless" and could not depend on "brusque" government bureaucrats for help in filling out forms, explaining programs, or producing necessary documents.[59] Birth and marriage certificates, tax records, and citizenship papers now became vital for eligibility

---

[55] LAB, "Annual Report of the Chicago Legal Aid Bureau, January 1939–1940" (unpublished copy), 5, Wigmore Papers, box 93, folder 5.

[56] Legal Aid Society of Minneapolis, *Annual Report 1939*, 2, United Way of Minn. Records, box 204, folder Legal Aid Society, 1931–1939.

[57] LAB, "Annual Report of the Legal Aid Bureau, January 1, 1939, to January 1, 1940," 4, Wigmore Papers. See, e.g., LAB, "Annual Report of the Legal Aid Bureau, January 1939–1940," 7, Wigmore Papers, box 93, folder 5.

[58] Tani, "Securing a Right to Welfare," 54–55.

[59] Abram Glaser to Henry Fleischman, October 20, 1934, Educational Alliance Papers, box 4, folder 67.

in New Deal programs. In the abstract, such documents should have been easy to produce, but often they were lost, destroyed, incorrect, or nonexistent. Many people had lived much of their lives unconcerned with official papers, but the availability of government benefits suddenly made those documents important – and the applicant now needed the help of some intermediary, whether a lawyer or social worker, to find or create them.

Recognizing the importance of legal aid to benefits programs, the federal government began to promote and subsidize legal aid. The Chicago Legal Aid Bureau was so immersed in relief work that the Federal Emergency Relief Administration paid the greater part of the salaries for two of its attorneys.[60] The U.S. Public Administration Service also engaged John Bradway to write a how-to manual for legal aid organizations; the agency published it as a bulletin in 1935.[61] Likewise, in at least some locations where legal aid organizations did not exist, federal agencies called on local bar associations to create them.[62] Clearly governments hoped bar associations would pick up the cost and provide the labor to help with New Deal programs. Such hopes were quickly dashed.

The Depression and New Deal created new roles for legal aid providers, and the federal government supported the expansion of legal aid. Elements of the private bar, however, instigated a concerted attack against legal aid organizations. In the past, lawyers and bar associations had expressed some concern about competition from legal aid organizations, but during the Depression their fears reached new heights. Now some members of the bar claimed that legal aid drained clients away from practitioners.[63] Before the Depression, the lawyers most threatened by legal aid were immigrant lawyers who served mostly immigrant communities; but the Depression made it increasingly difficult, especially for young lawyers, to attract new clients.[64] Segments of the bar became concerned not only with legal aid but also with competition from individuals and firms outside the legal profession, such as trust companies, collection

---

[60] LAB, *Annual Report for the Year 1934* (Chicago, 1934), 66.

[61] John S. Bradway, *Legal Aid Bureaus: Their Organization and Administration: A Manual of Practice* (Chicago: Public Administration Services, 1935).

[62] Ruth FitzSimons, "Law and Social Work," in NALAO, "Bulletin 90," August 2, 1938, UCC Papers, box 40.

[63] John S. Bradway, *The Work of Legal Aid Committees of Bar Associations* (Chicago: American Bar Association, 1938), 199.

[64] NYLAS, *Fifty-Ninth Annual Report of the Legal Aid Society of New York for the Year 1934* (New York: Manger and Son, 1935), 8.

agencies, realtors, and banks. A new genre of legal literature attacked the unauthorized practice of law. Exemplifying this new concern was the ABA's creation in 1930 of a special committee on the unauthorized practice of law. A key part of the ABA's national agenda by 1933 involved the eradication of unauthorized legal practice.[65]

Yet precisely what the unauthorized practice of law meant varied over time and from place to place. Each state had its own statutes and definitions. For the most part, bar associations' disciplinary committees had jurisdiction only over lawyers, making bar associations dependent on local prosecutors to enforce statutes against nonlawyers. In some states, definitions of the unauthorized practice of law were so overbroad as to lose all meaning. If one read such statutes liberally, neighbors, family members, friends, accountants, real estate brokers, bankers, social workers, and virtually anyone who provided any advice regarding any law to another person could be engaging in the unauthorized practice of law. Other statutes defined the practice of law as an exchange of legal services for financial gain, or as appearing in court in a representative capacity, seemingly exempting the free provision of legal services that did not include court appearances.[66] Still other states had no statute at all.

Remarkably, leaders of the ABA advised all states to enact statutes penalizing the unauthorized practice of law, and urged states not to define its meaning, as that would "invite evasion" and be "self-limiting."[67] They argued that it was generally "impossible to define the practice of law" in a statute and that any attempt would fail to fully encompass its meaning.[68] The ABA further advocated that only courts had the ability to define what constituted the unauthorized practice of law and that this had to be accomplished on a case-by-case basis. In part, the ABA

[65] Frederick C. Hicks and Elliott R. Katz, eds., *Unauthorized Practice of Law: A Handbook for Lawyers and Laymen* (Chicago: American Bar Association, 1934), 3–4; see also Frederick C. Hicks and Elliott R. Katz, "The Practice of Law by Laymen and Lay Agencies," *Yale Law Journal* 41 (1931–2): 69–100; Henry A. Shinn, "How to Deal with the Unlawful Practice of Law," *American Bar Association Journal* 17 (1931): 98–101; C. J. Roberts, "The Unlawful Practice of Law," *Lawyer and Banker Central Law Journal* 24 (1931): 80–84.

[66] Hicks and Katz, *Unauthorized Practice of Law*, 50–51.

[67] John G. Jackson, "Foreword," in Hicks and Katz, *Unauthorized Practice of Law*, 5. Jackson was the chairman of the ABA's Committee on the Unauthorized Practice of Law.

[68] Ralph T. Catterall, "The Unauthorized Practice of Law," *American Bar Association Journal* 19 (1933): 652.

and bar associations worried that legislators might be too sympathetic to nonlawyers in crafting a definition.[69]

Some lawyers sought to eliminate provisions in state law that specifically permitted legal aid organizations to practice law. In New York, the state assembly considered amending legislation that allowed charitable organizations to provide free legal services to the poor.[70] Equally alarming for legal aid societies, a handful of attorneys now brought charges for the first time targeting legal aid societies for the unauthorized practice of law. In one case, lawyers lodged a complaint against the Legal Aid Society of New York. At issue were two divorce cases in which the society accepted ten dollars from the clients. Such payments, the complainants argued, meant that the society was not a charitable organization that provided free legal advice. Although the bar association held hearings and then dismissed the complaint as without merit, this attack illustrated a new sense of desperation among lawyers.[71] Clearly, the fee that some legal aid lawyers had so steadfastly supported – because paying a fee made a legal aid society look more like a law office and less like a charity – now endangered legal aid organizations that depended on certain statutory exemptions from the unauthorized practice of law.[72]

Elements of the bar also claimed that legal aid organizations, *as corporations*, were prohibited from practicing law, as many state statutes specifically restricted lawyers from practicing law through a corporate entity.[73] NALAO and a number of local legal aid organizations, including the Chicago Legal Aid Bureau, responded – with some disingenuousness – that legal aid organizations were *not* corporations practicing law; instead a legal aid organization was simply an "administrative entity" that provided assignments to its attorneys. From this perspective, cases

---

[69] Laurel A. Rigertas, "Lobbying and Litigating against 'Legal Bootleggers': The Role of the Organized Bar in the Expansion of the Courts' Inherent Powers in the Early Twentieth Century," *Californian Western Law Review* 46 (2009): 66–136, 116–23.

[70] Section 280 of New York Penal Law; see Bruce Cobb to Hon. Burton Esmond, February 14, 1933, 1, Bradway Papers, box 8, vol. 38.

[71] See NYLAS, *Sixtieth Annual Report*, 11.

[72] NALAO, "Bulletin No. 1: Brief," Bradway Papers, box 6, vol. 29. In *In Re Axtell*, a New York appellate court affirmed the disbarment of a former NYLAS Seaman's Branch attorney who had gone into private practice, for soliciting clients and other unethical conduct. Although the lawyer was no longer affiliated with NYLAS and had not been for decades, his case was not good publicity for NYLAS. *In Re Axtell*, 229 A.D. 323 (S. Ct. N.Y., 1930).

[73] NALAO, "Bulletin No. 1: Brief."

actually belonged to individual attorneys, not the organization. Opponents of legal aid further asserted that law students who worked as legal aid volunteers or in the growing number of law school legal aid clinics were engaging in the unauthorized practice of law. In response, NALAO argued that nonlawyers working in legal aid offices and law school clinics were no more practicing law than were secretaries and clerks in large law firms who assisted and were under the control of a lawyer.[74]

Lawyers seeking to limit the role of legal aid organizations did not explicitly complain that social workers were engaged in the unauthorized practice of law. The closest they came to making such charges was in New Orleans, where the bar refused to allow laypeople on its advisory committee on the grounds that such work was "legal," "technical," and "tantamount to a lay person's practicing law."[75] Perhaps lawyers did not raise direct challenges to the role of social workers because lawyers assumed that female social workers could not be engaging in legal practice, nor could they be imagined as competition for "real" lawyers. The feminized field of social work, with its female clients, simply did not look like the stereotypical legal practice. To have acknowledged them would have been admitting that they were practicing law.

In this environment, many bar associations pressured legal aid societies to create and enforce strict eligibility guidelines for accepting clients. Before the 1930s, individual legal aid organizations had generally determined who qualified for legal aid services; now bar associations were increasingly involved in such issues. The Legal Aid Society of Denver entered into an agreement with the bar association in which it promised not to accept cases involving bankruptcy, estates or probate, divorce, cases in which the damages might exceed one hundred dollars, any work involving real estate titles or the transfer of property, and criminal cases.[76] Seeking to avoid specific prohibitions, the Legal Aid Society of New York explained that it recognized that the Depression was prompting lawyers to take cases that in the past they would have "scorned" for being too small.[77] It assured the bar that it would not accept clients who could pay even a small fee.[78] Such self-policing was designed to ward off direct interference.

---

[74] Ibid.
[75] Haskin, "A History of Legal Aid in New Orleans," 47 (citing personal interviews).
[76] "Agreement between the Legal Aid Association and the Denver Bar Association" (N.D.), Bradway Papers, box 6, vol. 31.
[77] NYLAS, *Fifty-Ninth Annual Report*, 8.
[78] Ibid.

Some scholars of legal aid have argued that legal aid organizations worked closely with the elite bar to keep cases from nonelite lawyers.[79] However, it is clear that this argument exaggerates the relationship between legal aid and the leaders of the profession, although it is true that Bradway and others had long sought bar association support. These arguments over the unauthorized practice of law first appeared with any force during the Depression, and a much larger swath of the bar, not just nonelite members, raised such complaints. In response, some bar associations bent over backward to mollify lawyers concerned about legal aid.[80] One officer of the Legal Aid Society of New York publically remarked that the Society had "to steer a course between Scylla and Charybdis . . . to keep on good terms with the bar."[81]

These efforts to restrict the provision of legal aid galvanized legal aid attorneys and social workers. NALAO charged that bar associations did not understand the work that legal aid conducted and that they needed to refrain from making rules for client eligibility: "When Bar Associations attempt to limit the work of the Societies, they . . . make their recommendations so meticulous that it often prohibits Legal Aid Societies from taking cases unless they can establish first, that the applicant is so impoverished that he is eligible to stand on a corner with a tin cup and ask for alms."[82] NALAO revived old tropes, invoking the specter of revolution among the poor unless legal aid was available. One letter from New York's Bruce Cobb to a New York legislator predicted that eliminating the statutory exception allowing charitable organizations to practice law would "cause untold misery to hundreds of thousands of poor persons" and would result in the dangerous escalation of their grievances.[83]

[79] Jerold S. Auerbach, *Unequal Justice: Lawyers and Social Change in Modern America* (New York: Oxford University Press, 1977).

[80] As Michael Powell writes, bar associations were heterogeneous. Even in New York, the elite Association of the Bar of the City of New York often was in disagreement with the less elite bar associations in the other New York City boroughs, as well as with upstate New York bar associations. Consensus among bar associations was difficult to achieve. Michael J. Powell, *From Patrician to Professional Elite: The Transformation of the New York City Bar Association* (New York: Russell Sage Foundation, 1988). See also Ronen Shamir, *Managing Legal Uncertainty: Elite Lawyers in the New Deal* (Durham, NC: Duke University Press, 1995).

[81] *Dinner Given in Honor of Allen Wardwell, Esq.*, December 2, 1936, 1, Wigmore Papers, box 83, folder 5.

[82] Richard J. Talbot (NALAO), "Report on Committee on Relations with the Bar," 60, Bradway Papers, box 6, vol. 31.

[83] See Bruce Cobb to Hon. Burton Esmond, February 14, 1933, Bradway Papers, box 8, vol. 38.

In a stunning paradox, legal aid organizations defended themselves on the ground that social workers first investigated clients, thus ensuring that all clients were both needy and poor. They claimed that legal aid involved "welfare work" and "social problems" that lawyers generally were not equipped to handle.[84] Now the presence of social workers marked a given case as rightfully belonging to legal aid rather than to a private lawyer. Thus, at the precise time when the Depression detached poverty from moral weakness, women, and the failure of a male breadwinner, NALAO emphasized that its clients were not self-sufficient, independent men. Such men could afford a private attorney; legal aid clients could not.

In combating more stringent eligibility rules, legal aid organizations wanted at least to be able to refer clients who did not qualify for legal aid to affordable and competent private lawyers, a practice many providers had followed informally for years. Bar associations, however, began claiming that it was their sole responsibility to create such referral lists. The lists produced strife, as nonelite lawyers – and essentially any lawyer who wanted to be on the list but was not included – charged the responsible committees with favoritism. In some places, bar associations became so mired in the politics of creating a list and so feared criticism from their members that they refused or failed to produce a list at all. Unable to create an official referral list, some bar associations directed legal aid organizations to cease making referrals altogether.[85]

In 1939, deeply frustrated with the bar, John Bradway announced his resignation as executive secretary of NALAO, having held the position for eighteen years. In his last report, he reflected on NALAO's initial hope that the expansion of legal aid would occur through bar associations. The organization had spent significant resources urging the bar to take responsibility for legal aid societies. After many years and brutal arguments over what constituted the unauthorized practice of law and the politics of referral lists, Bradway no longer had faith in bar associations.[86] He now believed that social service organizations were more willing than

---

[84] Richard J. Talbot (NALAO), "Report on Committee on Relations with the Bar," 59–60, Bradway Papers, box 6, vol. 31.

[85] John S. Bradway, "Work of Legal Aid Committees" in *Record of Proceedings at the Fifteenth Annual Meeting of the National Association of Legal Aid Organizations, Held at Pittsburgh, Pennsylvania, October 7 and 8, 1937* (1937), 34–36.

[86] John S. Bradway, "Report on the Work of the National Association of Legal Aid Organizations – Its Nature and the Methods of Conducting It," *National Association of Legal Aid Organizations, Reports of Committees, 1939–1940, for Discussion at the Conference in Jacksonville, Fla. October 31–November 1, 1940* (1936), 96.

the bar to support legal aid and would take the lead in creating new legal aid organizations. Equally discouraging, NALAO itself was so poor that it had not paid his salary for years and now owed him more than $40,000. Despite many appeals to wealthy lawyers, NALAO was unable to raise the full sum. In a bitter irony, Bradway had become a worker with a wage claim.[87]

Although legal aid providers were under assault from elements of the bar, the Depression era saw the dramatic liberalization of some legal aid organizations' policies regarding divorce. This change came in part from the new infusion of social workers and women attorneys into legal aid, as well as the from pressure that the Depression put on families. Female social workers and lawyers were often more accepting of divorce than male attorneys, and they had less patience with the hand-wringing of bar associations. Social workers also argued that poverty increased men's drinking and domestic abuse, and that such men squandered their family's relief checks.[88] These social workers recognized that the idea of keeping families together solely because husbands functioned as breadwinners (or at least potential breadwinners) no longer applied. The myth of the male breadwinner and the importance of family unity was cracking. In some situations, divorce could create more stability for women and children. Moreover, because of widespread impoverishment, individuals, primarily wives, simply could not afford private lawyers, so legal aid organizations began to see more applicants seeking a divorce.[89] Some legal aid organizations saw their number of divorce cases almost double, and divorce became the largest category of domestic relations cases.[90] The Legal Aid Society of New York remarked on its growing number of both domestic relations and divorce cases.[91] Before the Depression, domestic relations

---

[87] Despite Bradway's disappointment and what seemed like his genuine intent to leave NALAO, two years later he was elected president of the organization. NALAO was Bradway's baby; he could not abandon it.

[88] Sheldon D. Elliott, "Illustrations of Case Work Practice – With Marital Problems in Families, Legal Aspects," in NALAO, "Bulletin No. 90," August 2, 1938, (reprinting speech given at the meeting of the National Conference on Social Work, June 1938), UCC Papers, box 40.

[89] See Nancy F. Cott, *Public Vows: A History of Marriage and the Nation* (Cambridge, MA: Harvard University Press, 2002); Hendrik Hartog, *Man and Wife in America: A History* (Cambridge, MA: Harvard University Press, 2002).

[90] See the Legal Aid Society of Minneapolis, *Annual Reports* 1934, 1935, 1936, 1938, United Way of Minn. Records, box 204, folder Legal Aid Society, 1931–1939.

[91] NYLAS, *Fifty-Fifth Annual Report of the Legal Aid Society of New York for the Year 1930* (New York: Manger, Hughes, and Manger, 1931), 22.

cases constituted about 10 percent of its cases; in 1939 they represented 20 percent.[92] Rather than lamenting its role in the dissolution of families, the New York society boasted of its new and modern attitude toward divorce and condemned its own former "conservatism."[93] Its officers now admitted that "limited facilities" was an excuse for their earlier moralistic stance.[94] In Chicago, public relief agencies referred clients seeking a divorce to the Legal Aid Bureau, and at times even paid their court costs.[95] Many social workers and lawyers in legal aid now understood that failed male breadwinners could be a hindrance to family well-being. This recognition contrasted with other societal forces that attempted to prop up the male breadwinner ideal and return working women to the home.[96]

By the late 1930s, as social workers, women lawyers, and progressive male lawyers gained power within NALAO, the organization made it a priority to convince legal aid organizations to adopt more liberal divorce policies. A survey conducted by NALAO in the early 1930s explained: "The number of persons who seek assistance from legal aid organizations in divorce actions is very great, although the number of cases in which pleadings are filed and relief sought for clients through court actions is very small. One organization reported twenty-one court actions in the past *five years*; another 127; and another sixty."[97] NALAO found such numbers unacceptably small and sought to change the norms and framework governing legal aid lawyers' and organizations' approach to divorce. Attorney Ruth Miner, then the sole woman on NALAO's executive committee, suggested that legal aid organizations be urged, even ordered, not to refuse divorce cases.[98] Instead of asking whether it was ever appropriate for a legal aid organization to take a divorce case, Joel Hunter queried whether legal aid should ever *refuse* divorce cases when appropriate legal grounds existed. He implied that there was no valid reason to treat divorce cases differently from other cases.[99]

---

[92] NALAO, *Legal Aid News Letter* 8 (August 1, 1934): 3, Wigmore Papers, box 93, folder 5.

[93] NYLAS, *Ten Years of the Legal Aid Society 1927 to 1937*, 2.

[94] Ibid.

[95] UCC, "Memorandum Regarding Services of the Legal Aid Bureau in Securing Divorces for the Clients of Public Agencies," April 20, 1934, UCC Papers, box 40, folder 6.

[96] On such tensions see Abelson, "'Women Who Have No Men,'" 117–18.

[97] NALAO, *Reports of Committees, 1931–1932*, 44 (emphasis in original).

[98] NALAO, "Minutes of the Meeting of the Executive Committee," in *Reports of Committees, 1931–1932* (Rochester, NY: NALAO, 1932), 11.

[99] Ibid.

Despite this changed outlook, even progressive organizations still would not accept divorce cases simply because a potential client wanted a divorce. Almost all legal aid agencies, including the Chicago Legal Aid Bureau, required "social necessity," and social workers were the ones who made this determination.[100] In imposing the social-necessity requirement, the organizations treated divorce differently from every other legal claim. The dual authority of lawyers and social workers over divorce – something that early women's legal aid groups and then social workers had fought for – created two gatekeepers, as a lawyer and a social worker had to agree that a case should be accepted. Moreover, requiring social necessity resulted in a lack of uniformity among legal aid organizations, and even within the same organization, as what constituted social necessity in any individual case was highly subjective.[101]

Social necessity was a remarkably malleable concept, and during the 1930s it expanded to cover children born of a father who was not the (often long-departed) husband of the mother, mental or physical abuse, and desertion by a spouse. It could even include a wife's sense of emotional well-being and security. Some social workers began to view divorce as a potentially transformative event that could increase the welfare of mothers and children. In 1939 Mary Isham, a social worker with the San Francisco Legal Aid Bureau, wrote about the positive outcomes of divorce, including "escape from a tense home atmosphere," "mental release from the presence of a violent and fearsome person," "establishment of security and stability in the home," and "re-establishment of the self-respect of the woman."[102] Isham's report showed that some social workers considered domestic violence, even the fear of violence, as grounds for a legal aid organization to accept a divorce case. In an even greater rupture with the past, family stability was viewed as possible without a husband, and social workers began to talk about the importance of a wife's self-respect. Now divorce could be a narrative of new beginnings rather than a tragedy.[103] When the Chicago Legal Aid Bureau helped one woman divorce from

---

[100] Florence Nesbitt, "Bulletin No. 407: Regarding Services of the Legal Aid Bureau in Securing Divorces for the Clients of Public Agencies," April 20, 1934, UCC Papers, box 40, folder 16.

[101] See, e.g., NALAO, *Records of Proceeding at the Annual Meeting 1941–1942* (Rochester, NY: NALAO, 1942), 90.

[102] Mary Isham, "A Social Worker in a Legal Aid Society," *Annals of the American Academy of Political and Social Science* 205 (September 1939): 136.

[103] Alex Elson, "Divorce: A Study in Co-operation between Family Welfare Agencies and Legal Aid Bureaus," *Family* 16 (March 1935): 19–23.

her alcoholic husband, her son made a telling remark: "We aren't like gypsies anymore."[104] Divorce had allowed his mother to create a modest but stable home for her children.

This fresh approach to divorce, and NALAO's consistent urging, compelled at least some legal aid organizations to critically examine their policies on divorce. The Chicago Legal Aid Bureau became concerned that it was rejecting too many divorce cases because of lack of social necessity, prompting it to launch a study of all its rejected divorce cases between 1933 and 1936 to determine if any pattern emerged.[105] The bureau now recommended that its social workers interpret social necessity to include any positive development that might result from a divorce.[106] It further clarified its position on why social necessity existed at all: "It is impossible for Legal Aid to secure divorces in all cases where it is desirable and the Divorce Committee chose those where it is most urgent."[107] This change in definition challenged two former assumptions: first, that the divorces that it did not accept were those cases brought by selfish women, and second, that divorce itself was immoral. The bureau recognized a wide spectrum of need in divorce cases. Social necessity now meant balancing the applicant's urgency and the organization's resources. It was a question of funds, not morals. This, of course, was not an entirely valid explanation, as the bureau never examined a claimant's urgency or lack thereof in cases involving wage claims. How the organization used its resources revealed its priorities. The Legal Aid Society of New York conceded this point when it examined its own divorce policy and questioned why some types of cases received priority and others did not.[108] Although the rationale would change, legal aid providers' liberalization of the handling of divorce continued through World War II as soldiers and their wives sought to divorce.

During World War II, patriotism and war shaped legal aid services, its ideology, availability, and its definition of a worthy client. Depression-era conflicts between NALAO and bar associations receded as the ABA, NALAO, the Red Cross, and the Armed Forces worked to ensure that every serviceman and his dependents had access to some form of free legal aid. Legal aid organizations began to describe their work as part

[104] Ibid., 21.
[105] UCC, "Meeting of District Supervisors," November 9, 1936, UCC Papers, box 40, folder 6, 2–3.
[106] Ibid.
[107] Ibid.
[108] NYLAS, *Ten Years of the Legal Aid Society 1927 to 1937*, 2.

of the larger war effort, and many sought to relax or suspend eligibility requirements. For the first time, access to civil legal aid came close to being a legal right to which the soldier and his family were entitled. A corollary was that, by helping soldiers and their families, legal aid lawyers were no longer engaging in "charity" but were fulfilling their "patriotic duty."[109]

The Soldiers' and Sailors' Civil Relief Act of 1940 suspended enforcement of certain types of civil actions against servicemen.[110] Specifically, servicemen and their dependents could not be evicted summarily by landlords, and the act limited banks' ability to foreclose on homes and lenders' ability to enforce default provisions in installment contracts. Such proceedings were stayed automatically unless a court ordered them to go forward. The act also applied to dependents of men in the military, thereby providing many legal aid clients the ability to at least slow down the suits of lenders and landlords.[111]

Yet NALAO did not always support legislation intended to benefit the families, especially the wives, of soldiers. It opposed certain provisions in the Soldiers' and Sailors' Relief Act and the Servicemen's Dependents Allowance Act of 1942, both of which aided wives of servicemen because they automatically allotted enlisted mens' pay to their wives.[112] In contrast to past practice and especially earlier women's legal aid organizations (which emphasized a husband's financial responsibility to provide for women and children), NALAO opposed automatic allotments. It argued that "undeserving wives" who had abandoned or been unfaithful to their husbands might receive such benefits.[113]

The desire to protect servicemen also played off a fear of "Allotment Annies," women who married multiple servicemen in order to receive their allotments.[114] Although Allotment Annies were more misogynistic

---

[109] NALAO, *Reports of Committees 1942–1943* (Rochester, NY: NALAO, 1943), B-7.

[110] Article I, Section 100, of the Soldiers' and Sailors' Civil Relief Act of 1940, 50 U.S.C. App. § 501 (1940).

[111] See Karl R. Bendetson, "A Discussion of the Soldiers' and Sailors' Civil Relief Act of 1940," *Washington and Lee Law Review* 2 (1940): 10.

[112] NALAO, *Committee Reports and Proceedings 1941–1942* (Rochester, NY: NALAO, 1942), B-7; see the Servicemen's Dependents Allowance Act of 1942, 37 U.S.C. § 201 et seq. (1942); Doris Weatherford, *American Women during World War II: An Encyclopedia* (New York: Routledge, 2010), 19–20.

[113] NALAO, *Committee Reports and Proceedings 1941–1942* (Rochester, NY: NALAO, 1942), B-7.

[114] Ann Pfau, "Allotment Annies and Other Wayward Wives: Wartime Concerns about Female Disloyalty and the Problem of the Returned Veteran," in *The United States and the Second World War: New Perspectives on Diplomacy, War, and the Home Front*, ed. G. Kurt Piehler and Sidney Nash (New York: Fordham University Press, 2010).

fantasy than reality, the presumed need to protect soldiers from such women further liberalized legal aid organizations' divorce criteria for men and women alike; that is, it was believed that servicemen should be able to divorce wives who took unfair advantage of their military benefits. Divorce had previously been a woman's remedy, but now it was positioned as a remedy for the heroic husband and serviceman.[115]

Despite such rhetoric, the reality was that servicemen and their wives brought a wide array of domestic relations cases to legal aid, including cases that involved adoption, marriage, and divorce. At the Legal Aid Society of New York, domestic relations cases were the single largest category of cases, with the number of divorces dramatically rising from the prewar years.[116] At the war's beginning, families may have tried to formalize existing family arrangements, as military benefits created an incentive to do so.[117] Wives' allotments from their husbands' pay, death benefits, and pensions, as well as inheritance laws, made divorce and legal remarriage increasingly crucial for couples who may have long resided together but remained legally married to others. All of these people needed access to lawyers. As the war continued, it had a destabilizing effect as old families disintegrated and new families were created. The Legal Aid Society of Minneapolis explained, "We have been called upon in such widely varied situations as the problem of attempting to secure divorces for soldiers on overseas duty to the problem of working out a method of contracting a valid marriage between a soldier in North Africa and a prospective bride in Minneapolis."[118]

One might expect that legal aid's association with patriotism, the war effort, and the armed services, and the new emphasis on protecting soldiers from scheming women, would have masculinized legal aid. This was not the case. The reality was that legal aid organizations' clients

---

[115] On the symbol of the American GI, patriotism, citizenship, and entitlements, see James Sparrow, *Warfare State: World War II Americans and the Age of Big Government* (New York: Oxford University Press, 2011).

[116] NYLAS, *Statistical Supplement to the Sixty-Eighth Annual Report of the Legal Aid Society for the Year 1943* (New York, 1944), 4. In general, marriage rates rose between 1940 and 1941 and peaked in 1942. Divorce rates increased from 1940 to 1946 and then declined in 1947. Between 1930 and 1946 divorce rates more than doubled. Eliza Pavalko and Glen Elder, "World War II and Divorce: A Life Course Perspective," *American Journal of Sociology* 95 (March 1990): 1213–34, 1215. See also Sparrow, *Warfare State*, 115–17.

[117] On the role of military benefits and the creation of a welfare state, see Theda Skocpol, *Protecting Soldiers and Mothers: The Political Origins of Social Policy in the United States* (Cambridge, MA: Belknap Press of Harvard University Press, 1995).

[118] Legal Aid Society of Minneapolis, *Annual Report – 1942*, 3–4, United Way of Minn. Records, box 205, folder Legal Aid Society Annual Reports and Bulletins.

were often soldiers' wives and mothers, and it was women lawyers who provided them with such services.[119]

For some legal aid organizations, attracting women as clients was a deliberate and conscious strategy during the war. In 1944, the host of the Chicago radio program *For Women Only* introduced Marguerite Raeder Gariepy, head attorney of the Chicago Legal Aid Bureau, following a cooking segment on the differences among roasting, broiling, blanching, and sautéing. Gariepy explained that legal aid had originated with the Chicago Women's Club and its Protective Agency for Women and Children. She emphasized that she was the supervising attorney and that her legal staff consisted of seven women attorneys and three male attorneys, all of whom worked closely with social workers. She described one case involving a poor elderly woman whose Victory Garden was destroyed by a neighboring building's fumigation. The ten-dollar settlement that the woman received meant a great deal to her financially and symbolically, Gariepy stressed, and then she moved on to the bureau's procurement of divorces, and relief from creditors.[120]

Likewise, Chicago newspapers regularly published articles about and photographs depicting the bureau's women attorneys providing legal advice to soldiers' families. One article discussed a woman and her three children, whose beds were repossessed by lenders while the husband was serving in the Navy. Attorney Irene McCormick won the case in court under the Soldiers' and Sailors' Civil Relief Act.[121] Another photo captured Mrs. Virginia Smith, the mother of two sons in the Marines, with her lawyer, Frances D. Brown; Smith was seeking advice regarding benefits for two younger sons who were still at home.[122] A third image showed Gariepy working with Mrs. Burn, whose husband was in the Canadian air force. She had turned to the bureau for help in filling out papers that would allow her to receive compensation from the Canadian government that would help support her two children.[123]

These photographs showed women seeking benefits based on their status as mothers or wives of servicemen and are quite different from earlier images depicting well-kept but clearly poor women. In the World

[119] On gender and soldiers benefits during World War II, see Suzanne Mettler, *Soldiers to Citizens: The G.I. Bill and the Making of the Greatest Generation* (New York: Oxford University Press, 2005).

[120] Transcript of *For Women Only*, January 27, 1944, UCC Papers, box 42, folder 1.

[121] Martha Jane Smith, "Legal Aid Saves Grief for Soldiers," *Chicago Daily Times*, May 11, 1942, UCC Papers, box 42, folder 1.

[122] Untitled newspaper photograph, May 11, 1942, UCC Papers, box 42, folder 1.

[123] "Aid for Service Wives," *Chicago Daily Times*, May 11, 1942, UCC Papers, box 42, folder 1.

War II–era photographs, the bureau's women clients are well dressed, and the relationship between the client and attorney appears as one between equals. Attorney Frances Brown and her client, Virginia Smith, sit side by side at a table; together they are absorbed in the case.[124] Only the caption informs the reader which woman is the client. These newspaper photographs show clients who were neither the male independent bread-winners imagined by some lawyers nor the naïve and innocent women earlier depicted by women's legal aid organizations. Rather, they were female citizens who were now entitled to legal assistance – not by virtue of their poverty and helplessness but because of their relationship to the state. Likewise, it was the woman attorney who protected women and children on the domestic front.

Another photograph taken during this period is particularly striking and complex (Plate 6). It depicts attorney Edna Brown strolling through the Chicago Legal Aid Bureau's waiting room, where three fashionable white women, one with a beautifully dressed baby, sit waiting their turn to speak with an attorney. In the background, facing away from the camera and segregated in a corner, are two African American women applicants or clients, dressed neatly but more modestly than either Brown or the three white women.[125] This photograph shows that the bureau accepted African American clients, although they were not its primary focus.[126]

While the two African American women sit alone in semidarkness, the white women occupy and illuminate center stage, each perhaps repre-senting a different female stereotype. The first woman, dressed in a cloth coat and comfortable shoes, represents the working woman, perhaps a waitress or a factory worker. The second woman is clothed more elabo-rately. Sporting a hat and heels, and striking a confident pose, she seems to represent the single woman, perhaps an office worker or a sales clerk. The third woman is simply dressed and holds a baby on her lap. As she looks at the child, she conveys a sense of concern and worry; perhaps she is a mother seeking advice regarding a domestic relations problem.

[124] Smith, "Legal Aid Saves Grief for Soldiers," UCC Papers, box 42, folder 1.
[125] "Poor Man's Portia," *Chicago Daily News*, November 20, 1943, 4, UCC Papers, box 42, folder 1, photograph no. ICHi-68715, Chicago History Museum.
[126] Even in the South, legal aid organizations increasingly served African Americans. By 1944, African Americans comprised 47 percent of the clients of the Legal Aid Society of Atlanta. In addition, a woman was the head attorney for the society, as was the case in New Orleans. "Mrs. Dwyer Heads Atlanta Legal Aid Society for 1944," *Atlanta Daily World*, February 3, 1944, 2; "Mary Pallotta Counsel with Legal Aid Unit," *Atlanta Daily World*, October 5, 1949, 3.

These World War II–era newspaper photographs depict clients who appear content with the legal assistance provided to them. But from extant archival sources it is difficult, if not impossible, to know how most clients experienced their encounters with legal aid. Were clients' objectives fulfilled? Did they perceive that lawyers condescended to them or listened to them? Did they care whether an attorney was a man or a woman? Did they believe that law had the ability to deliver justice? Was a lawyer able to put them at ease, or did they leave the legal aid office full of worry that their problems could not be solved? Were questions such as these even important to them?

Clients' letters give a fleeting impression that at least some of the women who received legal assistance from the Chicago Legal Aid Bureau during the war were grateful for and satisfied with the help provided: "Last summer your Mr. Proctor handled a case between the Local Loan Company and me. It really was remarkable how fine Mr. Proctor was at all times. Cool and calm, and brought up various points, all to my advantage. . . . I feel Mr. Proctor deserves a tremendous lot of praise."[127] Another client, Henrietta Wilson, wrote, "This is to express my sincere thanks, and to try in my most humble way to express my gratitude & appreciation. You have made possible the happiest Xmas I've known for me & my two children. . . . May God Bless you and may you live long to carry on your good work for people like me."[128] Emma Ware wrote in 1945, "Thank to you and Legal Aid Bureau fore your Kind[ness]. I have received my $25.50 and many thank to you. I wont fore get you."[129] Another woman, who received assistance from the bureau in connection with the adoption of a child, wrote, "We want to thank you . . . for your tireless efforts and your patience all those months and the unlimited help you have given to us."[130] Client after client wrote letters such as these, although whether such appreciation and satisfaction was the norm is impossible to say.

From the Depression through the end of World War II, the provision of legal aid changed dramatically. Women, either as social workers or as lawyers – were increasingly assimilated into the provision of legal aid.

[127] Alice E. Kossenjons to Legal Aid Bureau, December 15, 1944, UCC Papers, box 42, folder 1.
[128] Mrs. Henrietta Wilson to Attorney Arthur K. Young, December 21, 1944, UCC Papers, box 42, folder 1.
[129] Emma Ware to Mrs. B. Schieble, April 3, 1945, UCC Papers, box 42, folder 1.
[130] Mildred Patsones to Mrs. M. J. Warning, April 2, 1950, UCC Papers, box 42, folder 1.

Together, lawyers and social workers assisted clients applying for a variety of New Deal benefit programs and served as intermediaries between the client and the state, working to puzzle out the contours of eligibility for such programs. At other times they challenged the programs' denial of benefits. Just as important, social workers came close to being treated as the professional equals of lawyers rather than their assistants. The Depression and World War II also separated legal aid from poverty, while simultaneously situating legal aid as an integral part of social welfare. This reformulation occurred while the newly poor, often homeowners, made use of legal services, and legal aid organizations struggled to differentiate their work from the private practice of law. The closest analogy to legal aid became other forms of social welfare, not the private practice of law.

The war further distanced legal aid from poverty as it made legal aid part of the entitlements – even rights – of soldiers and their families. The mass mobilization that accompanied the war silenced the complaints of bar associations and individual lawyers about the threat of competition from legal aid. Like much on the home front, legal aid became feminized once again, as women lawyers handled cases for female clients. Women clients brought cases involving domestic relations, and legal aid providers demonstrated a new willingness to accept these cases. By the war's end, it appeared as if a permanent truce, even a partnership, had been formed between legal aid lawyers and social workers. Yet this truce proved ephemeral.

Conclusion

By the mid-1960s many of Arthur von Briesen and Reginald Heber Smith's greatest ambitions for legal aid had been realized. President Lyndon Johnson's War on Poverty included expanding legal aid to the poor through federal grants to a variety of legal aid organizations, old and new. These programs generated debates and contestation among politicians, American Bar Association officers, state governors, Supreme Court justices, and even United States presidents.

For decades, beginning in the 1960s, Earl Johnson Jr. was in the midst of these developments as the second director of the Office of Economic Opportunity's Legal Service Program. He remained one of legal aid's greatest proponents, as well as a chronicler of its history. I eagerly awaited his three-volume history of legal aid, *To Establish Justice for All* (2014), which promised a comprehensive analysis of legal aid from the nineteenth century through the 1980s. But instead it offered the standard early history of legal aid, tracing its beginnings to the Legal Aid Society of New York, heralding Reginald Heber Smith, missing the work of women's organizations and social workers, and offering little discussion of the forty-year period between the 1920s and the 1960s. With the best of intentions, Johnson also replicated Smith's assumptions, measuring the success of legal aid according to traditional ideas of prestige and status in the legal profession, noting the Ivy League–educated lawyers, large law firms, and high-ranking politicians who worked in and supported legal aid.[1] As in the past, professional prestige in legal aid was still closely associated with masculinity.

---

[1] See Earle Johnson Jr., *To Establish Justice for All: The Past and Future of Civil Legal Aid in the United States*, vol. 1 (Santa Barbara, CA: Praeger, 2014).

Women and Justice for the Poor moves away from that standard narrative and demonstrates how a multitude of actors with diverse agendas and institutional interests – men and women, lay lawyers, social workers, and professional lawyers – created and then fought for control over legal aid. Much of the heterodoxy associated with legal aid ended after World War II. In 1945, the National Association of Legal Aid Organizations counted a total of 142 legal aid organizations in operation nationwide, including 32 independent legal aid societies, 16 departments of social service agencies, 55 volunteer bar committees, and 4 public bureaus.[2] Smith's vision of legal aid was gaining ground: even when a legal aid organization was associated with a social service agency, its staff members were mostly lawyers. Those few social workers who were still part of a legal aid organization worked primarily on domestic relations cases. By the late 1950s, NALAO had found its place beside bar associations, its leadership interchangeable with that of the ABA.[3] Legal aid was now firmly situated in the world of professional lawyers.

At this point, lawyers again began demonizing social workers. Calling up old misogynies, male leaders of legal aid criticized social workers as meddling women.[4] One legal aid attorney compared social workers with nurses who, even with medical training, did not have the authority to write prescriptions.[5] Raynor Gardiner, general counsel of the Legal Aid Society of Boston and longtime executive officer of NALAO, labeled social workers "monstrosities" and claimed: "Our clients do not wish to see a social worker. They are thoroughly washed up with social workers."[6] Such condemnation of social workers who provided legal assistance paralleled lawyers' fight for control of legal aid in the 1920s.

---

[2] NALAO, *1945 Committee Reports and Proceedings of NALAO* (Rochester, NY: 1945), A-5.

[3] The National Association of Legal Aid Organizations went through a number of name changes.

[4] On misogyny in the years of the Cold War, see Elaine Tyler May, *Homeward Bound: American Families in the Cold War Era* (New York: Basic Books, 1988); Daniel Horowitz, *Betty Friedan and the Feminine Mystique: The American Left, the Cold War, and Modern Feminism* (Amherst: University of Massachusetts Press, 1998). On social workers during the Cold War, see Karen M. Tani, "Securing a Right to Welfare: Public Assistance and the Rule of Law, 1935–1965," PhD diss., University of Pennsylvania, 2011; Daniel J. Walkowitz, *Working with Class: Social Workers and the Politics of Middle-Class Identity* (Chapel Hill: University of North Carolina Press, 1999).

[5] NALAO, *Committee Reports and Proceedings of NALAO* (Rochester, NY: NALAO, 1947), B-12–13.

[6] National Legal Aid and Defenders Association, *Proceedings of the Annual Conference, National Legal Aid and Defenders Association* (Chicago, 1953), 86.

One reason that NALAO had earlier learned to tolerate social workers was that philanthropic organizations interested in social work and social reform, such as the Russell Sage Foundation, had provided funding. In the period after World War II the Russell Sage Foundation went through dramatic changes, with elite attorney Eli Whitney Debovoise – who had been on the board of directors of the Legal Aid Society of New York – presiding over its restructuring. The much smaller foundation, now with a male board of directors, downplayed social work and made medicine and law its prime areas of focus, thus removing the funding incentive that had prompted NALAO to court social workers.[7]

The field of social work underwent changes as well. Freudian psychology became the dominant approach to understanding human behavior, and social reform faded into the background. Increasingly, social workers identified, diagnosed, and treated their clients' individual pathologies. As a result, many social workers came to view women who required assistance with domestic problems as neurotics with personality disorders. Other social workers became bureaucrats, gatekeepers to welfare benefits who strictly policed the behavior of their female beneficiaries.[8]

Even the Chicago Legal Aid Bureau worked to sever legal aid from social work, viewing social workers as conservative and rule bound – an accusation that social workers had previously directed at lawyers. Divorce was the lone area in which social workers and lawyers continued to collaborate. By the mid-1950s, the Chicago Legal Aid Bureau's attorneys sought to discard the requirement that a social worker find "social necessity" in order to accept a divorce case. These lawyers explained that the requirement violated clients' "equal protection rights," because those who could afford a private attorney did not have to meet a similar precondition.[9] The bureau not only eliminated the requirement but also removed social workers from making legal determinations of any sort.

[7] David C. Hammack and Stanton Wheeler, *Social Science in the Making: Essays on the Russell Sage Foundation, 1907–1972* (New York: Russell Sage Foundation, 1994), 87–93.

[8] Walkowitz, *Working with Class*; Linda Gordon, *Heroes of Their Own Lives: The Politics and History of Family Violence* (New York: Penguin Books, 1988); Eileen Boris and Jenifer Klein, *Caring for America: Home Health Workers in the Shadow of the Welfare State* (New York: Oxford University Press, 2012).

[9] "Report of Cases Handled by the Legal Aid Bureau of United Charities of Chicago under Procedures Approved by the Legal Aid Committee of United Charities," October 7, 1958, United Charities of Chicago Papers, folder Legal Aid Bureau, 1958–1961, Chicago History Museum (hereinafter UCC Papers).

New procedures provided that lawyers or law students – not social workers – should conduct all intake interviews. In addition, social workers were no longer to determine whether applicants were eligible for legal aid. Even offering a referral to an outside lawyer was a function reserved for the bureau's lawyers.[10] A Legal Aid Bureau memorandum explained the change with nonchalance: "The social worker feels more comfortable operating in her area of competence. She is relieved of the responsibility of making the decision as to whether [the bureau] should handle the case."[11]

The postwar period also saw the retirement of leading women attorneys who had spent most of their careers in legal aid. Marguerite Raeder Gariepy retired after twenty-five years as an attorney with the Chicago bureau, and her fellow bureau attorney, Irene McCormick, resigned after twenty-one years.[12] Marjorie Hurd, the first women attorney hired by the Legal Aid Society of Boston, who began her career at Boston's Women's Educational and Industrial Union, retired after thirty-five years. These women had not complained publicly about their lack of mobility in their jobs; they were "firsts" who had supervised large legal aid societies, including staffs of male lawyers, and who had devoted their entire careers to such work. Their departures, however, further severed the institutional links between lawyers and social workers, and erased the institutional memory of women's role in legal aid.

It is tempting to argue that the conservatism and domesticity of the 1950s diminished the ranks of women working as providers of legal aid, but the reality is less clear. One scholar of legal aid calls the staffs of postwar legal aid organizations "demographically bizarre." Women lawyers constituted little more than 3 percent of practicing lawyers in Chicago in 1950, yet in 1955 eight of the fourteen lawyers employed by the Chicago bureau were women. Even more exceptional was the fact that three African American women lawyers worked for the bureau in the early 1950s, for they represented approximately 33 percent of the city's African American women lawyers.[13] Forty-eight years after Rosalie Loew

---

[10] Ibid., 14. See also United Charities of Chicago, "Bulletin No. 281," November 20, 1957, folder Legal Aid Bureau, UCC Papers.

[11] "Report of Cases Handled by the Legal Aid Bureau of United Charities of Chicago under Procedures Approved by the Legal Aid Committee of United Charities."

[12] Grace H. Harte, "Women's Bar: Personal Views and Notes," *Chicago Law Bulletin*, November 23, 1945.

[13] Jack Katz, *Poor People's Lawyers in Transition* (New Brunswick, NJ: Rutgers University Press, 1982), 48. See also Marina Zaloznaya and Laura Beth Nielsen, "Mechanisms and

left the Legal Aid Society of New York, Mary Tarcher was appointed in 1951 to serve as the society's acting head attorney, the second woman to hold that position. Moreover, seven out of seventeen NYLAS attorneys were women, and domestic relations matters still made up the largest category of cases.[14] Although scholars have seen this period as marking the marginalization of women lawyers, legal aid organizations were in fact remarkably diverse in the 1950s. Yet when a cadre of new lawyers came to legal aid in the 1960s, they must have seen such staffing as another indication that legal aid was a professional backwater that held little interest for ambitious male lawyers.[15]

Perhaps one of the largest differences between early women's legal aid organizations and postwar legal aid organizations was the unwillingness or inability of later legal aid lawyers to listen to clients' stories. As I learned in New Orleans after Hurricane Katrina, listening to people's narratives was crucial to their capacity to regain a sense of control – something that women's legal aid organizations had long recognized. In contrast, in 1945 one legal aid lawyer advised that "the responsibility of the attorney is to allow the client enough conversation to tell the essential facts, and as much more as will be required to reasonably satisfy him, and at the same time, not to permit too much time to be consumed."[16] Other legal aid lawyers counseled that client interviews should not exceed five or ten minutes. A few were more draconian, such as the one who used a variety of watches and clocks in his office and attempted to limit client appointments to three to five minutes.[17] Legal aid lawyers complained about the "bulk handling" of routine cases that legal aid work required, but what constituted routine for the lawyers was not routine for most clients.[18]

Continuities and discontinuities also existed in regard to the kinds of claims that dominated in legal aid organizations' caseloads. Wage and domestic relations cases had long been the two largest categories, but

Consequences of Professional Marginality: The Case of Poverty Lawyers Revisited," *Law and Social Inquiry* 36 (Fall 2011): 919–44.

[14] See, e.g., NYLAS, *Eighty-Fourth Annual Report of the Legal Aid Society of New York for the Year 1959* (New York, 1960); *Seventieth Annual Report of the Legal Aid Society of New York for the Year 1945* (New York, 1946).

[15] Johnson, *Justice and Reform*, 6–14.

[16] NALAO, *Committee Reports and Proceedings of NALAO 1947* (Rochester, NY: NALAO, 1947), A-43.

[17] Ibid., B-13.

[18] See Katz, *Poor People's Lawyers in Transition*; Zaloznaya and Nielsen, "Mechanisms and Consequences of Professional Marginality."

wage claims dropped dramatically, in part because of new federal and state labor laws and the states' ability to prosecute employers for labor violations. Now, across legal aid organizations, domestic relations claims became the largest category of cases. In 1959 the Legal Aid Society of New York handled almost 13,000 domestic relations cases out of a total of 40,478 cases.[19] As in the past, legal aid leaders seldom publicly discussed this fact.

Long-standing issues involving legal aid, lay lawyers, and the reproduction of hierarchy continued to be themes that occupied legal aid after the 1960s. The civil rights movement led to innovations in legal aid that began with a series of neighborhood projects established in cities with large minority populations, including New Haven, Connecticut; Washington, D.C.; and New York City. These grassroots projects incorporated social workers along with lawyers, with the idea of creating one-stop neighborhood centers that offered a wide variety of social services, including legal assistance. Much like the earliest legal aid organizations, these new groups took a holistic approach to their clients' problems.[20] In New York City, for example, the organization Mobilization for Youth (MFY) focused on a variety of social issues, including housing, job creation, and welfare benefits. MFY's lawyers worked closely with social workers and community organizers in a relatively nonhierarchical fashion.[21] In many senses, this restructuring represented a return to older models, even though few of the people involved understood the history behind their actions.

These new grassroots organizations gave rise to massive changes in the conception and delivery of legal aid that occurred in the 1960s with the federal government's creation of the Office of Economic Opportunity (OEO). The OEO made millions of federal dollars in grants available to legal aid projects.[22] Lawyers within the OEO, and a new crop of young attorneys, believed that legal aid societies had long been complacent and passive.[23] These new 'lawyers envisioned aggressive, litigation-oriented

---

[19] New York Legal Aid Society, *Eighty-Forth Annual Report for the Year 1959* (New York, 1959), 3.

[20] Edgar S. Cahn and Jean C. Cahn, "The War on Poverty: A Civilian Perspective," *Yale Law Review* 73 (July 1964): 1317–52.

[21] Earl Johnson Jr., *Justice and Reform: The Formative Years of the OEO Legal Services Program* (New York: Russell Sage Foundation, 1974); Tamar Carroll, *Mobilizing New York: Community Activism from the War on Poverty through the AIDS Epidemic* (Chapel Hill: University of North Carolina Press, 2015).

[22] Johnson, *Justice and Reform*, 43, 49–50.

[23] Katz, *Poor People's Lawyers in Transition*, 40–41; Johnson, *Justice and Reform*, 46–47.

cases that would dismantle the inequalities that kept the poor entrenched in poverty. Simultaneously, the federal government and others saw legal aid as a way to address injustice and popular discontent and thus perhaps avoid more radical collective action, especially on the part of minorities.[24]

From its inception, however, the OEO was mired in conflict. The OEO's director, Sargent Shriver, announced in 1964 that he intended to create "supermarkets" of social services that would include legal assistance, mirroring what was already occurring on the grassroots level. This announcement fueled a firestorm within the ABA and other professional organizations, which complained that OEO "lawyers would be working under non-lawyers and as just another social service, not as members of an honored and licensed profession."[25] The possibility that nonlawyers would supervise lawyers provoked claims that such laypeople would be engaging in the unauthorized practice of law.[26]

The OEO Legal Services Program (OEO-LSP), like NALAO before it, soon concluded that legal aid needed the support of the established bar. The ABA eventually agreed to support the OEO-LSP in exchange for control of its advisory board, and with the understanding that lawyers would be in charge of all OEO legal services programs. Earl Johnson Jr. writes that the reaction by lawyers to the mere possibility of lay control was "almost violent" and that the "bar took the position that legal services programs should be free from lay control locally, regionally, and nationally."[27] Reginald Heber Smith had taken a similar stance more than forty years earlier.

Such arguments served to veil a move toward further professional monopolization and legal autonomy and hampered community participation. Laypeople had a long history of providing legal aid, but this history had been buried and thus could not serve as precedent. Likewise, lawyers in the OEO-LSP even refused to submit to the control of other parts of the OEO.[28] When OEO leaders proposed such a structure, the ABA quickly intervened, charging that having nonlawyers supervise lawyers would be a breach of the ABA and OEO's gentlemen's agreement: "We had to represent to lawyers and we did represent to lawyers ... that this was going to be a professional program, run by lawyers. Lawyers were going to be

---

[24] Johnson, *To Establish Justice*, 149.

[25] Ibid., 69

[26] Johnson, *Justice and Reform*, 50.

[27] Ibid., 154; Alan Houseman, "Political Lessons: Legal Services for the Poor – A Commentary," *Georgetown Law Journal* 83 (April 1995): 1669, 1674.

[28] Johnson, *To Establish Justice*, 182–5.

on top of it. . . . And, up and down the line, lawyers would be running the Program."[29] Reporting to nonlawyers or even cooperating with them, the ABA argued, would prevent the recruitment of the best lawyers, because no attorney worth his salt would accept having his judgment or priorities questioned by a layperson.[30]

The OEO was particularly interested in test cases that involved innovative constitutional arguments for creating new rights for the poor. Such litigation was well suited for the ambitious, aggressive, and idealistic men from the best law schools that the OEO recruited into its "Reggie" fellowship program, named after Reginald Heber Smith.[31] The recruitment program was intended to resemble that of a large law firm, with a goal of creating "Wall Street lawyers for the poor."[32] Unsurprisingly, the OEO often selected men with the highest grades from Ivy League law schools, or from large corporate law firms, to receive Reggie fellowships and new legal aid positions, making it increasingly difficult for women and minorities to be hired by legal aid organizations.[33] Counterintuitively, as the women's right movement and feminism were gaining traction, the proportion of women lawyers in legal aid declined in the mid-1960s and early 1970s.[34] The assumption that a combination of top law schools, high grades, law review positions, and prestigious federal clerkships made elite male lawyers particularly suitable to be legal aid attorneys, or that Wall Street law firms constituted the model of success that needed to be replicated, rested on unexamined premises. The masculinization of legal aid – which had occurred in fits and starts since the turn of the century – thus continued through what is understood to be the heyday of legal aid.

The OEO favored cases involving high-impact legislation, but the reality of clients' more mundane issues often took precedence. Providers from the 1860s onward knew that as legal aid offices opened, clients would flock to them with their immediate legal problems, as well as their other needs. Young lawyers in OEO-LSP programs soon learned that the real work of legal aid was not purely legal – that legal aid lawyers often functioned as intermediaries between clients and a variety of institutions,

[29] Johnson, *Justice and Reform*, 157, citing Orison Marden, National Advisory Committee meeting, September 21, 1967.
[30] Johnson, *Justice and Reform*, 108–12.
[31] Katz, *Poor People's Lawyers in Transition*, 68.
[32] Johnson, *Justice for All*, 119–20, 140, 149.
[33] Cynthia Fuchs Epstein, *Women in Law* (Urbana: University of Illinois Press, 1994), 124.
[34] Katz estimates that the proportion of women among legal aid lawyers went from 35 percent to 12 percent. Katz, *Poor People's Lawyers in Transition*, 71.

including community organizations, schools, businesses, and government agencies.[35] The OEO-LSP had committed itself to projects that were purely legal, but in actuality, real clients needed more than pure law. As legal aid lawyers learned, and as I discovered at the disaster recovery center in New Orleans, poor people needed help from those who can flexibly perform a variety of roles.

Many scholars, commentators, and legal professionals recognize that the bar, legal aid, and legal education are currently in crisis. Law schools produce thousands of graduates each year, but enormous legal and social needs remain unmet. To address these needs, we must rethink what it means to be a lawyer, as well as who has legal skills, what constitutes a legal problem, and what legal aid encompasses. Our answers to these questions are not preordained but socially constructed; they are the result of a nonlinear history that involved many individual actors and institutions and played out over decades.

The long and rich history of nonlawyers providing legal assistance to the poor was buried by those who wished to rewrite it. Women lay lawyers and social workers represented a threat to lawyers, particularly in how some saw justice as based in substance rather than procedure. As women lay lawyers in the past understood, legal need could not be separated from the other needs of the poor – whether for funds, housing, food, or the benefit of telling stories and having someone listen. Many legal aid organizations today understand this truth in theory, but true cooperation, equal partnership, and cross-training among professionals remains rare. As we go about rethinking the legal profession we must remember that even with lawyers' repeated attempts to prevent others from providing legal advice, lawyers have not had and do not have a true monopoly over what we imagine to be the practice of law.[36]

The story in this book could be told only by looking at the history of legal aid from a different perspective and placing different protagonists, women lay lawyers and social workers, at its center. This required unraveling the canon on the history of legal aid. Women were expelled from both the *practice* of legal aid and then the *writing* of its history. Using the rich body of scholarship on women's organizations, along with

---

[35] See, e.g., Katz, *Poor People's Lawyers in Transition*, 67–68; Johnson, *Justice and Reform*, 97–99.

[36] Deborah L. Rhode and Lucy Buford Ricca, "Protecting the Profession or the Public? Rethinking Unauthorized-Practice Enforcement," *Fordham Law Review* 82 (2014): 2587–610; Jack Sahl, "Cracks in the Profession's Monopoly Armor," *Fordham Law Review* 82 (2014): 2635–63.

new archival documents, I have interrogated the fields of women's history and legal history from a new angle, with the goal of ending the intellectual segregation that dominates legal history. When we do not question underlying assumptions, legal history appears to be populated primarily by male actors. We thus assume that there were few women legal aid providers, or that women reformers were engaged in politics, reform, or the creation of a civic sphere unrelated to law, or even that historians of women have already explored and answered all of the necessary questions. When we expand our frame of reference, a multitude of actors we did not expect to see become fundamental to our understanding of legal institutions and legal history. At the very least, they may change the stories that we choose tell and illuminate a past that sheds light on the present.

Index

ABA (American Bar Association), 150–53, 191, 200, 221–22
Abbott, Edith, 131–32, 133n42
Abelson, Elaine, 185n2
Addams, Jane, 53, 72, 131, 141–42
Adler, Felix, 72n135
African Americans: domestic labor and, 23, 117n142, 119–22, 144; Draft Riots and, 20–21; as lawyers, 11, 178, 193, 218–19; legal aid and, 10–11, 62, 68–69, 83, 162–63, 177–79, 190–94, 212; sterilization laws and, 162–63. *See also* race and racialization
"Allotment Annies," 209–10
American Association for Organizing Family Social Workers, 181n100
American Association of Law Schools, 183
American Seaman's Friend Society, 101
Anthony, Susan B., 19, 50n12
anti-Semitism, 92, 93n23, 95–96. *See also* Jews and Jewishness
Arthur, Helen, 115n134
assimilationism, 91–100, 104, 120–22, 139, 172
Associated Charities of Columbia, 165
Associated Charities of Knoxville, 165
Association of the Bar of the City of New York, 12, 88
Atlanta, 191n28, 212n126
Atlantic World, 193

bar associations: legal aid's services and, 8, 68–69, 81–84, 143–44, 147–48, 150–53,

159–60, 174–84, 199–201, 201n72, 216, 222; New Deal programs and, 199; race and racialization issues in, 190–94; unauthorized practice of law claims of, 176, 183, 200–4, 221; women's relation to, 5–6, 9–10, 17
Barthleme, Mary, 132
Basch, Norma, 33n75
Batlan, Felice, 1–3, 223
Beach, Moses S., 20
Bignall, Louise, 165
BLAS (Legal Aid Society of Boston), 124, 126, 135–37, 136n52, 140, 148, 188, 218
BoJ (Chicago Bureau of Justice), 72–81, 90–91, 101. *See also* CLAS (Legal Aid Society of Chicago)
Boris, Eileen, 7n10
Boston Associated Charities, 136
Boston Women's Educational and Industrial Union (WEIU). *See* WEIU (Boston Women's Educational and Industrial Union)
Bowie, J. F., 138
Boyes, Maud Parcells, 82–84, 126–27, 127n13, 128–29, 132, 142
Bradway, John, 147, 147n108, 148–65, 170, 174, 181–84, 199, 203–5, 205n87
Brady, James, 21
Brandeis, Louis D., 135
Breckinridge, Sophonisba, 12, 131, 133n42, 135, 179, 179n93, 180–81, 181n100, 183

Briesen, Arthur von, 88–92, 96–99, 107–8, 115–19, 124–27, 143, 215
Brown, Caroline M., 47–48, 50–51, 54, 59–60
Brown, Edna, 212, *plates*
Brown, Frances D., 211–12, *plates*
Brown, John, 38
Bureau of Personal Service, 141, 164, 188

Caring for America (Boris and Klein), 7n10
Carle, Susan D., 7n10
Carnegie Foundation, 138–39, 142, 146–47, 150, 172
charitable organizations: community chests and, 187, 190, 192; gender and, 4, 4n3, 8–9, 36–37, 47–49; immigrants and, 91–93, 95–97; legal aid as, 4–5, 12, 20–46, 87, 128–29, 136, 138, 140–43; poverty's causes and, 129–31
Charn, Jeanne, 13
chattel mortgage cases, 51, 63, 82, 194n40
"Chicago Attorney Sets Example for Professionals" (*Atlantic World*), 193
Chicago Board of Education, 48
Chicago Bureau of Justice (BoJ). *See* BoJ (Chicago Bureau of Justice)
Chicago Legal Aid Bureau. *See* Legal Aid Bureau (Chicago)
Chicago Protective Agency for Women and Children (PAWC). *See* PAWC (Protective Agency for Women and Children)
Chicago School of Civics and Philanthropy, 131–32
Chicago Women's Club. *See* CWC (Chicago Women's Club)
Chicago Working Women's Union, 55, 55n35
Chinese Americans, 99–100
citizenship: class and, 12–13, 129–33, 144, 204, 208; immigrant disciplining and, 91–100, 104, 120–22, 139, 172; masculine ideal and, 13, 18, 22, 30, 62–64, 89, 100–6, 111, 128–31, 143–44, 149–50, 169, 197, 204–5, 209; women's legal rights and, 32, 32n72, 33, 35–38, 47–49, 111, 120, 128–29, 149–50. *See also* class; gender; race and racialization
Civil Rights Movement, 12, 132, 162, 178–79, 220
Civil War, 17, 20–21, 36–37, 50
Claghorn, Kate Holladay, 172–74, 176

CLAS (Legal Aid Society of Chicago), 10–11, 73, 81–84, 126–32, 141, 143n85, 148, 153, 169, 180–81, *plates*
class: Civil War unrest and, 17–18; community chests and, 187; domestic servant cases and, 13, 23, 114–16; gender and, 10, 20–21, 35–36, 38, 52, 54–55, 57, 59, 83–84, 108–9; *Justice and the Poor* and, 145–46; legal aid providers and, 3–4, 36–46, 66–67, 72–84, 91, 203, 220–21; morality and, 129–33, 144, 204, 208; philanthropy and, 36–46, 50; procedural justice and, 161–62; race's intersections with, 22–23, 185n2. *See also* charitable organizations; legal aid; women
Clephine, Beatrice, 190
Clisby, Harriet, 37
Cobb, Bruce, 186, 203
Cohen, Andrew, 63n85
Colcord, Joanna, 165
Cole, Rebecca, 45n134
Columbia Law Review, 146n102
Columbian Exhibition, 79, 79n160
Commission on Interracial Cooperation, 192n32
Committee on Relations with Social Service Agencies (NALAO), 166, 183
community chests, 187, 190, 192
"Complaint Day" (image), *plates*
contracts. *See* gender; law; wage claims
Cook, Carolina, 124
Cook County Bar Association, 178
Cook County Suffrage Association, 50
Cooper, Peter, 21
Coudert, Fredric, 26
coverture, 33, 33n75
Crane, Mary Potter, 68, 70
Creating a Female Dominion in American Reform (Muncy), 4n3
CWC (Chicago Women's Club), 12, 46–49, 51–52, 52n17, 79, 84, 211

Daly, Charles, 21, 21n23, 24
Darrow, Clarence, 72
Dauber, Michele Landis, 194n42
Davis, Georgina, 29, *plates*
Davis, Noah, 26
Debovoise, Eli Whitney, 217
dependence discourses, 130–31, 143–44, 149–50, 168, 185

Der Deutsche Rechts-Schutz Verein, 87–88

desertion (at sea), 102–5, 120

desertion (of wives), 63, 71, 77, 109n109, 207. *See also* divorce cases; gender; masculinity

Dillingham, Alice, 107

divorce cases, 13, 60, 64–66, 78, 81–82, 205–8, 210n116, 217–18. *See also* domestic relations cases

Domestic Employment (NYLAS), 115–18

domesticity (trope), 29–30, 64–65, 83–84, 103, 114–22

domestic relations cases: "Allotment Annies" and, 209–10; BLAS and, 136n52; BoJ and, 78; class and, 62n81; Depression's economic havoc and, 205–8; gender and, 5–6, 108–9, 126; legal aid's goals and, 13, 68–69, 125, 220; NYLAS and, 108, 111–13, 128; paternity cases and, 45; PAWC and, 62–64; social workers and, 126–27, 159, 168–69, 210; violence and, 56–58, 111, 207; WWPU and, 23–24

domestic relations courts, 7, 47–49, 53, 71, 84, 113, 113n125

domestic servants: employment agencies for, 42, 42n116; NYLAS and, 13, 114–22, 144–45; termination issues and, 41–46, 114–16; wage claims of, 13, 24, 36–46, 119–20, 144, 173

Douglas, Mildred, 196–97

Draft Riots (New York), 20

Duffy, Mary, 82

Educational Alliance, 98, 187

Equal Protection Clause (14th Amendment), 149

Errant, Joseph, 72–73, 76–77

The Family and the State (Breckinridge), 180

Family Welfare in a Metropolitan Community (Breckinridge), 180

fees (for legal aid), 44, 74, 81, 128–29, 136–37

FEMA (Federal Emergency Management Agency), 1–3

feminism, 222; PAWC and, 47–49, 54–56; substantive justice aims of, 56–63. *See also* social workers; women

Ferrer, Martha W., 28

Fisk, Annette, 107

Flexner, Abraham, 133

Flower, Lucy, 70, 79

For Women Only (program), 211

Fourteenth Amendment (to the Constitution), 10, 149

Frankfurter, Felix, 134

Freudian psychology, 217

Freund, Ernst, 181, 181n99

Friedman, Lawrence, 33n74

Friend, Ida Weis, 191, 192n32

Front Desk attorneys, 90. *See also* lawyers

Gardiner, Raynor, 216

Gariepy, Marguerite Raeder, 166–68, 175, 181n100, 183, 194, 211, 218

gender: case typologies and, 5–6, 12n26, 34–35, 39, 62–64, 114–22; charitable organizations and, 4, 4n3, 8–9, 73–75; class and, 10, 35–36, 38, 41–46, 50, 52, 54–55, 59, 83–84, 108–9, 129–31; definitions of, 8–9; domestic relations cases and, 13, 108–9, 109n109, 126, 168; domestic servants' labor and, 114–22, 173; familial economic unit and, 13, 18, 22, 29–30, 128, 130–31, 169–75, 197, 204–9; immigration and, 95–96; labor activism and, 17–36, 75; legal aid histories and, 3–10, 91, 123–27, 139–40, 159–60, 215–16; legal aid leadership and, 79, 82–84, 123, 125, 213–14; listening and, 1–3, 43, 169–70, 219; moral panic and, 21–22, 144–45; procedural *versus* substantive justice and, 7, 108, 139, 142, 157; professionalization impulses and, 4–5, 8–10, 123–25; race's intersections with, 118–19; Seaman's Branch clients and, 100–5; social workers and, 6–7, 123, 129, 133, 133n42, 149, 157–58, 160–64, 176–77, 184, 202; wage claims and, 17–18, 22, 32–46, 89, 159. *See also* bar associations; lawyers; masculinity; professions and professionalization; social workers; women

General Federation of Women's Clubs, 53, 192n32

German Society, 92

Gordon, Linda, 62n81, 169n47, 185n2

Gordon, Robert W., 30

Great Depression, 184–87, 191, 194–205, 213–14
Green Bag (journal), 127
Grossberg, Michael, 30

Hale, Robert, 138
Ham, Charles, 74–76
Harding, Warren G., 150n124
Harlem Branch (NYLAS), 119–22
Harlem Lawyers Association, 193
Harper's Monthly, 30
Harvard Law Review, 146
Hayes, Melisa, 59
HOLC (Home Owners' Loan Corporation), 195–97
Holt, Charlotte, 54, 56n37, 65, 67
Houston, Charles Hamilton, 178
Howe, Fanny, 81
Howe, Julia Ward, 37
Huggins, Macon, 193
Hughes, Charles Evans, 12, 145–46, 150, 150n124, 152
Hull House, 49, 53, 131, 135
Hunter, Joel, 71, 153, 170, 181n100, 186, 206
Hunter, Tera, 117n142
Hurd, Marjorie, 218
Hurricane Katrina, 1–3, 219, 223

Illinois State Industrial School for Girls, 50
Illinois Women's Press Association, 50
immigrants: domestic labor and, 144; legal aid's services and, 5, 62, 87–100, 172; racialization of, 34; social workers and, 176–77; WWPU and, 23
The Immigrant's Day in Court (Claghorn), 172–73, 176
Isham, Mary, 207

Jews and Jewishness: as lawyers, 107n97; legal aid and, 71; NYLAS and, 87–100; philanthropy and, 192n32; racialization of, 91n15, 120–22. *See also* anti-Semitism
Jim Crow South, 162–63
Johnson, Earl, Jr., 215
Johnson, J. Augustus, 101–2
Johnson, Lyndon B., 215
Joint Committee for the Study of Legal Aid, 175–84
Jordon, Gwen, 56n37

justice: access to, 13; definitions of, 12–13; gendered corruption and, 56–57, 209–10; procedural emphases and, 7, 12, 73–81, 105, 112, 139, 160, 175–76, 223; race and racialization and, 190–94; substantive emphases and, 7, 24, 52, 54–58, 62–63, 70, 76, 96, 142, 157, 159–75, 180, 220–22
Justice and the Poor (Smith), 5–6, 123, 128, 135–53, 158–59, 172, 176
"Justice for the Friendless and Poor" (Errant), 72
juvenile courts, 7, 47, 53, 70–71, 84, 160

Katz, Michael, 97, 222n34
Kelso, Robert, 160–61
Klein, Jennifer, 7n10
Knupfer, Anne Meis, 70n131

labor activism, 17–36, 55, 55n35, 72, 75
Laddey, Paula, 127n13
Laing, Margaret, 165
law: contracts and property and, 22–25, 32–36, 38–42, 78, 94, 115–18, 160–61, 182; procedural justice and, 7, 12, 73–81, 105, 112, 139, 160, 175–76, 223; professional knowledge and, 131–34, 160–63, 172. *See also* bar associations; legal aid; professions and professionalization; social workers
Law and Social Work (Bradway), 181–82
lawyers: African Americans as, 11, 178, 193, 218–19; Chicago's corruption and, 56–58; definitions of, 7–8, 8n11; education and, 134–35, 153; lay lawyers and, 5–8, 13–14, 27–36, 43–46, 72–84, 89–90, 100, 123–26, 193, 223; legal aid agencies and, 1–3, 20–36, 87, 136, 145, 158–75, 199–201, 216; masculinity and, 5, 54, 105–6, 108–9, 172–75, 180–84, 202–3; morality of, 68–69, 69n123; NYLAS structure and, 89–90, 106–10; professionalization discourses and, 4–8, 134–53, 160, 188; social workers and, 123, 137, 157–75, 216–17; women as, 5–6, 8–10, 17–18, 107, 110–11, 173, 176–77, 186, 189–90, 210–11, 218
legal aid: bar associations and, 143–44, 147–48, 150–53, 159–60, 174–84, 199–200, 201n72, 216, 222; benefit

eligibility and, 1–3, 194–205, 213–14, 218; civil rights work and, 7n10, 12, 132, 162, 178–79; class disparities and, 3–4, 12, 38, 51–57, 66–67, 72–84, 91; educational functions of, 5–6, 91–100, 114–22; eligibility requirements of, 10–13, 22–23, 26, 62, 81, 95–99, 114, 176–77, 186, 208–13; fee-charging issues in, 44, 67, 128–29, 188; gender and, 18–26, 54, 91, 100–8, 114–22, 124–25, 139–40, 176–77, 213–16, 222; governmental funding of, 13, 187–88, 199, 213–15; histories of, 3–7, 127, 174–84, 223–24; holistic approaches to, 66, 70, 101–6, 135–36, 153, 158–84, 220–23; immigrants and, 5, 62, 71, 87–100, 172, 176–77; *Justice and the Poor* and, 135–53; lawyers and, 1–3, 161–62, 187–89, 216, 221–22; professionalization discourses and, 5–7, 87–88, 123–25, 133, 135–53, 157–58, 165–66; race and racialization in, 10, 12, 62, 177–79, 190–94, 212; social workers and, 6–7, 126, 133, 147–49, 157–90, 194n40, 204–5; unauthorized practice of law claims and, 176, 183, 199–204, 221; World War II and, 208–13
Legal Aid Bureau (Chicago), 153, 165–68, 181, 188, 194–98, 206–13, 217, *plates*
Legal Aid Society of Atlanta, 212n126
Legal Aid Society of Chicago (CLAS). *See* CLAS (Legal Aid Society of Chicago)
Legal Aid Society of Denver, 202
Legal Aid Society of Minneapolis, 195, 210
Legal Aid Society of New York (NYLAS). *See* NYLAS (Legal Aid Society of New York)
Legal Aid Society of Philadelphia, 125, 128, 147, 173, 187
Legal Aid Society of Pittsburgh, 127
Leuz, Albert, 89–90
listening, 1–3, 27–29, 38–39, 43, 66–67, 169–70, 189, 219
Loew, Rosalie, 107, 107n97, 108, 111, 173, 218–19
Louisiana Bar Association, 191
Low, Minnie, 71, 141–42, 164, 171, 192n32

Maguire, John MacArthur, 173
Maine, Guy (Yee Kai Man), 100

market inefficiency, 31–32, 40, 136
masculinity: abstract reasoning and, 160–63; breadwinner expectation and, 13, 18, 22, 30, 62–64, 89, 100–6, 111, 128–31, 143–44, 149–50, 197, 204–5; class and, 83–84, 185; immigrants' legal aid use and, 95–96; law's practice and, 105–6, 112, 123–26, 172–75, 184; legal aid leadership and, 22–27, 29, 43–44, 46, 61, 87, 108–9, 123–27, 136–37, 222; professionalization discourses and, 5–7, 133–34, 222; Seaman's Branch and, 100–6; Social Gospel movement and, 73–74; violence and, 55–60, 207; wage claims and, 18–20. *See also* citizenship; domestic relations cases; gender; women
Massachusetts Law Review, 143n85
Massachusetts Society for the Prevention of Cruelty to Children, 136, 169n47
master and servant (law), 115
Matsell, George, 20
Matz, Rudolph, 127
McCook, Phillip J., 112n121
McCormick, Irene, 211, 218
McGee, Leonard, 118–19, 157–58
Mobilization for Youth (MFY), 220
mortgage moratoriums, 195, 197
Mother's Pensions, 113–14
Muncy, Robyn, 4n3, 133n42
Murphy, J. Prentice, 175

NALAO (National Association of Legal Aid Organizations): bar associations and, 151–53; leadership of, 204–5, 205n87; naming of, 147; race and racialization and, 179; social workers and, 157–66, 174–75, 182–84, 186, 189, 207–8, 216–17; state benefit eligibility and, 209–10; unauthorized practice of law claims and, 201–2; women's participation in, 190
National Alliance, 127
National Bar Association, 193
National Conference on Social Work, 160–61
National Legal Aid Conference (1911), 123–27
National Proceeding of Social Workers (1927), 175
Negro Fellowship League, 178

New Deal programs, 185, 194–205, 220–22
New Left, 12
New Orleans, 1–3, 190–92, 219, 223
New Orleans Bar Association, 191–92
New Orleans Legal Aid Society, 191–94
New Orleans Urban League, 192n32
New Republic, 173
New York Amsterdam News, 193
New York Earnings Act, 32, 33n75
New York State Bar Association, 151
New York Sun, 20
New York Times, 106
New York Working Women's Protective Union (WWPU). *See* WWPU (Working Women's Protective Union)
notice (in domestic servants' claims), 114–22, 144
NYLAS (Legal Aid Society of New York): domestic relations cases and, 108, 111–13, 144–45, 205–8, 210; domestic servants and, 114–22; Harlem Branch of, 119–22; historical place of, 127, 143n85, 215–16; images of, 114, *plates*; immigrants and, 84, 87–101; Joint Committee report on, 175–84; Seaman's Branch of, 100–6, 109–10, 119–20, 122; social workers and, 186, 188–89, 217; unauthorized practice of law and, 201–2; women's involvement with, 106–14, 128, 158, 172–73, 218–19; work routines of, 125–26

Odem, Mary E., 67n113
OEO (Office of Economic Opportunity), 215, 220–23
Ottendorfer, Oswald, 92

Palmer, Alice, 136
Parsons, Lucy, 55, 55n35
paternity cases, 45
PAWC (Protective Agency for Women and Children), 49–81; BoJ's relation to, 72–73, 79–81; caseload of, 54; Chicago corruption and, 56–61; Chicago Women's Club and, 46–49, 51, 52n17, 70; divorce cases and, 60, 64–66, 109, 111; eligibility for, 62; historical place of, 127, 127n14; mission of, 49–51, 53, 56, 66, 69–70; social workers and, 129, 211; wage claims and, 62; WWPU's

relation to, 53–54, 56. *See also* CLAS (Legal Aid Society of Chicago)
People's Law Firm, 111
Perry, Bertha, 178
Philadelphia Committee for the Protection of Women and Children, 125
The Political Status of Women in the United States (Rembaugh), 110
"Poor Man's Portia" (image), *plates*
Portia Club, 178
Potter, Henry, 75
Pound, Roscoe, 12, 134–35, 146
poverty. *See* class
Powell, Michael, 203n80
Prison Aid League, 191
professions and professionalization: abstract thinking and, 160–63, 172; education and, 131–34; fees and damages and, 44, 74, 81, 128–29, 136–37; gender and, 4–10, 43–46, 123–25, 180–84; *Justice and the Poor* and, 135–53; labor activism and, 18–36; legal aid's philanthropic history and, 87–90, 139–43, 145, 147–48, 151–53, 165–66, 185; legal monopolies and, 4–8, 13–14; social workers and, 131–35, 157, 166–67, 179, 191, 221
progressivism: legal reform and, 134–35, 139, 146, 164, 170, 175–83, 206–7; social work and, 130, 166; women's organization and, 28, 37, 50–56; World War I and, 139. *See also specific organizations*
prostitution, 21–22
Protestant Episcopal Church Missionary Society for Seamen, 101
Pue, W. Wesley, 8n11

Quackenbos, Mary, 107, 111, 173

race and racialization: assimilationist impulses and, 91–100, 104, 120–22; Civil War and, 20–21; class's intersections with, 22–23, 185n2; domestic servants and, 23, 117n142, 119–22; feminist movement and, 51–53; gender's intersections with, 118–19, 122; immigrants and, 34, 91–100; legal aid clients and, 9–10, 83, 177–79, 190–94, 212, 218–19; seamen and, 102–3; social workers and, 190–94; WWPU's work

and, 20–21. *See also* African Americans; citizenship; immigrants; justice
Railroad Retirement Act of 1935, 198
rape. *See* sexual violence
Reed, Alfred Z., 142–43, 146–47
Reggie fellowship program, 222
"Regulate the Loan Sharks" (advertisement), 84, *plates*
Rembaugh, Bertha, 107, 110, 173
Richmond, Mary E., 133n42, 165, 170–71, 172n56
Roberts, William, 21
Robinson, Leila, 43–44
Rochester Women's Educational and Industrial Union, 141
Roosevelt, Eleanor, 194n42
Root, Elihu, 139
Rothschild, A. M., 79
Rothschild, Sadie Frances, 107
Russell Sage Foundation, 165, 175, 217

Sabine, William, 126
Sage, Olivia, 165n32
The Sailor's Log (NYLAS), 106, 115
Sampson, Edith, 178
San Francisco Legal Aid Bureau, 207
Schiff, Jacob, 92–93
School of Social Science Administration (U of Chicago), 181
Schwartz, Maude, 176n74
Scoville, Samuel, 125, 128
Seaman's Branch (NYLAS), 100–6, 109–10, 114, 119–20, 122
Servicemen's Dependents Allowance Act of 1942, 209
settlement house movement, 49, 53, 93, 99, 130, 178
Sewall, Harriett, 38, 43
Sewall, Samuel, 38
sexual violence, 51, 56–62, 66
Shriver, Sargent, 221
slavery: domestic servants and, 42, 118; prostitution as, 21–22; seamen and, 102–3; wage labor's opposition to, 37–38
small-loan claims, 194, 194n40
Smith, Julia Holmes, 79
Smith, Reginald Heber, 5–6, 123, 128, 135–53, 157–61, 168–76, 182, 215, 221–22
Smith, Virginia, 211–12, *plates*

Social Gospel, 37, 72n135, 73–74, 74n140, 75, 87, 91
Social Security Act, 197n54, 198
social workers: dependence discourses and, 130–31, 143–44, 168; domestic relations cases and, 126–27, 159, 168–69, 205–8, 217–18; Freudian psychology and, 217; gendering of, 6–9, 123, 129, 133, 133n42, 149, 162–65, 202; immigrants and, 176; *Justice and the Poor* and, 140–43, 158; lawyers' relations with, 137, 147–49, 157–76, 180–84, 216–17; legal aid's relation to, 6–7, 126, 133, 136–37, 147–48, 166–90, 204–5, 216–17; origins of, 129–31; professionalization of, 131, 131n36, 132–35, 149–50, 157, 159–75, 179, 191, 221; race and racialization and, 190–94; state benefits and, 166–68, 194–205, 210, 213–14, 218; substantive justice and, 142, 159–84
Society for Ethical Culture (Chicago), 72–73
Society for Ethical Culture (New York), 72n135
Soldiers' and Sailors' Civil Relief Act of 1940, 209, 211
Staats-Zeitung, 98
Stanley, Amy Dru, 33n74
Stary, Josephine, 107, 109–10
St. Bartholomew's Chinese Guild, 99–100
sterilization laws, 162–63
Stoiber, Louis, 125
Stokes, Elizabeth, 82
Stone, Harlan F., 146n102
Sugarman, David, 8n11

Tani, Karen, 160n9, 198
Tarcher, Mary, 219
Taylor, Graham, 131
Tobey, Frank, 73
To Establish Justice for All (Johnson), 215
"To Tramps" (Parsons), 55n35
Truth Church Institute, 192
Tweed, Harrison, 152

UCC (United Charities of Chicago). *See* United Charities of Chicago
United Charities Building (NYC), 108, 170
United Charities of Chicago, 71, 153, 170, 186
United Way, 174

University Settlement House (NYC), 93, 93n24
U.S. Public Administration Service, 199
U.S. Shipping Commission, 105

Volunteer Defenders Office (New York), 166

wage claims: BLAS's caseload and, 136n52; domestic servants and, 13, 24, 36–46, 114–22, 144; gender and, 5–6, 17–18, 20–36, 50, 83, 89, 125, 159; NYLAS's involvement with, 88–89, 97; PAWC and, 62; slavery's opposition to, 21–22, 39, 102–6, 118–19; state regulations and, 89, 105, 185, 219–20
"The Waiting Room in the Building of the Workingwoman's Protective Union" (image), *plates*
Waldo, Alice, 158–60, 160n7, 166
Walford, Daniel, 20
Walkowitz, Daniel, 123n1
Wardwell, Allen, 189–90
Ware, Emma, 213
War on Poverty (program), 215
Washington Council of Social Agencies, 190
WEIU (Boston Women's Educational and Industrial Union), 12, 36–46, 124, 140, 142–43, 218. *See also* BLAS (Legal Aid Society of Boston); specific people
Welfare Council of New York City, 175
Wells, Ida B., 132, 178
Wentworth, Edward C., 75
Wheaton v. Higgins, 117n145
whitemailing, 62, 63n85
whiteness, 3, 10–11, 22–23, 91, 91n15, 120, 190–94
Wigmore, John, 143n85, 153, 181n100
Willard, Frances, 50n12
Willrich, Michael, 57, 69n123, 170
Wilson, Henrietta, 213
Witt, John Fabian, 11
Woman's Homeopathic Society, 50
women: bar membership and, 5–6, 9–10, 43–44, 110–11, 173, 186, 210–11; BoJ's relation to, 79–81; civilizing force of, 21–22, 49, 60–61, 103, 205–8; domestic servants' claims and, 114–22; dressmaking industry and, 34, 34n79,

35, 35n85, 39; gendered portrayals of, 18–36, 43, 52, 60–61, 92, 133, 162–64, 209–10; lay lawyering and, 27–46, 68, 81–84, 123–26, 223; legal aid histories and, 3–7, 123–29, 135–53, 159–60, 174–84, 215–16, 223–24; legal rights of, 32–33, 32n72, 35–36, 38, 47–49, 111, 120, 128–29, 149–50; listening and, 1–3, 66–67, 133n42, 169–70, 219; NYLAS and, 106–14; philanthropy and, 36–46, 51, 187–88; reform movements and, 47–49, 51–81, 84, 129–31, 139, 176; social work and, 6–9, 123, 127–33, 133n42, 149, 162–65, 176–77, 202; substantive justice and, 7, 12–13, 24–25, 36–46, 44n131, 45, 52, 54–58, 62–63, 70, 96, 142. *See also* bar associations; domestic relations cases; domestic servants; gender; lawyers; legal aid; social workers; wage claims
Women Lawyers' Journal, 189–90
Women's Branch (of NYLAS), 108, 110
Women's Christian Temperance Union, 49–50, 50n12
Women's Committee (of CLAS), 81–83
Women's Directory, 45n134
Women's Physiological Institute of Chicago, 49
women's suffrage, 10–11, 49
Women's Trade Union League, 53, 111, 176, 176n74
Working Women's Union (precursor to the WWPU), 18–20
workmen's compensation, 114, 160, 176–77
World's Fair (1893), 79n160
World War II, 208–13
WPA (Works Progress Administration), 197–98
WWPU (Working Women's Protective Union): founding of, 17–20, 88; images of, 28–30, *plates*; lawyers' charitable works and, 29–36, 96–97; lay lawyers of, 27–36, 89–90; male leaders of, 20–21; omissions of, from later histories, 148–49; PAWC's debt to, 53–54, 56; raced and gendered qualifications for, 20–27, 89; recognitions of, 176; WEIU's debt to, 37–40, 45–46

Yiddish, 93, 98–99